Call of the Night

〈2〉

KOTOYAMA

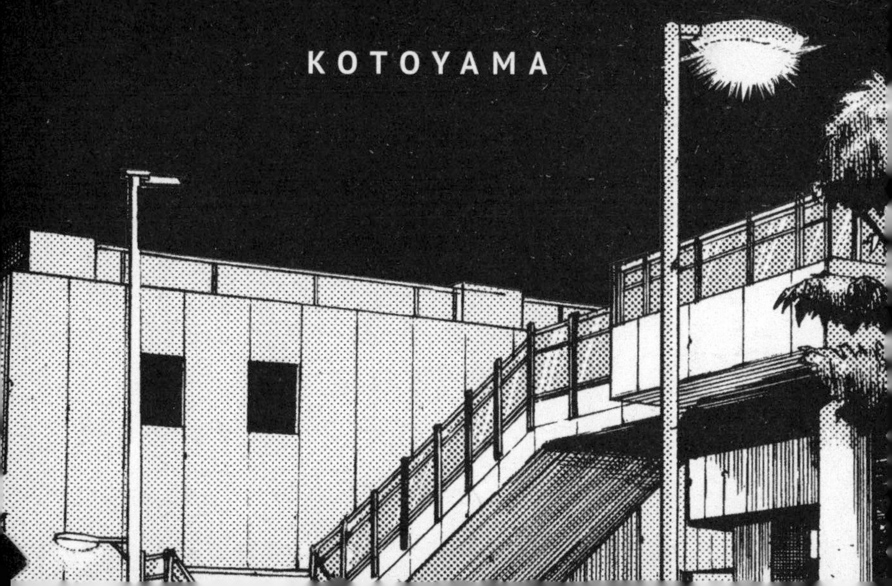

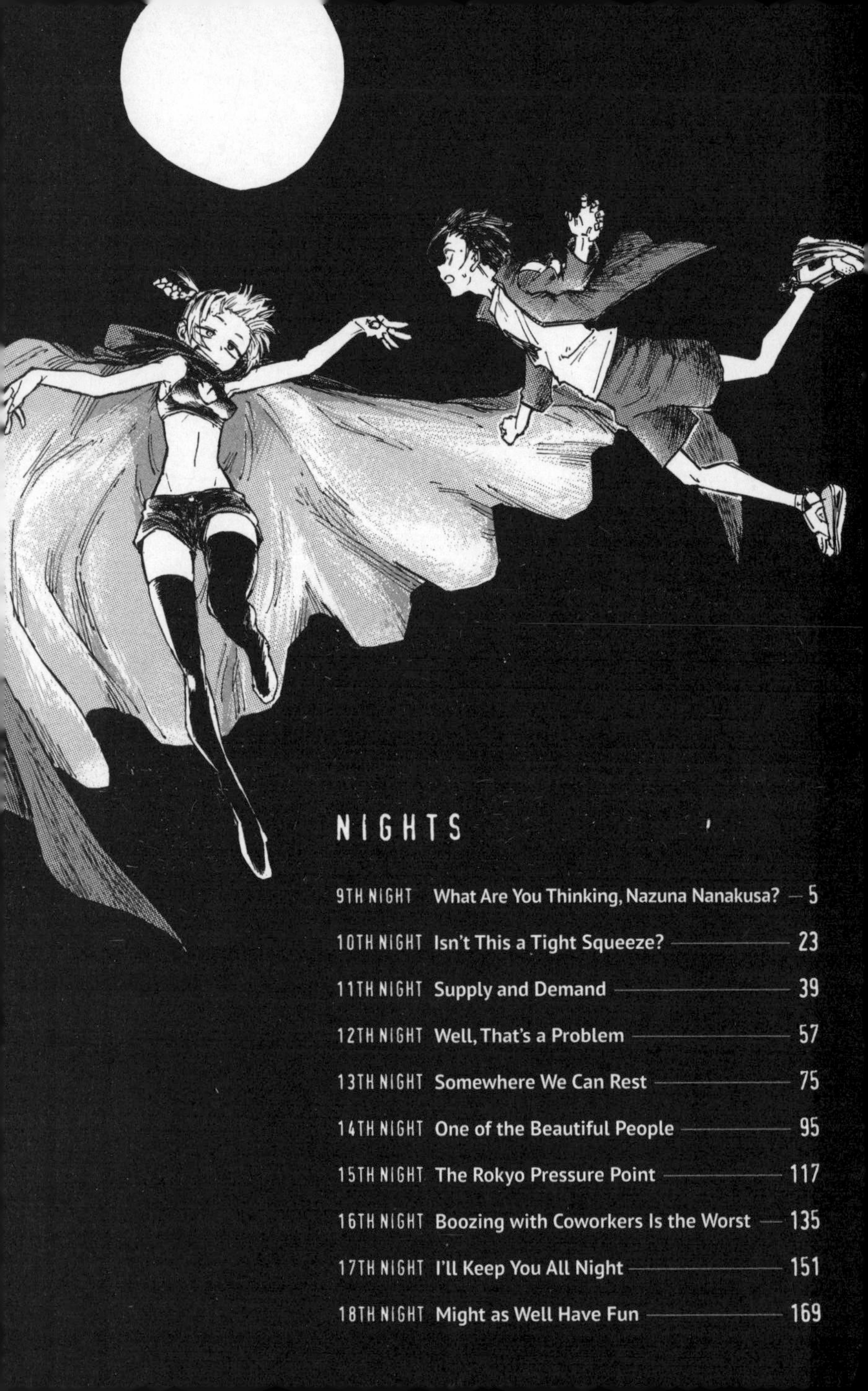

NIGHTS

NIGHT 9: WHAT ARE YOU THINKING, NAZUNA NANAKUSA?

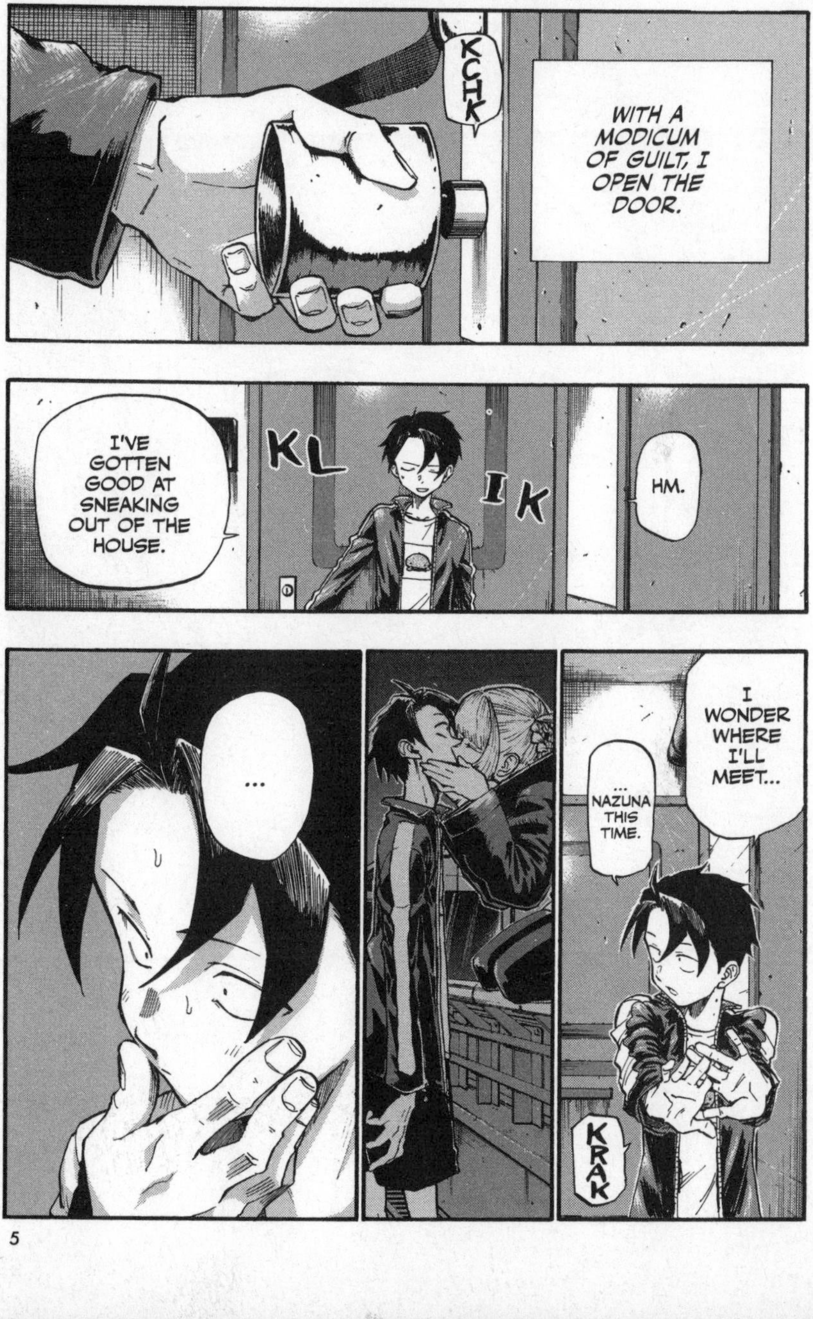

WITH A MODICUM OF GUILT, I OPEN THE DOOR.
KCHK
HM.
KLIK
I'VE GOTTEN GOOD AT SNEAKING OUT OF THE HOUSE.
I WONDER WHERE I'LL MEET...
...NAZUNA THIS TIME.
KRAK
...

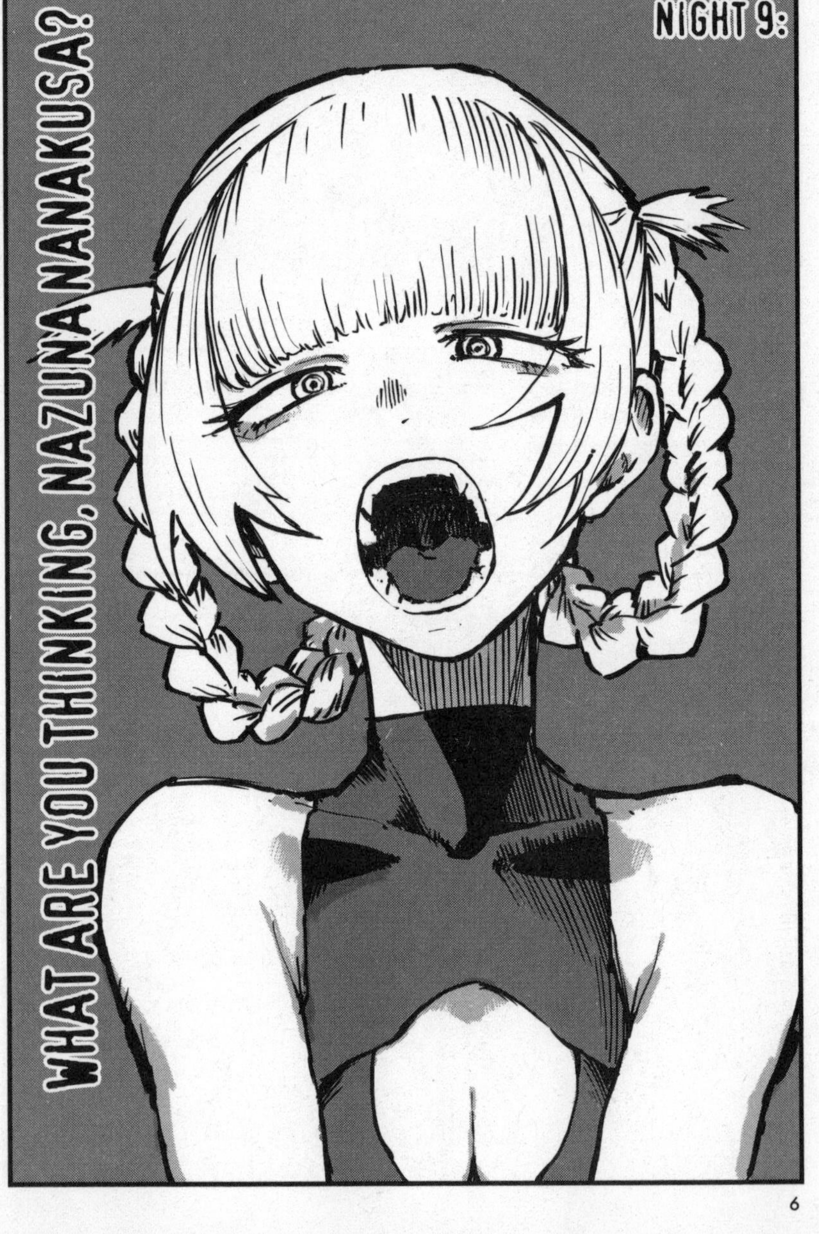
NIGHT 9:
WHAT ARE YOU THINKING, NAZUNA NANAKUSA?

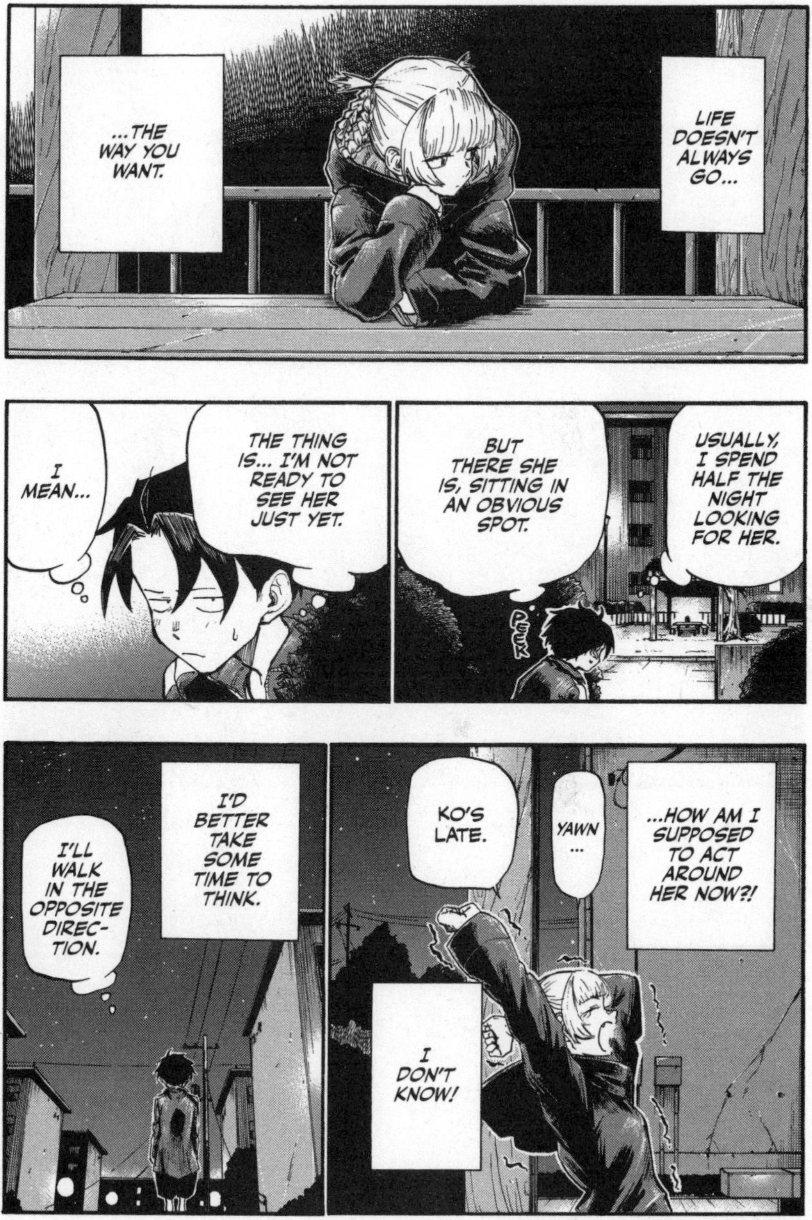
LIFE DOESN'T ALWAYS GO...
...THE WAY YOU WANT.
USUALLY, I SPEND HALF THE NIGHT LOOKING FOR HER.
BUT THERE SHE IS, SITTING IN AN OBVIOUS SPOT.
PEEK
THE THING IS... I'M NOT READY TO SEE HER JUST YET.
I MEAN...
...HOW AM I SUPPOSED TO ACT AROUND HER NOW?!
YAWN...
KO'S LATE.
I DON'T KNOW!
I'D BETTER TAKE SOME TIME TO THINK.
I'LL WALK IN THE OPPOSITE DIRECTION.

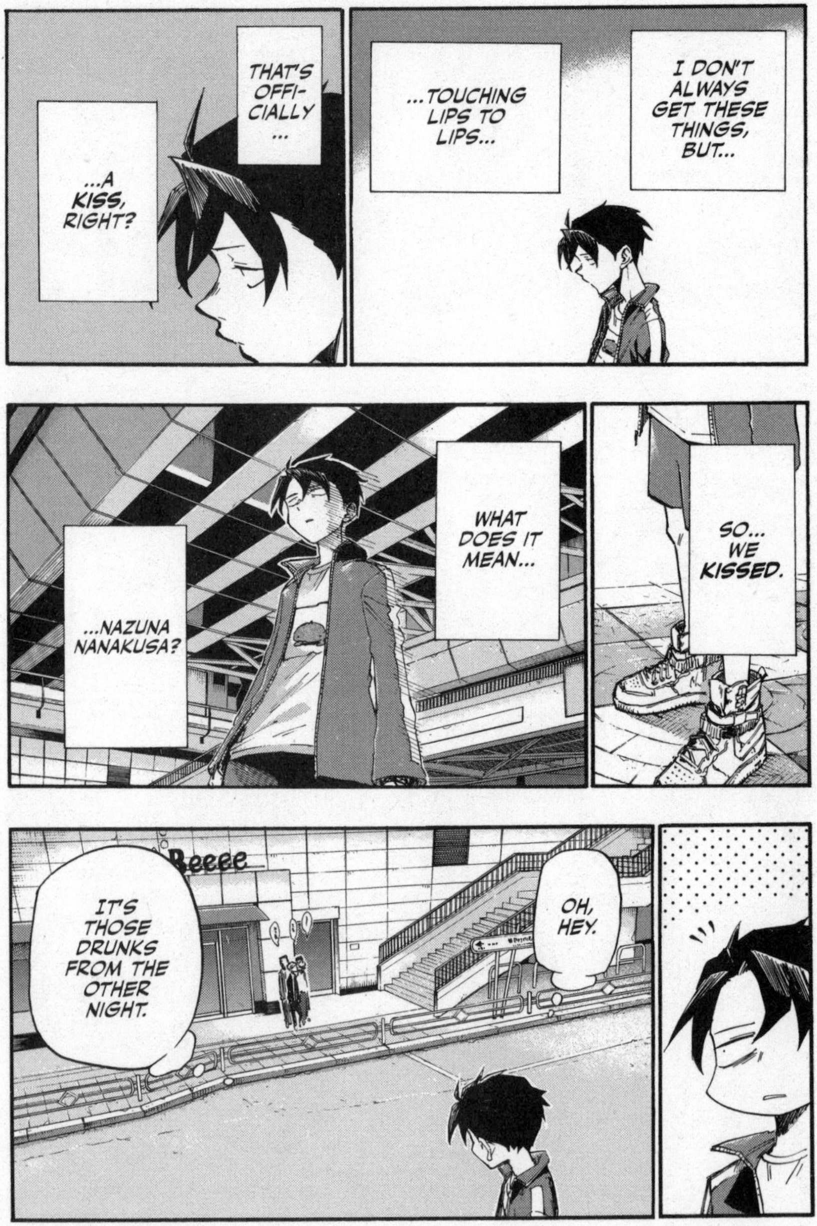
I DON'T ALWAYS GET THESE THINGS, BUT...
...TOUCHING LIPS TO LIPS...
THAT'S OFFI-CIALLY ...
...A KISS, RIGHT?
SO... WE KISSED.
WHAT DOES IT MEAN...
...NAZUNA NANAKUSA?
OH, HEY.
IT'S THOSE DRUNKS FROM THE OTHER NIGHT.

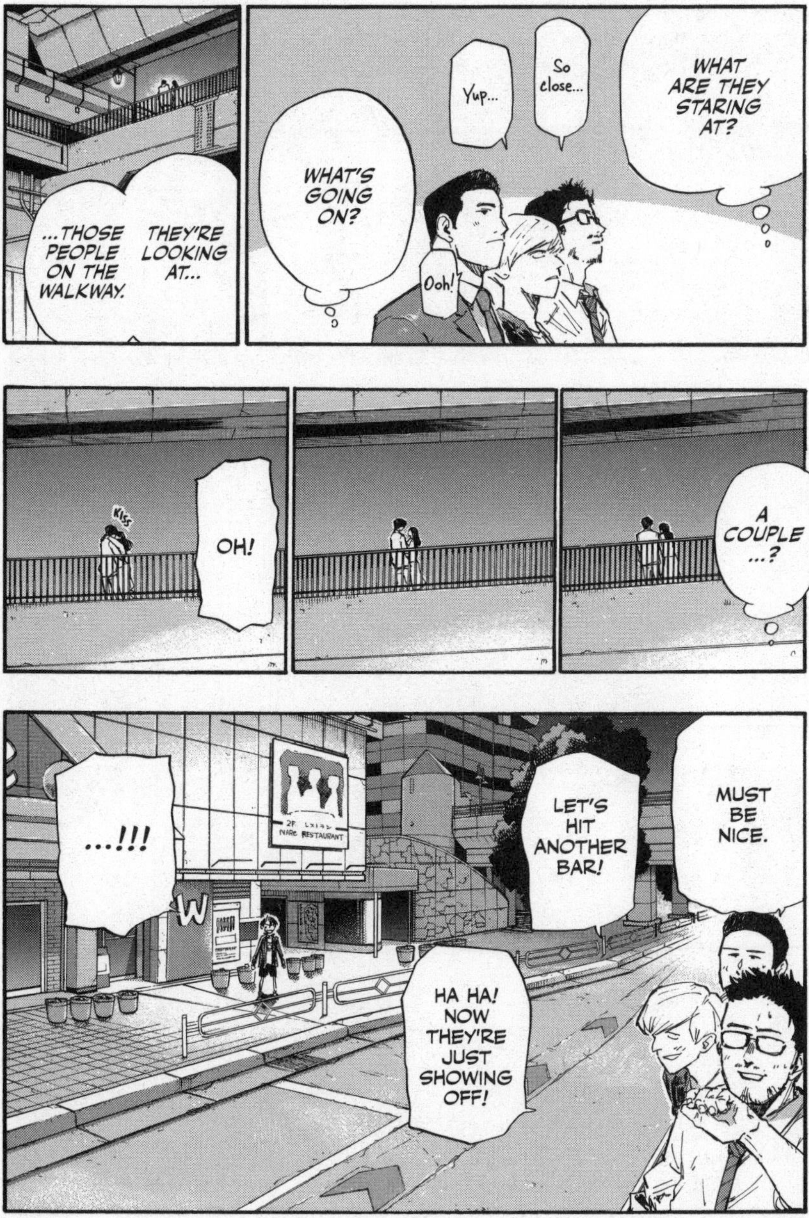
WHAT ARE THEY STARING AT?
So close...
Yup...
WHAT'S GOING ON?
Ooh!
THEY'RE LOOKING AT...
...THOSE PEOPLE ON THE WALKWAY.
A COUPLE ...?
KISS
OH!
MUST BE NICE.
LET'S HIT ANOTHER BAR!
HA HA! NOW THEY'RE JUST SHOWING OFF!
...!!!

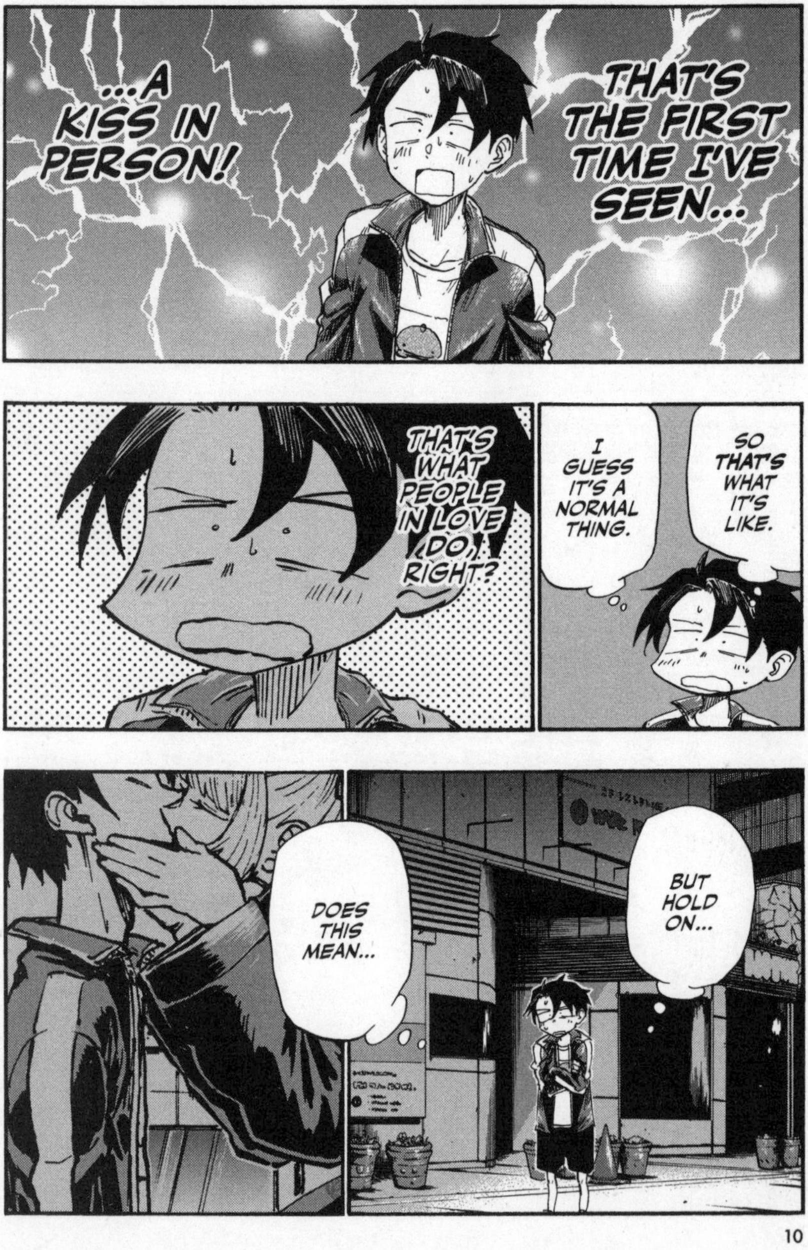
THAT'S THE FIRST TIME I'VE SEEN...
...A KISS IN PERSON!
SO THAT'S WHAT IT'S LIKE.
I GUESS IT'S A NORMAL THING.
THAT'S WHAT PEOPLE IN LOVE DO, RIGHT?
BUT HOLD ON...
DOES THIS MEAN...

... NAZUNA AND I...
...ARE IN LOVE?!
My heart's going a mile a minute!
THAT MEANS I'VE ACHIEVED MY GOAL!
TWIRL
TWIRL
I'VE FALLEN IN LOVE WITH A VAMPIRE!
WHOA !!
POKE
I DID IT!
NOW I CAN TURN INTO A VAMPIRE!
GOODBYE, OLD LIFE! GOODBYE, NORMAL! GOODBYE, MISERY!
SAY HELLO TO THE NEW ME!
TP

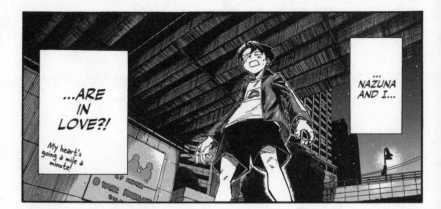

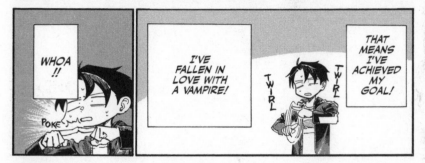

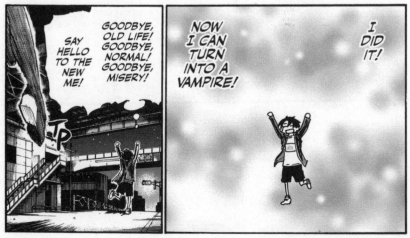

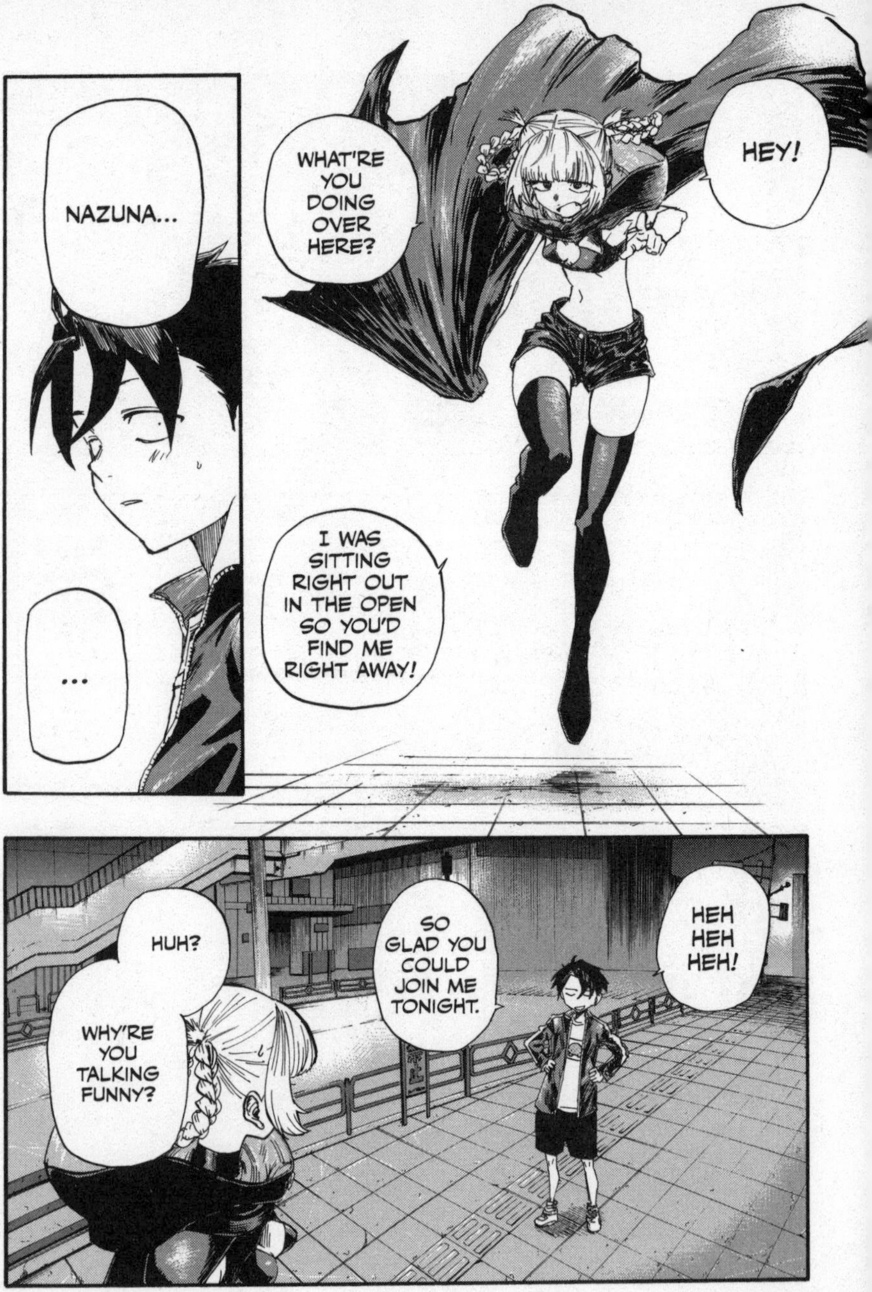
HEY!
WHAT'RE YOU DOING OVER HERE?
I WAS SITTING RIGHT OUT IN THE OPEN SO YOU'D FIND ME RIGHT AWAY!
NAZUNA...
...
HEH HEH HEH!
SO GLAD YOU COULD JOIN ME TONIGHT.
HUH?
WHY'RE YOU TALKING FUNNY?

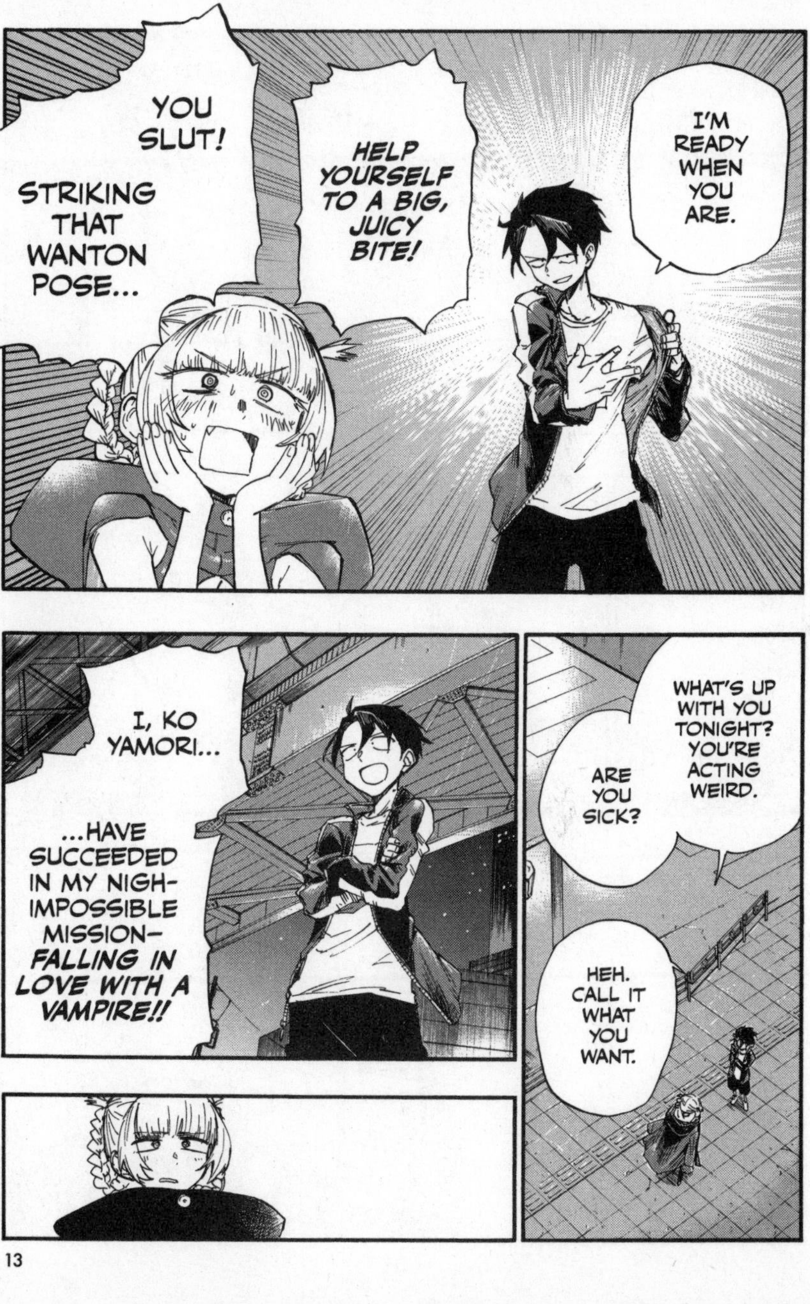
I'M READY WHEN YOU ARE.
HELP YOURSELF TO A BIG, JUICY BITE!
YOU SLUT!
STRIKING THAT WANTON POSE...
WHAT'S UP WITH YOU TONIGHT? YOU'RE ACTING WEIRD.
ARE YOU SICK?
HEH. CALL IT WHAT YOU WANT.
I, KO YAMORI...
...HAVE SUCCEEDED IN MY NIGH-IMPOSSIBLE MISSION—FALLING IN LOVE WITH A VAMPIRE!!

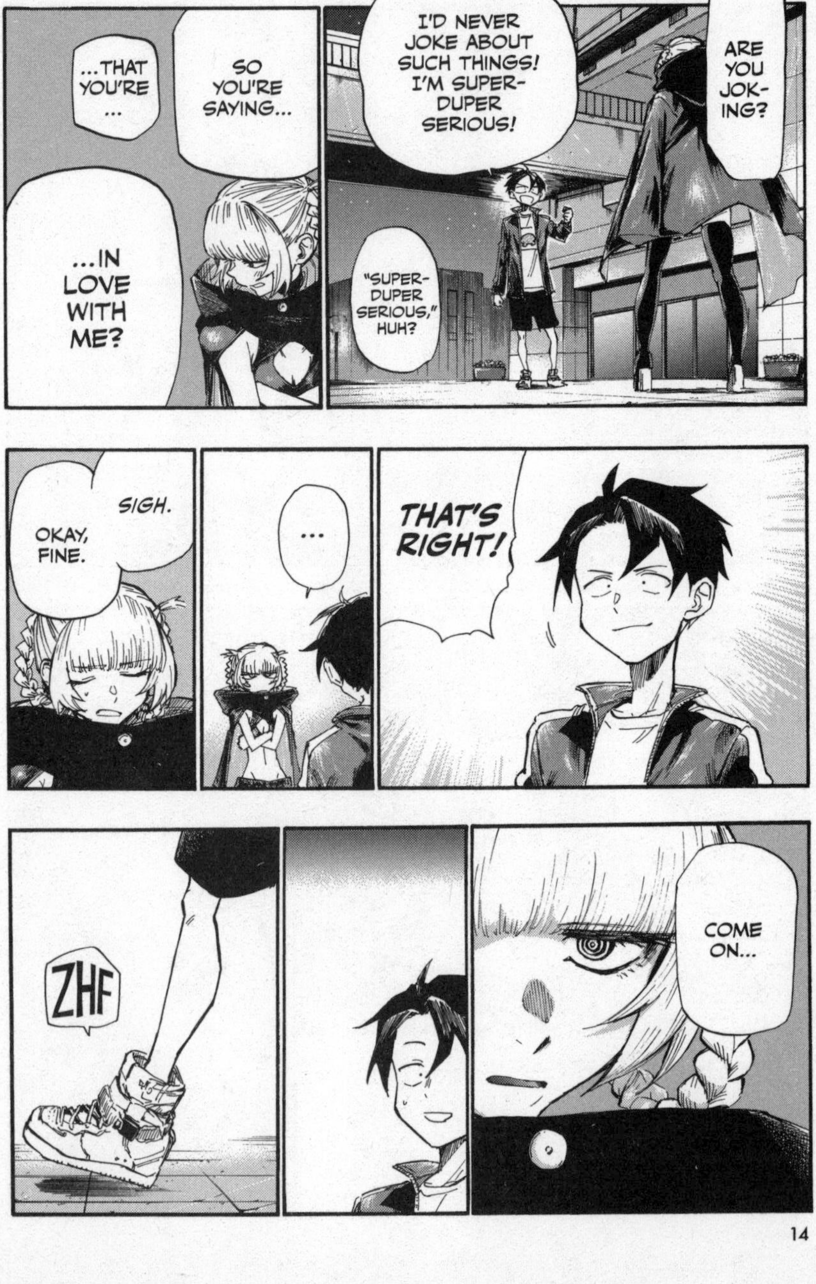
ARE YOU JOK-ING?
I'D NEVER JOKE ABOUT SUCH THINGS! I'M SUPER-DUPER SERIOUS!
"SUPER-DUPER SERIOUS," HUH?
SO YOU'RE SAYING...
...THAT YOU'RE ...
...IN LOVE WITH ME?
THAT'S RIGHT!
...
SIGH.
OKAY, FINE.
COME ON...
ZHF

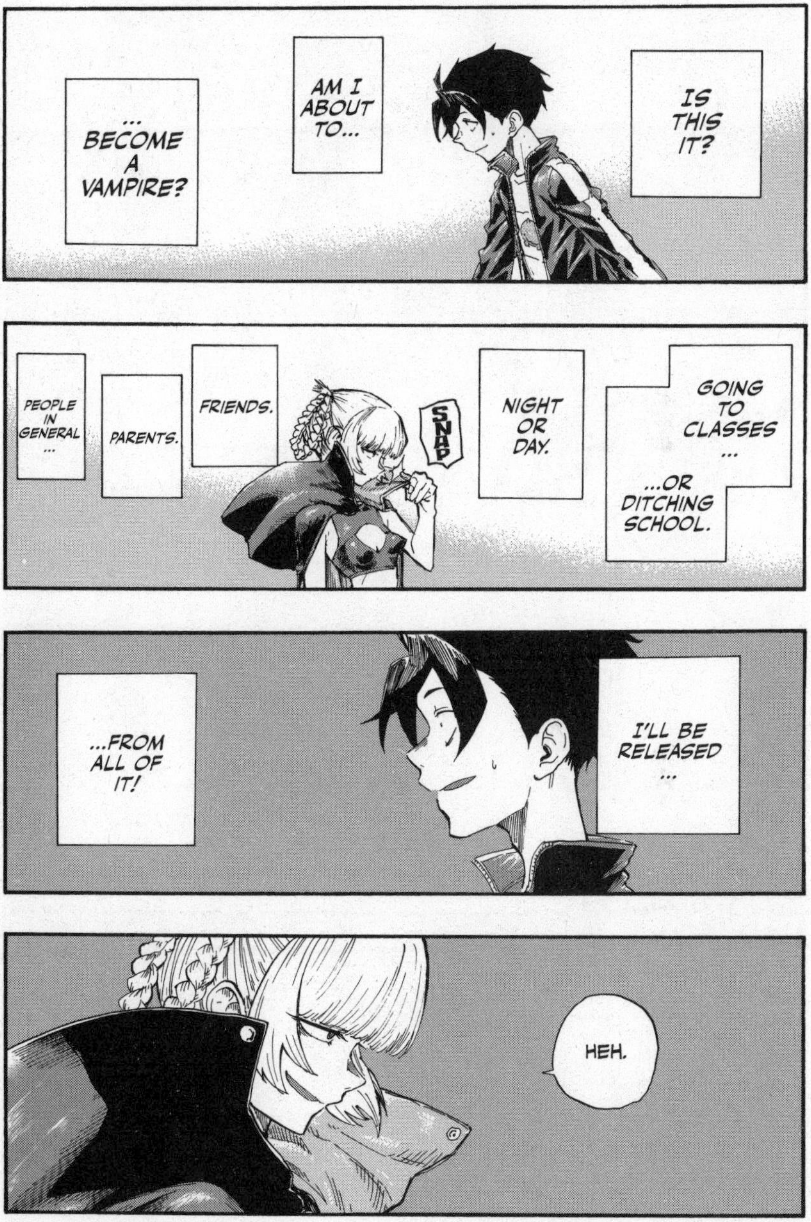
IS THIS IT?
AM I ABOUT TO...
...BECOME A VAMPIRE?
GOING TO CLASSES ...
...OR DITCHING SCHOOL.
NIGHT OR DAY.
SNAP
FRIENDS.
PARENTS.
PEOPLE IN GENERAL ...
I'LL BE RELEASED ...
...FROM ALL OF IT!
HEH.

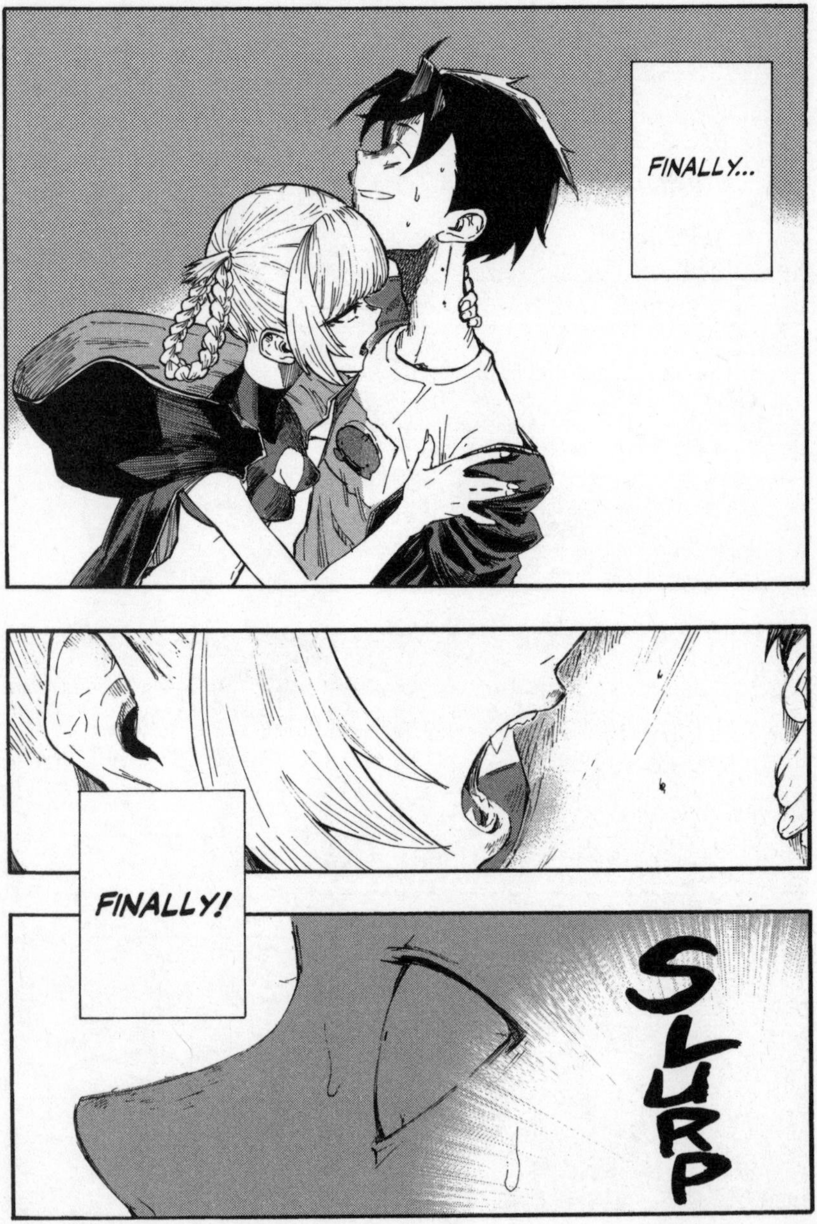
FINALLY...
FINALLY!
SLURP

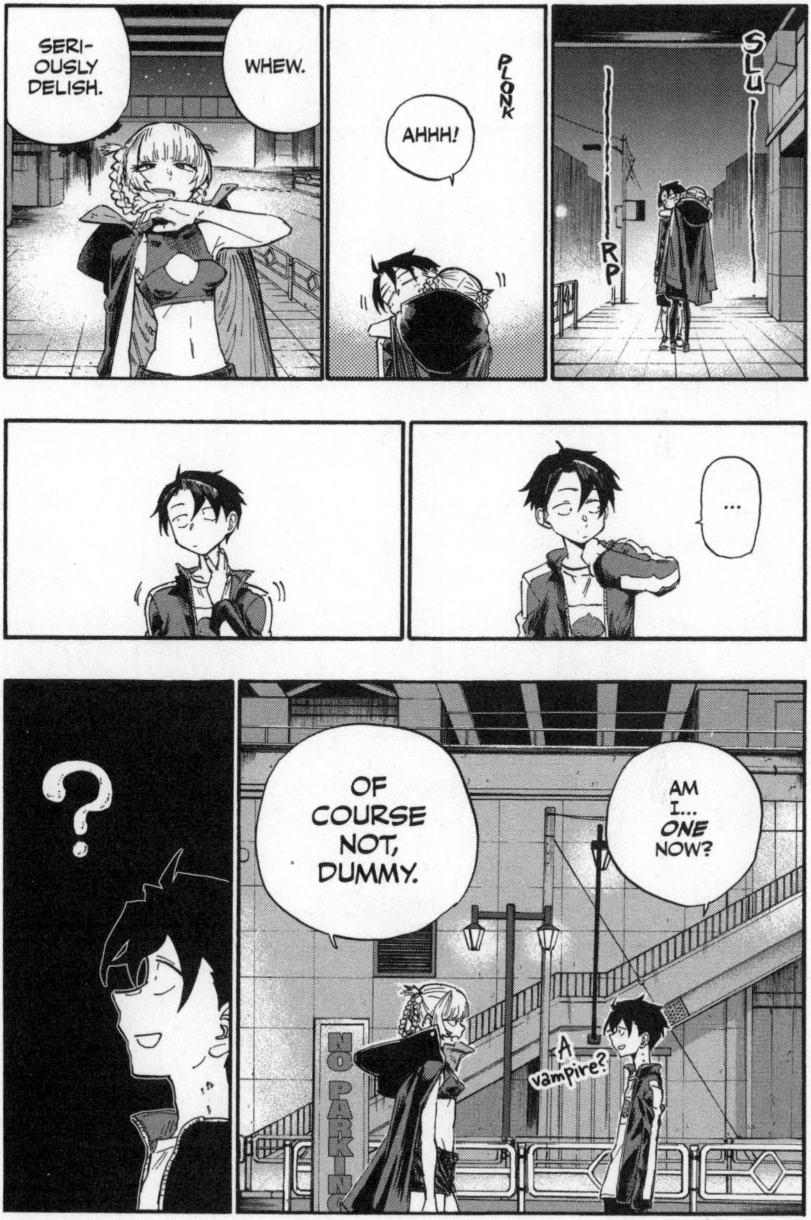
SLURP
PLONK
AHHH!
WHEW.
SERI-OUSLY DELISH.
...
AM I... ONE NOW?
A vampire?
OF COURSE NOT, DUMMY.
NO PARKING
?

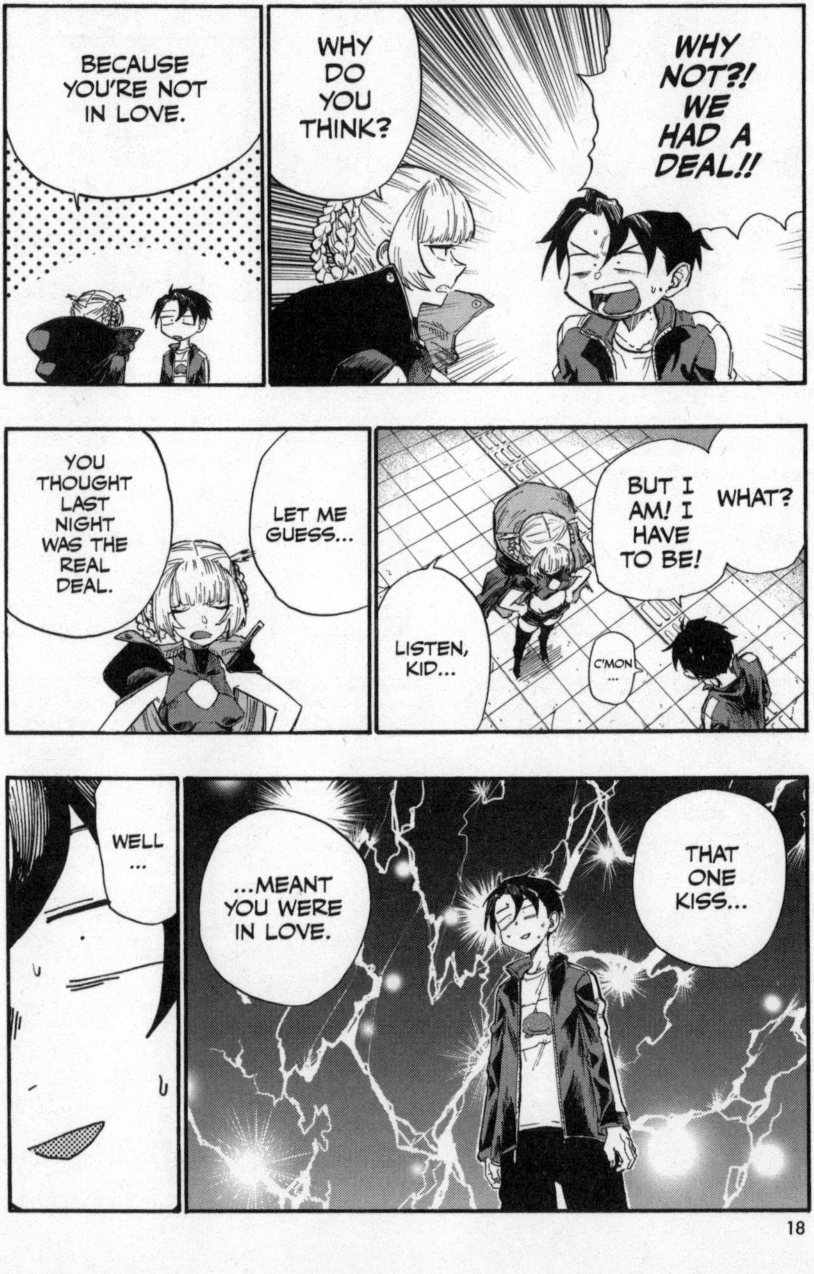
WHY NOT?! WE HAD A DEAL!!
WHY DO YOU THINK?
BECAUSE YOU'RE NOT IN LOVE.
WHAT?
BUT I AM! I HAVE TO BE!
C'MON...
LISTEN, KID...
LET ME GUESS...
YOU THOUGHT LAST NIGHT WAS THE REAL DEAL.
THAT ONE KISS...
...MEANT YOU WERE IN LOVE.
WELL...

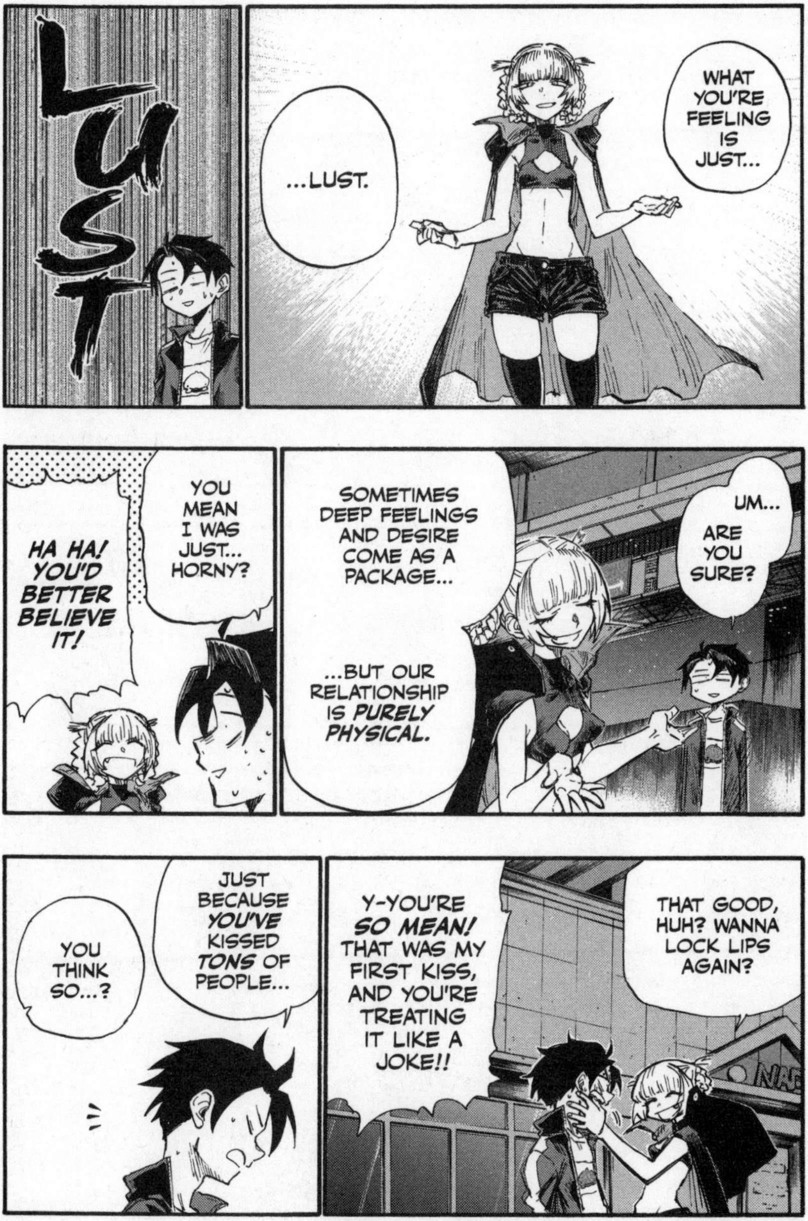
WHAT YOU'RE FEELING IS JUST...
...LUST.
LUST
UM...
ARE YOU SURE?
SOMETIMES DEEP FEELINGS AND DESIRE COME AS A PACKAGE...
...BUT OUR RELATIONSHIP IS *PURELY PHYSICAL.*
YOU MEAN I WAS JUST... HORNY?
HA HA! YOU'D BETTER BELIEVE IT!
THAT GOOD, HUH? WANNA LOCK LIPS AGAIN?
Y-YOU'RE *SO MEAN!* THAT WAS MY FIRST KISS, AND YOU'RE TREATING IT LIKE A JOKE!!
JUST BECAUSE *YOU'VE* KISSED *TONS* OF PEOPLE...
YOU THINK SO...?

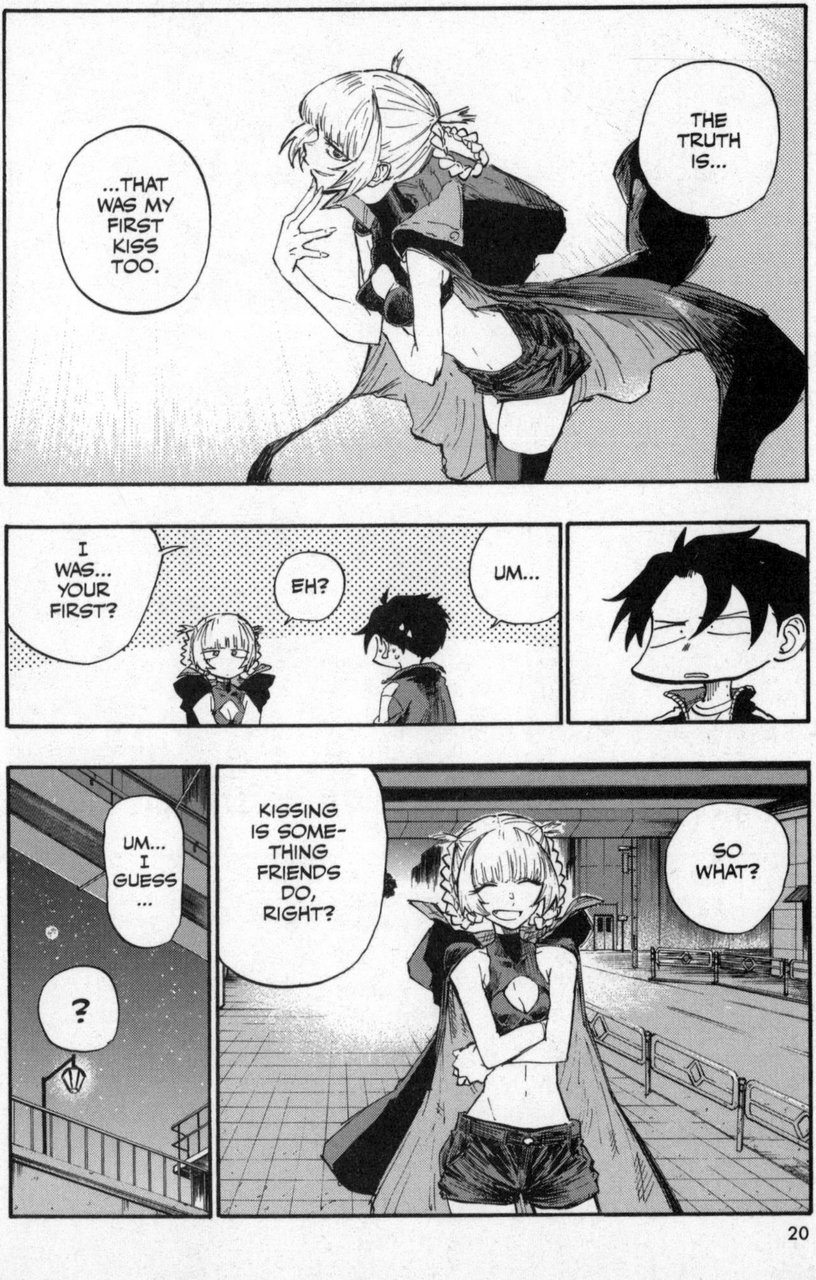
THE TRUTH IS...
...THAT WAS MY FIRST KISS TOO.
UM...
EH?
I WAS... YOUR FIRST?
SO WHAT?
KISSING IS SOME-THING FRIENDS DO, RIGHT?
UM... I GUESS ...
?

Call of the Night

Call of the Night

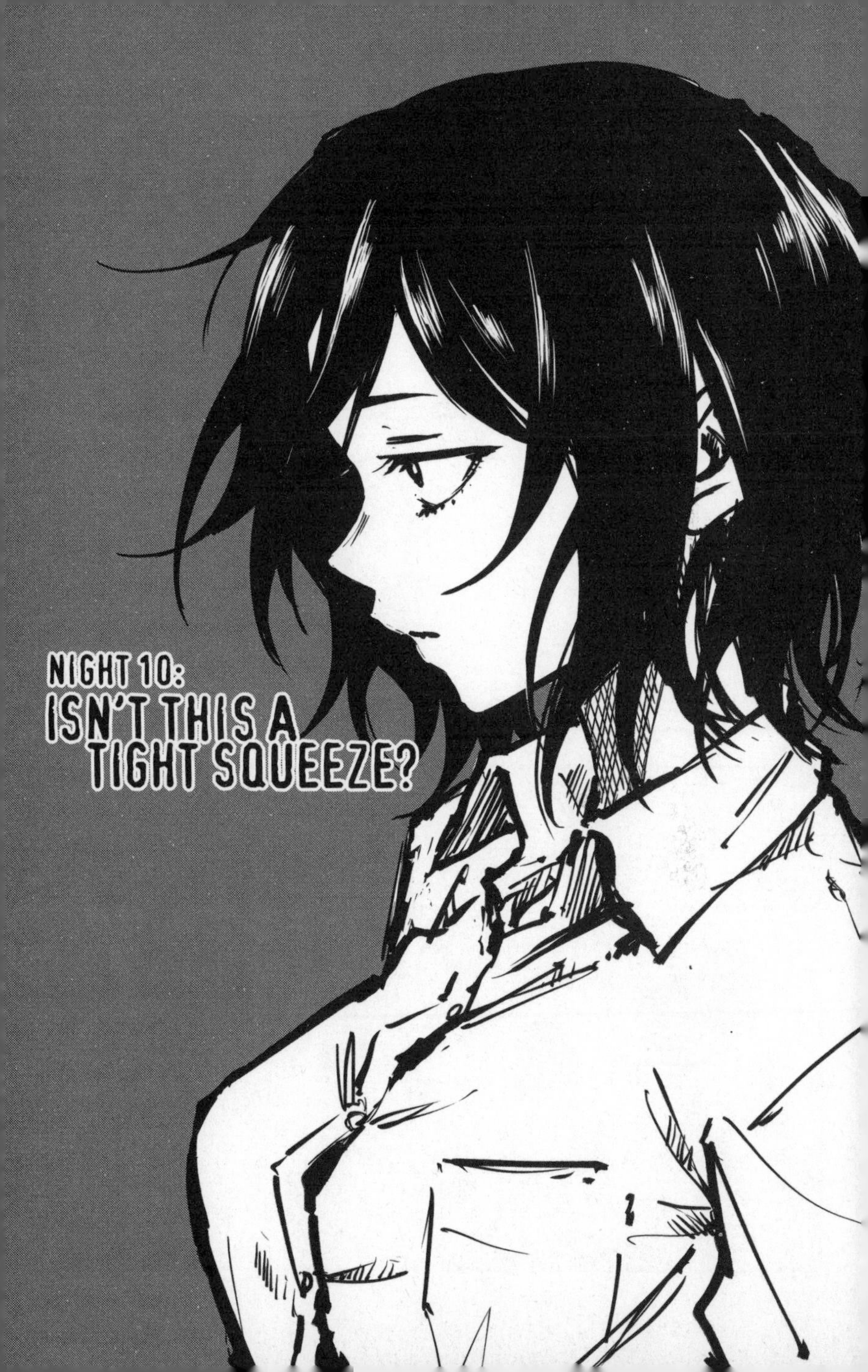
NIGHT 10:
ISN'T THIS A TIGHT SQUEEZE?

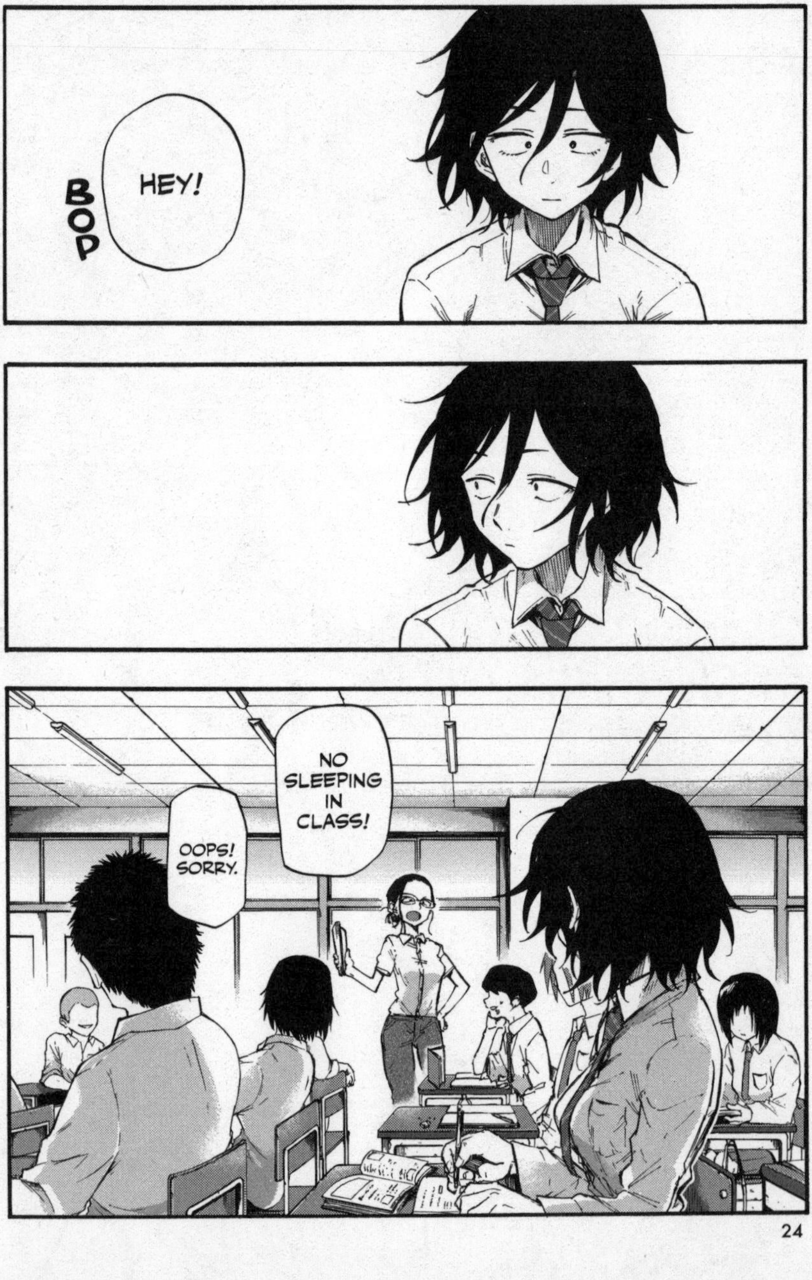
HEY!
BOP
NO SLEEPING IN CLASS!
OOPS! SORRY.

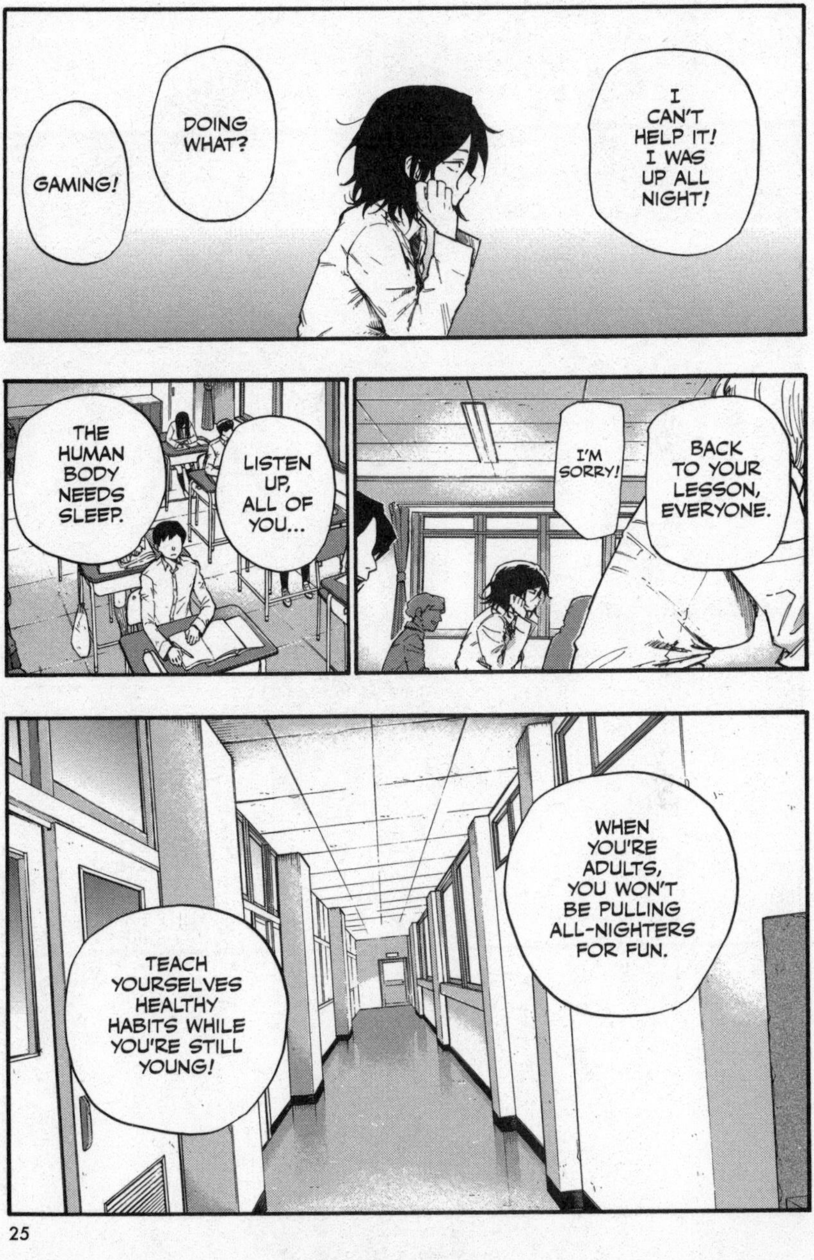
I CAN'T HELP IT! I WAS UP ALL NIGHT!
DOING WHAT?
GAMING!
BACK TO YOUR LESSON, EVERYONE.
I'M SORRY!
LISTEN UP, ALL OF YOU...
THE HUMAN BODY NEEDS SLEEP.
WHEN YOU'RE ADULTS, YOU WON'T BE PULLING ALL-NIGHTERS FOR FUN.
TEACH YOURSELVES HEALTHY HABITS WHILE YOU'RE STILL YOUNG!

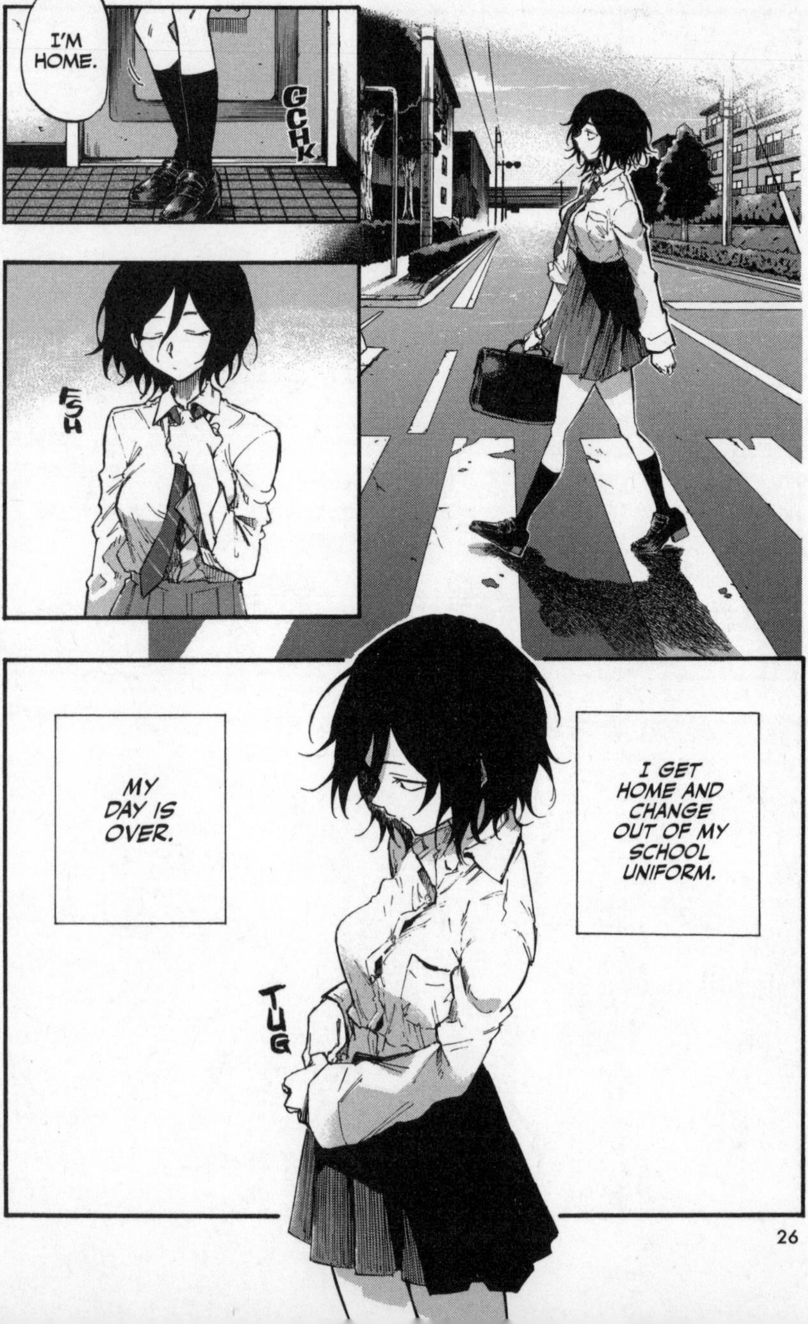
I'M HOME.
GCHK
FSH
I GET HOME AND CHANGE OUT OF MY SCHOOL UNIFORM.
MY DAY IS OVER.
TUG

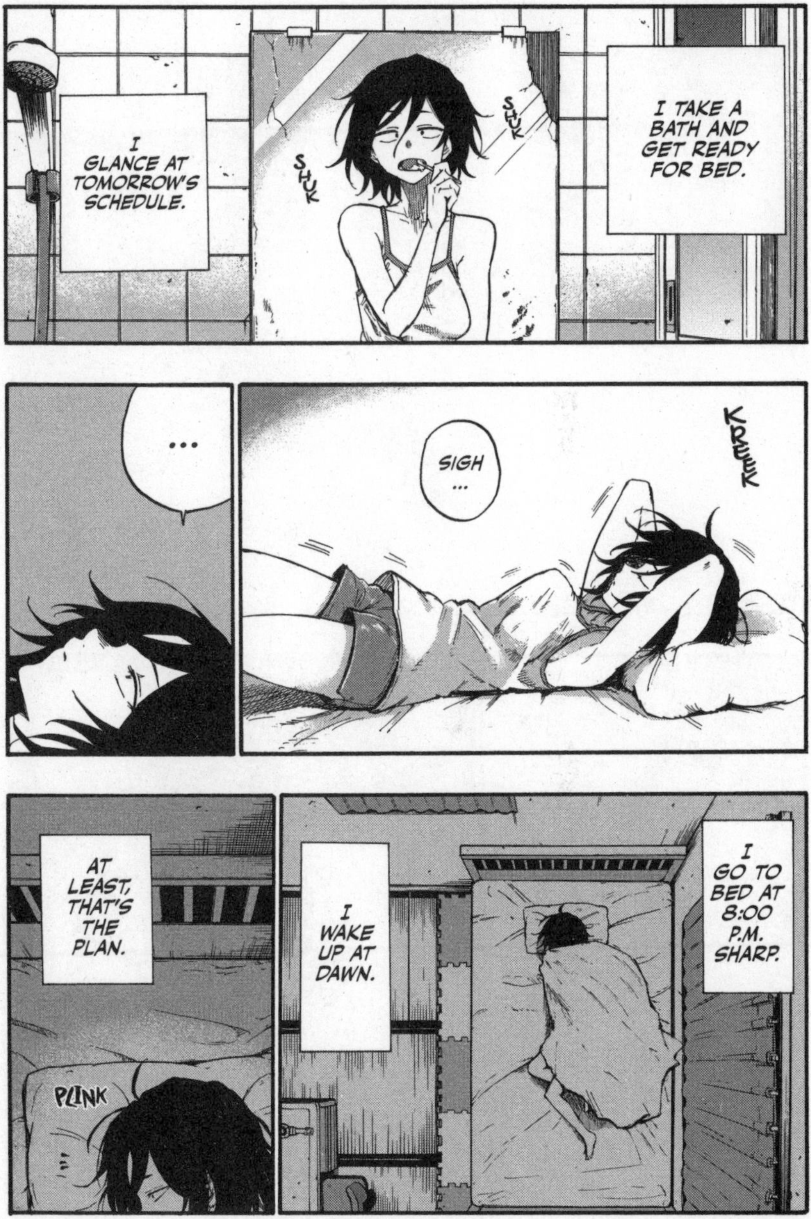
I TAKE A BATH AND GET READY FOR BED.
SHUK
SHUK
I GLANCE AT TOMORROW'S SCHEDULE.
KREEK
SIGH ...
...
I GO TO BED AT 8:00 P.M. SHARP.
I WAKE UP AT DAWN.
AT LEAST, THAT'S THE PLAN.
PLINK

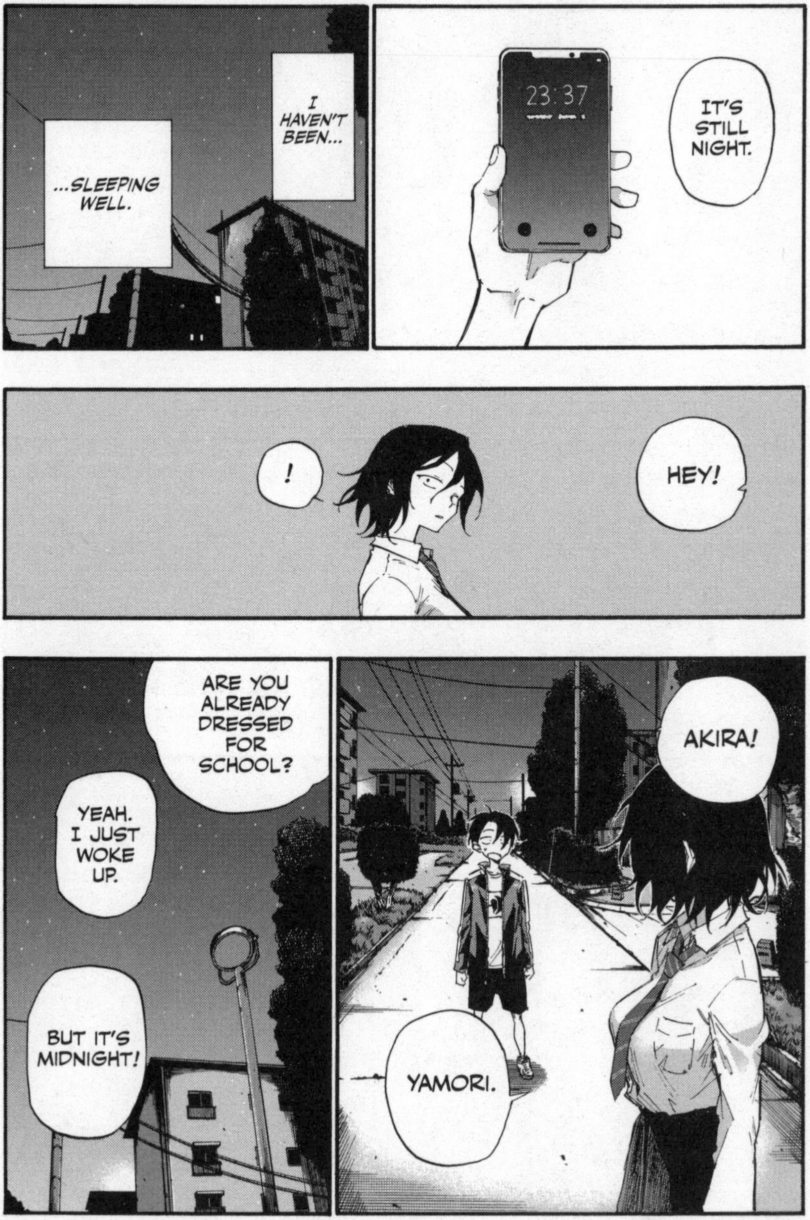
23:37
IT'S STILL NIGHT.
I HAVEN'T BEEN...
...SLEEPING WELL.
HEY!
!
AKIRA!
YAMORI.
ARE YOU ALREADY DRESSED FOR SCHOOL?
YEAH. I JUST WOKE UP.
BUT IT'S MIDNIGHT!

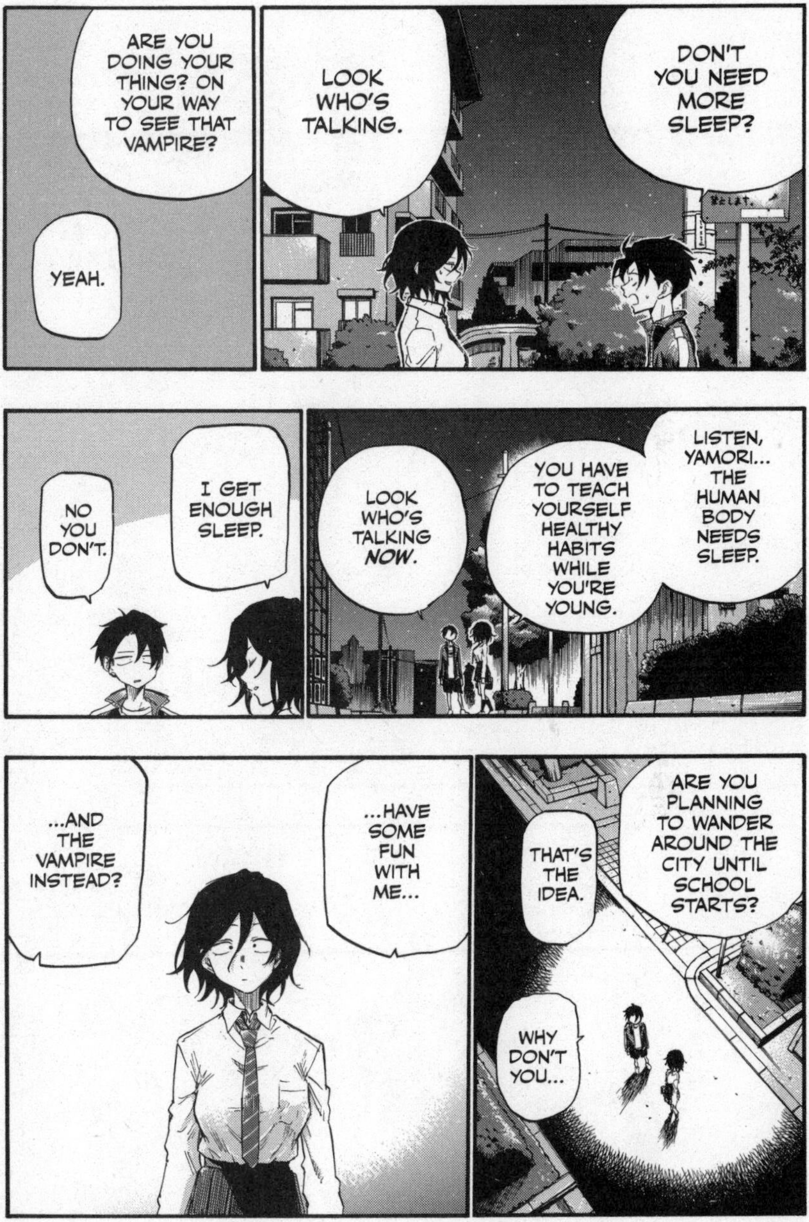
DON'T YOU NEED MORE SLEEP?
LOOK WHO'S TALKING.
ARE YOU DOING YOUR THING? ON YOUR WAY TO SEE THAT VAMPIRE?
YEAH.
LISTEN, YAMORI... THE HUMAN BODY NEEDS SLEEP.
YOU HAVE TO TEACH YOURSELF HEALTHY HABITS WHILE YOU'RE YOUNG.
LOOK WHO'S TALKING *NOW*.
I GET ENOUGH SLEEP.
NO YOU DON'T.
ARE YOU PLANNING TO WANDER AROUND THE CITY UNTIL SCHOOL STARTS?
THAT'S THE IDEA.
WHY DON'T YOU...
...HAVE SOME FUN WITH ME...
...AND THE VAMPIRE INSTEAD?

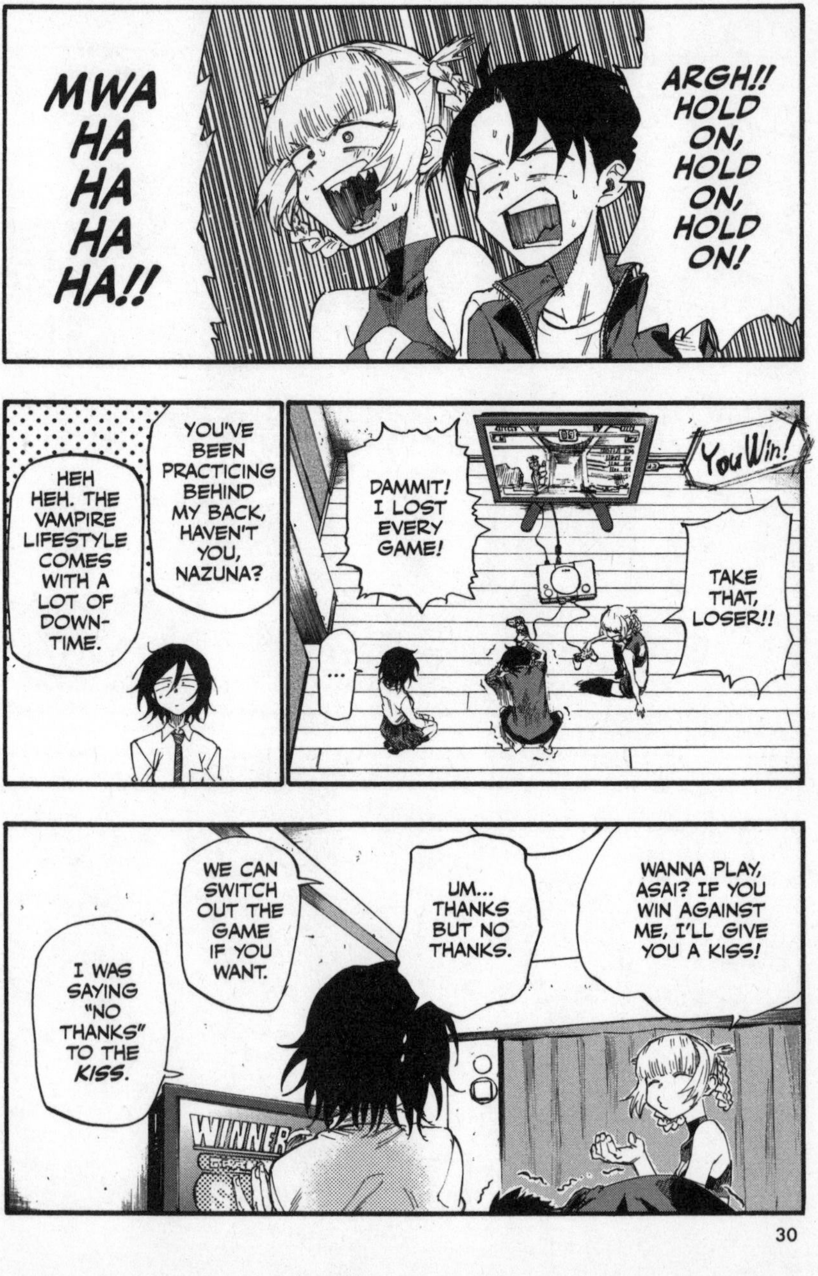
ARGH!! HOLD ON, HOLD ON, HOLD ON!
MWA HA HA HA HA!!
You Win!
TAKE THAT, LOSER!!
DAMMIT! I LOST EVERY GAME!
...
YOU'VE BEEN PRACTICING BEHIND MY BACK, HAVEN'T YOU, NAZUNA?
HEH HEH. THE VAMPIRE LIFESTYLE COMES WITH A LOT OF DOWN-TIME.
WANNA PLAY, ASAI? IF YOU WIN AGAINST ME, I'LL GIVE YOU A KISS!
UM... THANKS BUT NO THANKS.
WE CAN SWITCH OUT THE GAME IF YOU WANT.
I WAS SAYING "NO THANKS" TO THE *KISS*.
WINNER

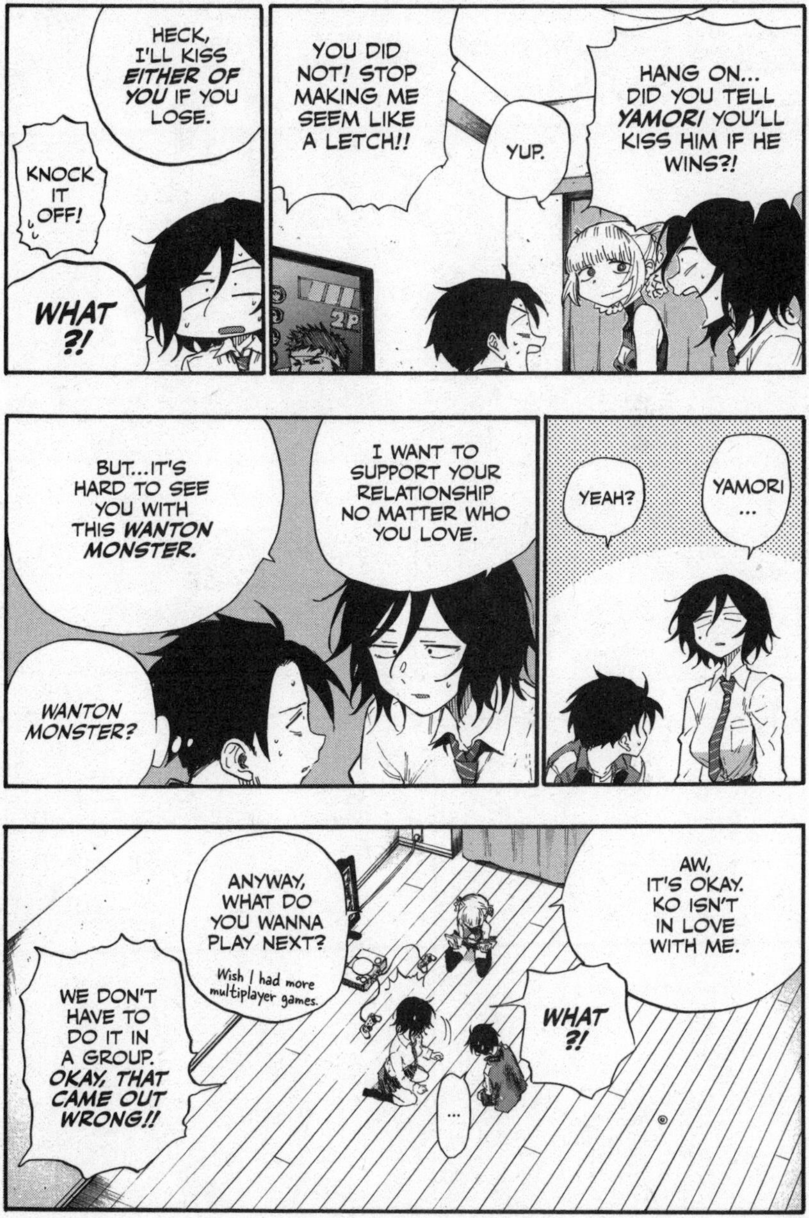
HANG ON... DID YOU TELL YAMORI YOU'LL KISS HIM IF HE WINS?!
YUP.
YOU DID NOT! STOP MAKING ME SEEM LIKE A LETCH!!
2P
HECK, I'LL KISS EITHER OF YOU IF YOU LOSE.
KNOCK IT OFF!
WHAT?!
YAMORI ...
YEAH?
I WANT TO SUPPORT YOUR RELATIONSHIP NO MATTER WHO YOU LOVE.
BUT...IT'S HARD TO SEE YOU WITH THIS WANTON MONSTER.
WANTON MONSTER?
AW, IT'S OKAY. KO ISN'T IN LOVE WITH ME.
WHAT?!
...
ANYWAY, WHAT DO YOU WANNA PLAY NEXT?
Wish I had more multiplayer games.
WE DON'T HAVE TO DO IT IN A GROUP. OKAY, THAT CAME OUT WRONG!!

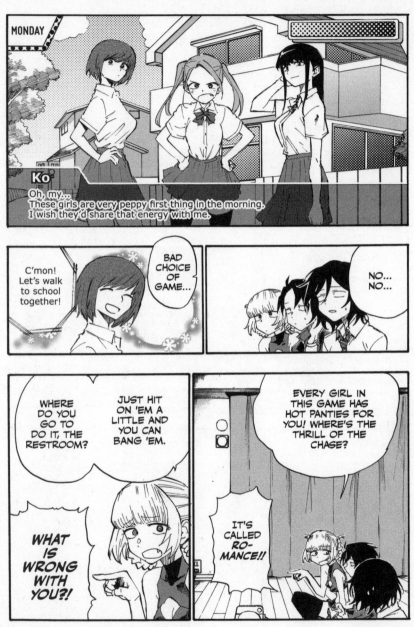

MONDAY
Ko
Oh, my...
These girls are very peppy first thing in the morning.
I wish they'd share that energy with me.
NO... NO...
BAD CHOICE OF GAME...
C'mon! Let's walk to school together!
EVERY GIRL IN THIS GAME HAS HOT PANTIES FOR YOU! WHERE'S THE THRILL OF THE CHASE?
IT'S CALLED RO-MANCE!!
JUST HIT ON 'EM A LITTLE AND YOU CAN BANG 'EM.
WHERE DO YOU GO TO DO IT, THE RESTROOM?
WHAT IS WRONG WITH YOU?!

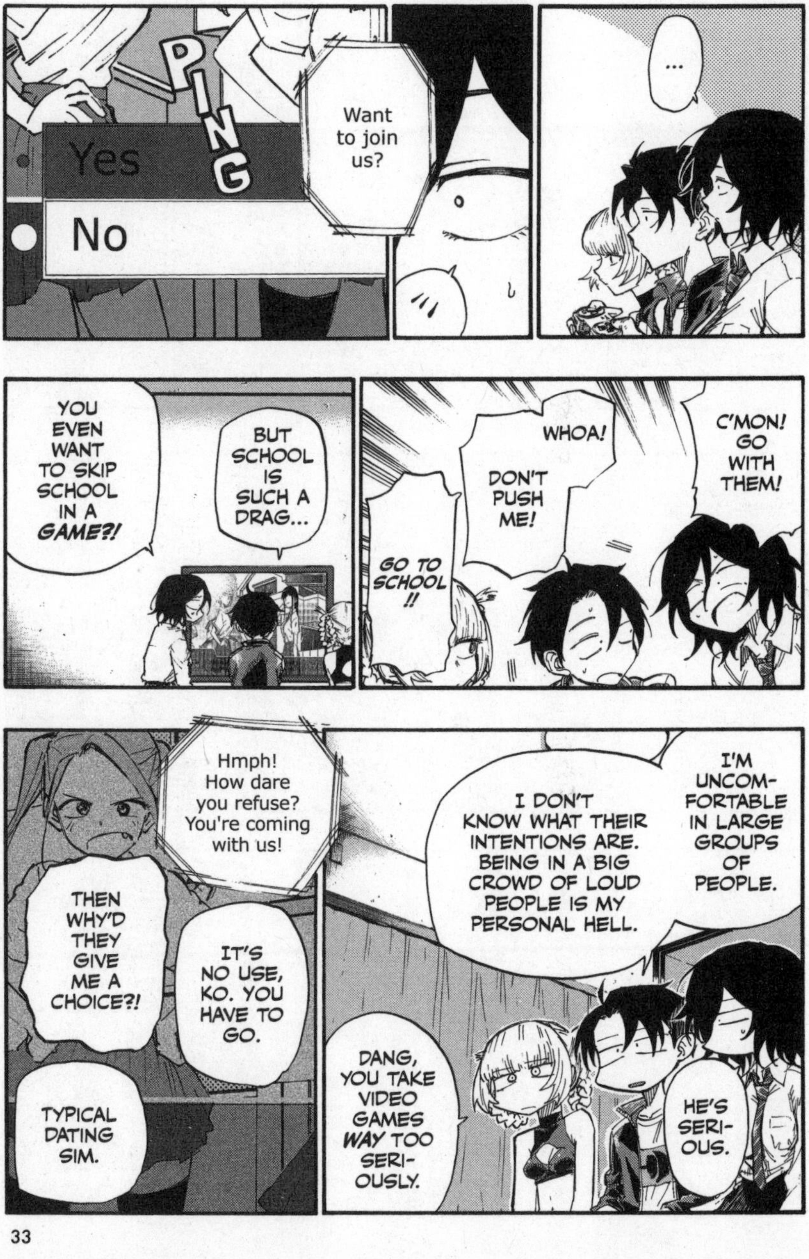
...
Want to join us?
PING
Yes
No
C'MON! GO WITH THEM!
WHOA!
DON'T PUSH ME!
GO TO SCHOOL!!
BUT SCHOOL IS SUCH A DRAG...
YOU EVEN WANT TO SKIP SCHOOL IN A GAME?!
I'M UNCOM-FORTABLE IN LARGE GROUPS OF PEOPLE.
I DON'T KNOW WHAT THEIR INTENTIONS ARE. BEING IN A BIG CROWD OF LOUD PEOPLE IS MY PERSONAL HELL.
HE'S SERI-OUS.
DANG, YOU TAKE VIDEO GAMES WAY TOO SERI-OUSLY.
Hmph! How dare you refuse? You're coming with us!
IT'S NO USE, KO. YOU HAVE TO GO.
THEN WHY'D THEY GIVE ME A CHOICE?!
TYPICAL DATING SIM.

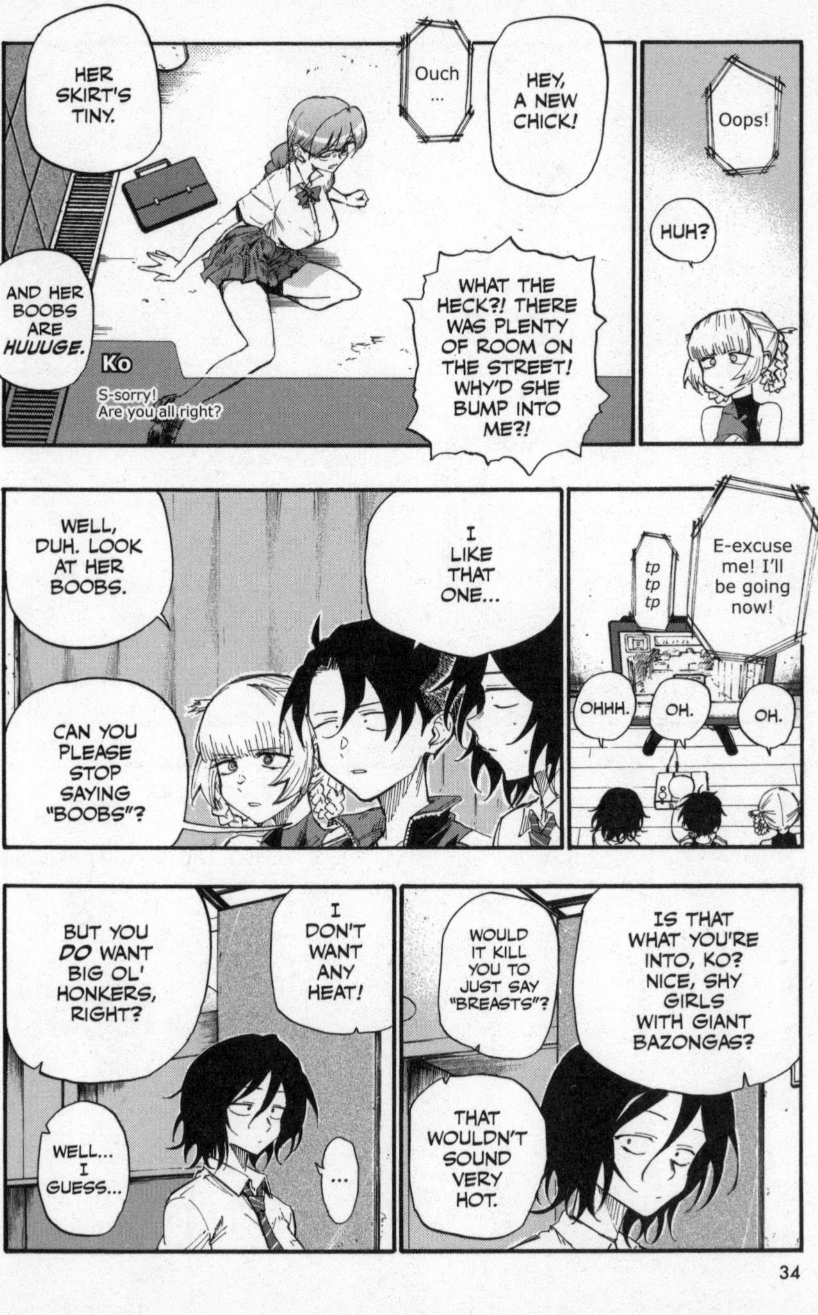
Oops!
HUH?
HEY, A NEW CHICK!
Ouch ...
WHAT THE HECK?! THERE WAS PLENTY OF ROOM ON THE STREET! WHY'D SHE BUMP INTO ME?!
HER SKIRT'S TINY.
AND HER BOOBS ARE *HUUUGE.*
Ko
S-sorry! Are you all right?
E-excuse me! I'll be going now!
tp tp tp
OH.
OH.
OHHH.
I LIKE THAT ONE...
WELL, DUH. LOOK AT HER BOOBS.
CAN YOU PLEASE STOP SAYING "BOOBS"?
IS THAT WHAT YOU'RE INTO, KO? NICE, SHY GIRLS WITH GIANT BAZONGAS?
WOULD IT KILL YOU TO JUST SAY "BREASTS"?
THAT WOULDN'T SOUND VERY HOT.
I DON'T WANT ANY HEAT!
BUT YOU *DO* WANT BIG OL' HONKERS, RIGHT?
...
WELL... I GUESS...

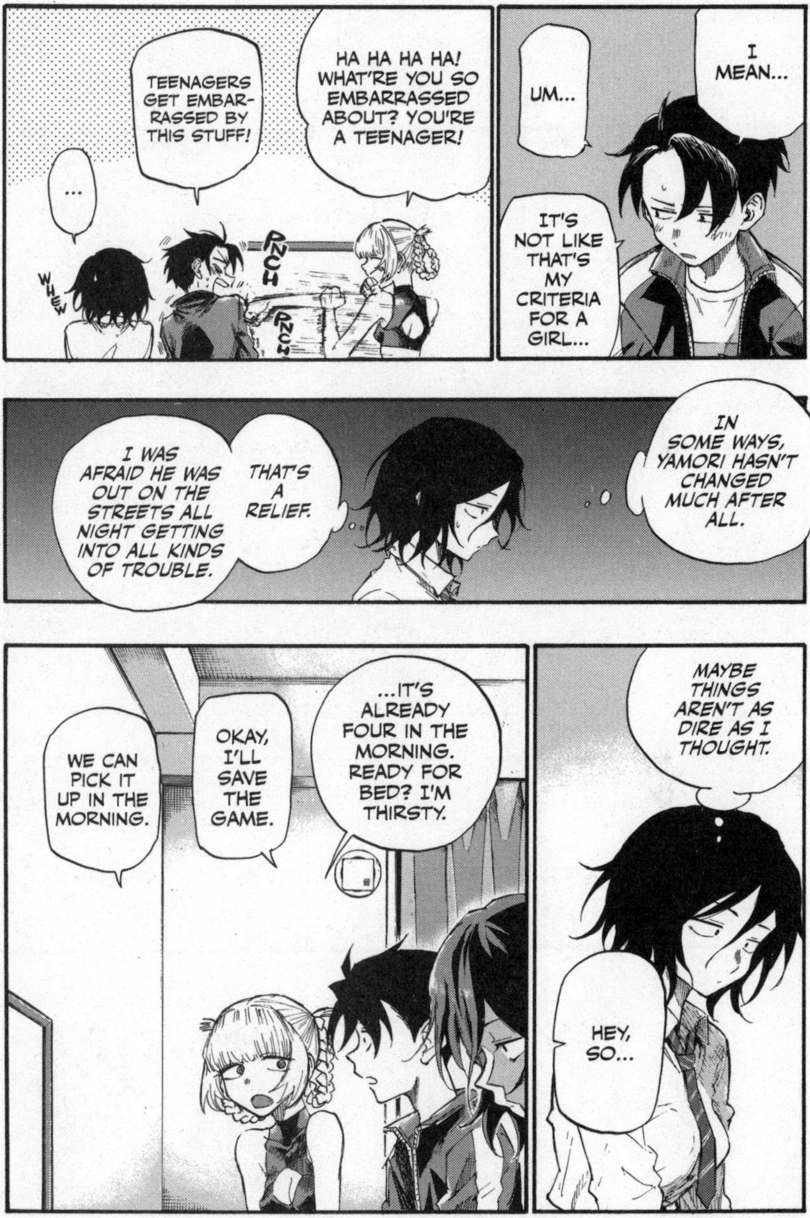
I MEAN...
UM...
IT'S NOT LIKE THAT'S MY CRITERIA FOR A GIRL...
HA HA HA HA! WHAT'RE YOU SO EMBARRASSED ABOUT? YOU'RE A TEENAGER!
TEENAGERS GET EMBARRASSED BY THIS STUFF!
...
PNCH
PNCH
WHEW
IN SOME WAYS, YAMORI HASN'T CHANGED MUCH AFTER ALL.
THAT'S A RELIEF.
I WAS AFRAID HE WAS OUT ON THE STREETS ALL NIGHT GETTING INTO ALL KINDS OF TROUBLE.
MAYBE THINGS AREN'T AS DIRE AS I THOUGHT.
HEY, SO...
...IT'S ALREADY FOUR IN THE MORNING. READY FOR BED? I'M THIRSTY.
OKAY, I'LL SAVE THE GAME.
WE CAN PICK IT UP IN THE MORNING.

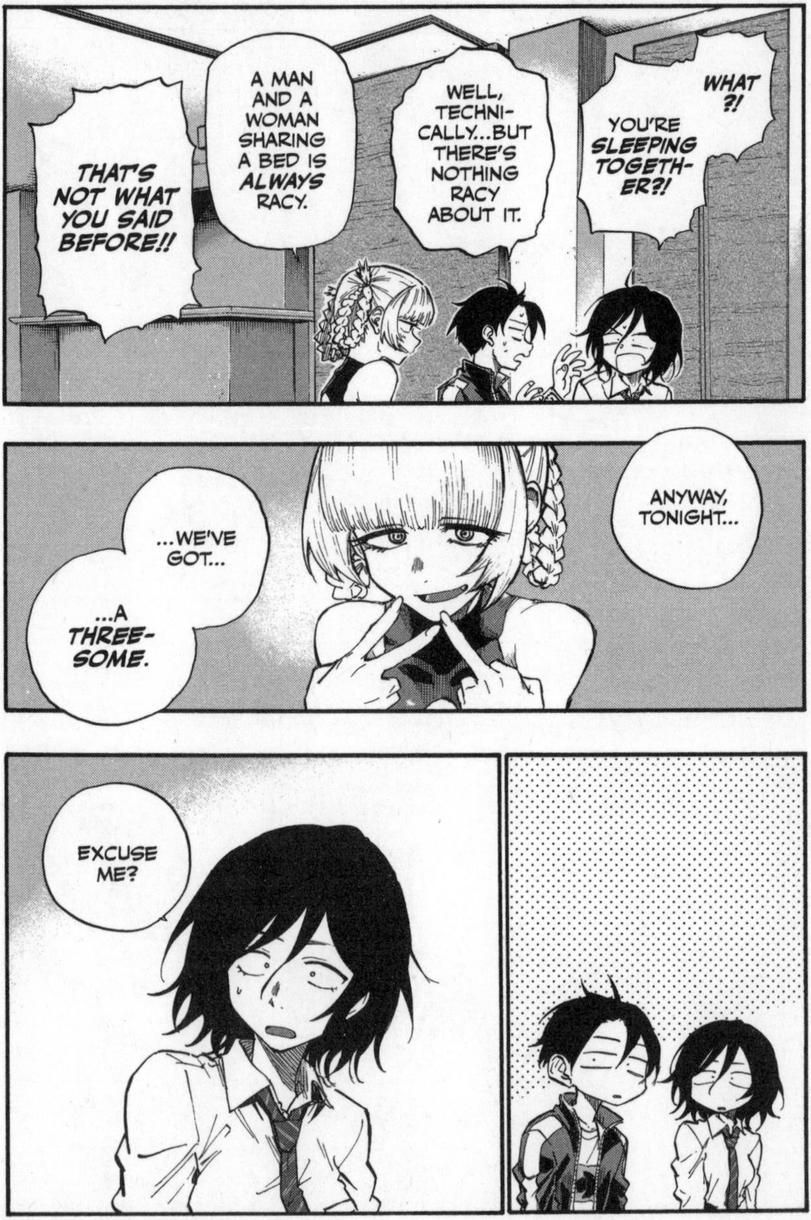
WHAT?!
YOU'RE SLEEPING TOGETHER?!
WELL, TECHNICALLY...BUT THERE'S NOTHING RACY ABOUT IT.
A MAN AND A WOMAN SHARING A BED IS ALWAYS RACY.
THAT'S NOT WHAT YOU SAID BEFORE!!
ANYWAY, TONIGHT...
...WE'VE GOT...
...A THREESOME.
EXCUSE ME?

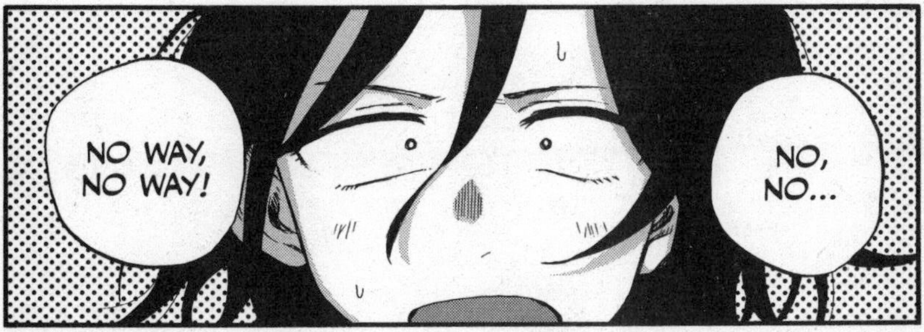
NO, NO...
NO WAY, NO WAY!

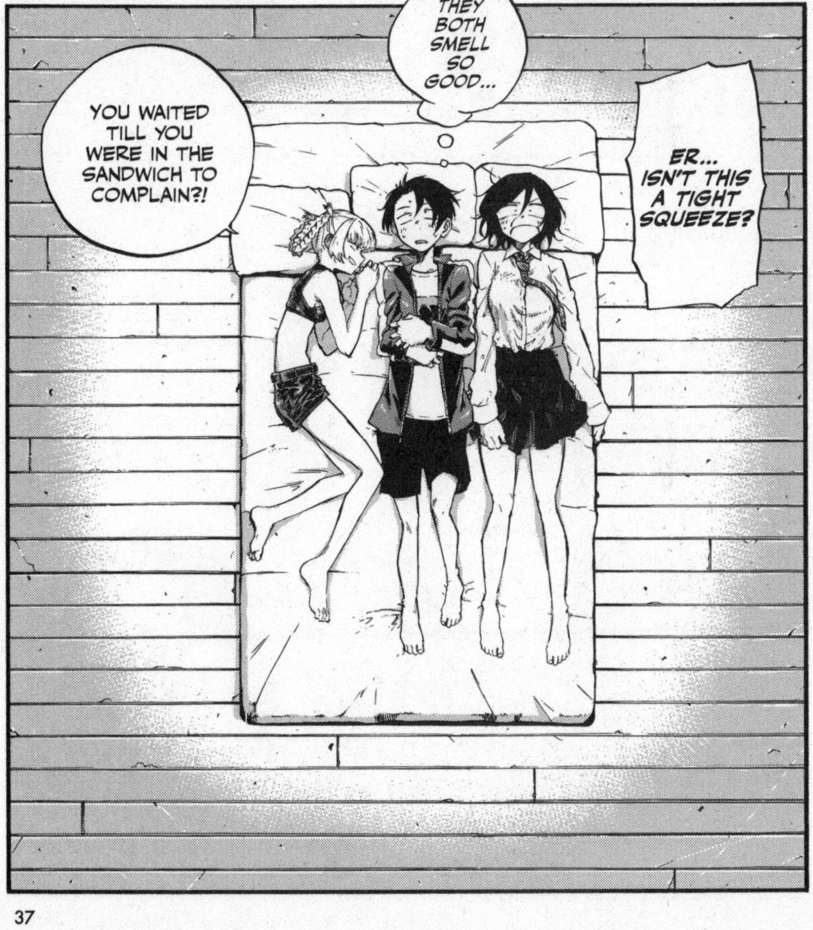
ER... ISN'T THIS A TIGHT SQUEEZE?
THEY BOTH SMELL SO GOOD...
YOU WAITED TILL YOU WERE IN THE SANDWICH TO COMPLAIN?!

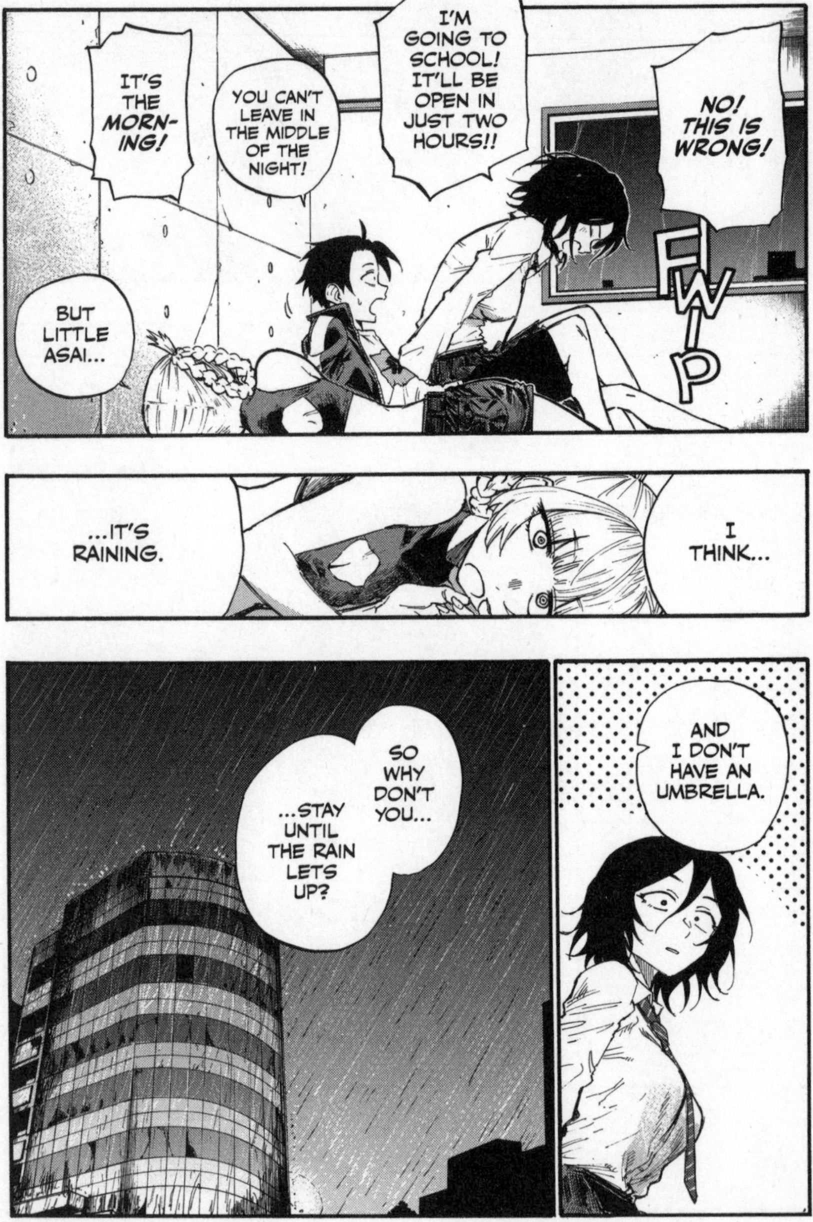
NO! THIS IS WRONG!
FWIP
I'M GOING TO SCHOOL! IT'LL BE OPEN IN JUST TWO HOURS!!
YOU CAN'T LEAVE IN THE MIDDLE OF THE NIGHT!
IT'S THE MORNING!
BUT LITTLE ASAI...
I THINK...
...IT'S RAINING.
AND I DON'T HAVE AN UMBRELLA.
SO WHY DON'T YOU...
...STAY UNTIL THE RAIN LETS UP?

NIGHT 11: SUPPLY AND DEMAND

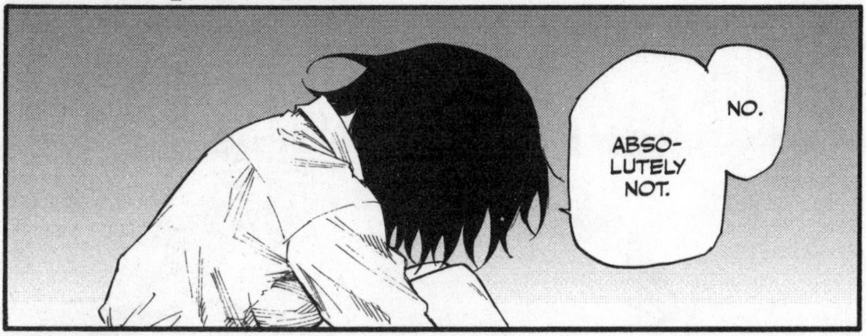
NO.
ABSO-LUTELY NOT.

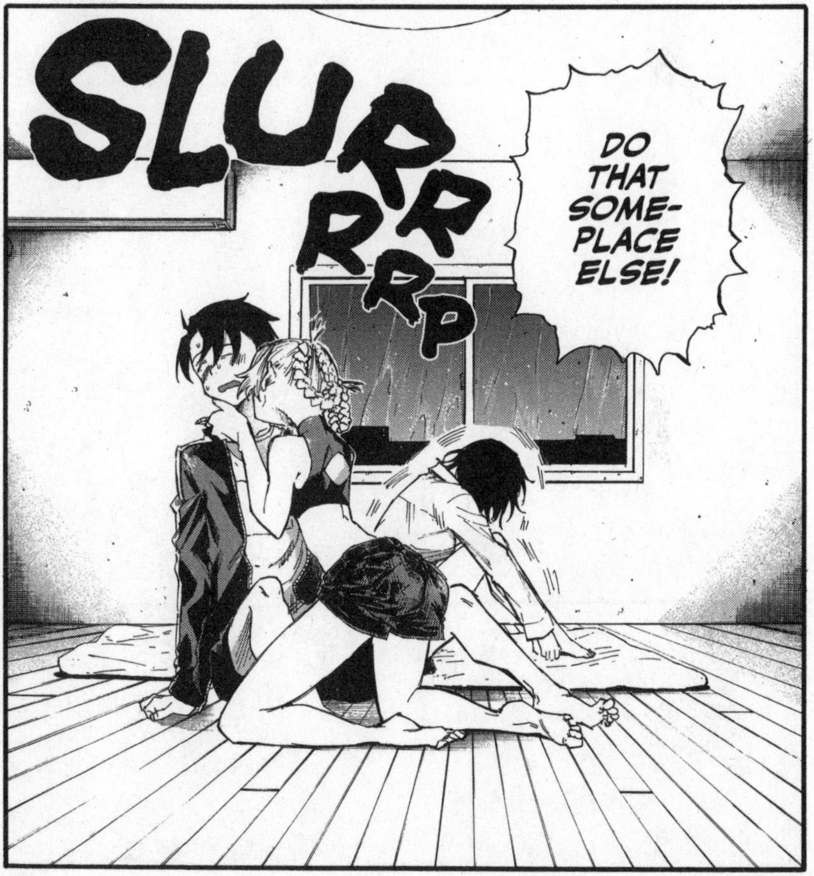
DO THAT SOME-PLACE ELSE!
SLURRRRP

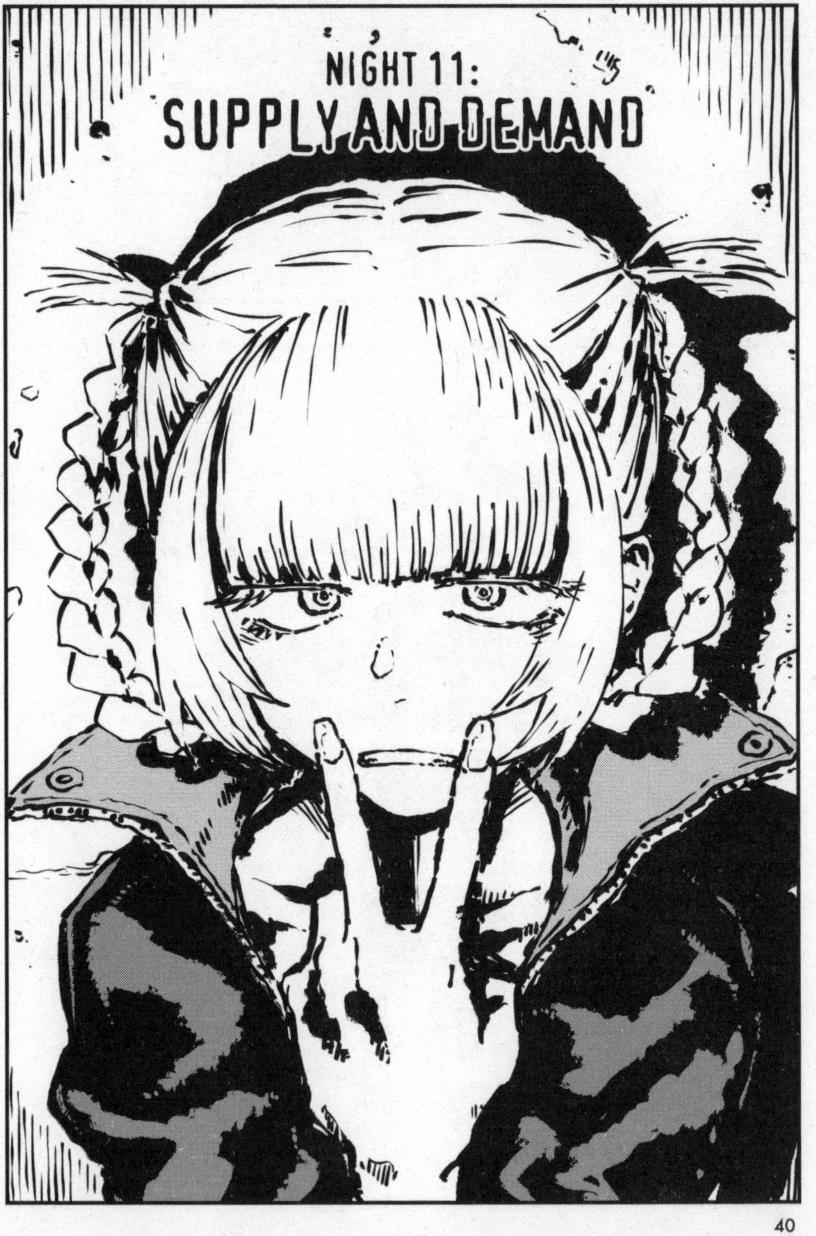
NIGHT 11:
SUPPLY AND DEMAND

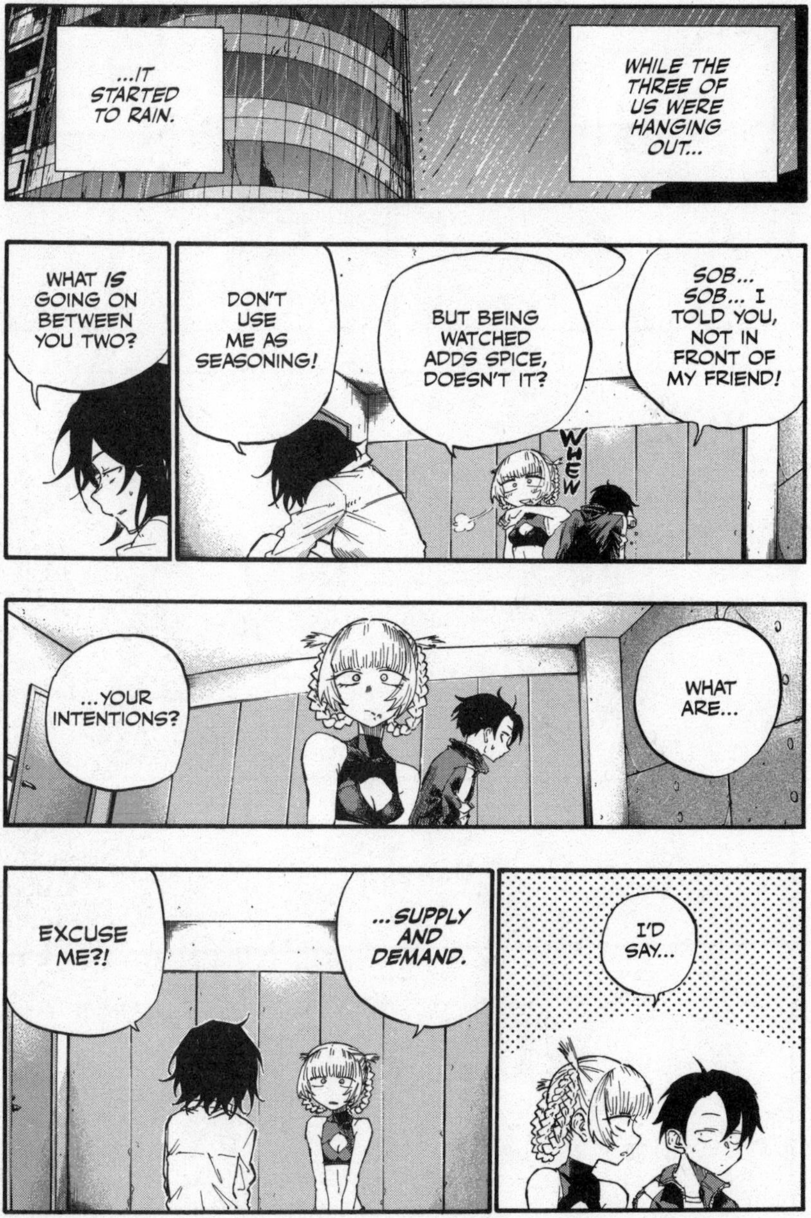
WHILE THE THREE OF US WERE HANGING OUT...
...IT STARTED TO RAIN.
SOB... SOB... I TOLD YOU, NOT IN FRONT OF MY FRIEND!
BUT BEING WATCHED ADDS SPICE, DOESN'T IT?
WHEW
DON'T USE ME AS SEASONING!
WHAT *IS* GOING ON BETWEEN YOU TWO?
WHAT ARE...
...YOUR INTENTIONS?
I'D SAY...
...SUPPLY AND DEMAND.
EXCUSE ME?!

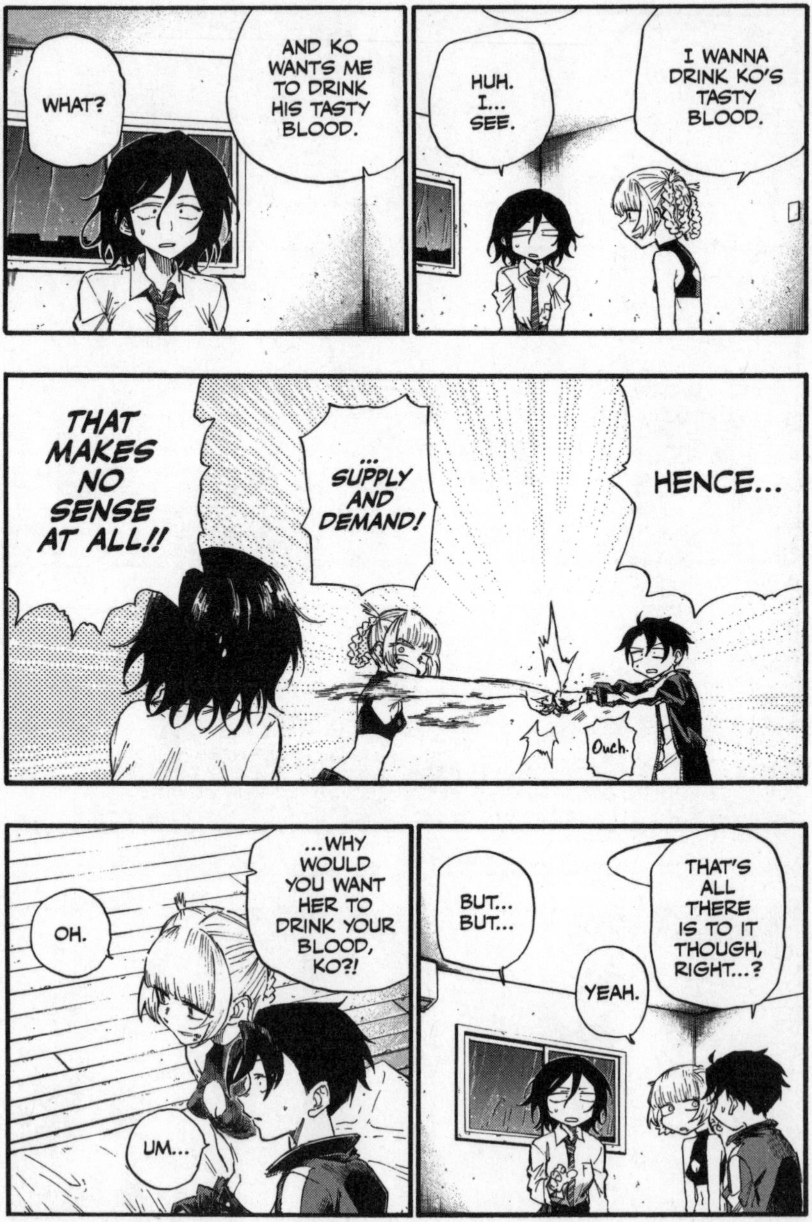
I WANNA DRINK KO'S TASTY BLOOD.
HUH. I... SEE.
AND KO WANTS ME TO DRINK HIS TASTY BLOOD.
WHAT?
HENCE...
... SUPPLY AND DEMAND!
THAT MAKES NO SENSE AT ALL!!
Ouch.
THAT'S ALL THERE IS TO IT THOUGH, RIGHT...?
YEAH.
BUT... BUT...
...WHY WOULD YOU WANT HER TO DRINK YOUR BLOOD, KO?!
OH.
UM...

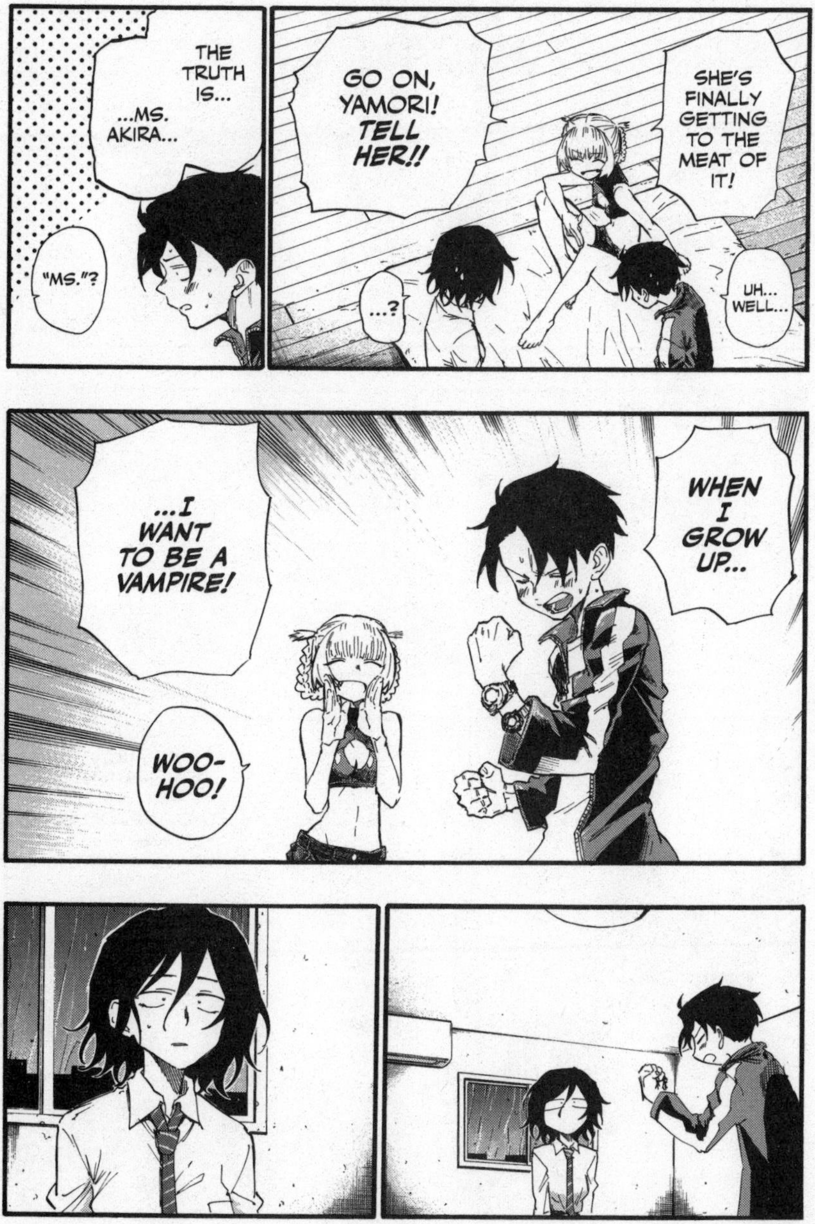
SHE'S FINALLY GETTING TO THE MEAT OF IT!
GO ON, YAMORI! TELL HER!!
UH... WELL...
...?
THE TRUTH IS... ...MS. AKIRA...
"MS."?
WHEN I GROW UP...
...I WANT TO BE A VAMPIRE!
WOO-HOO!

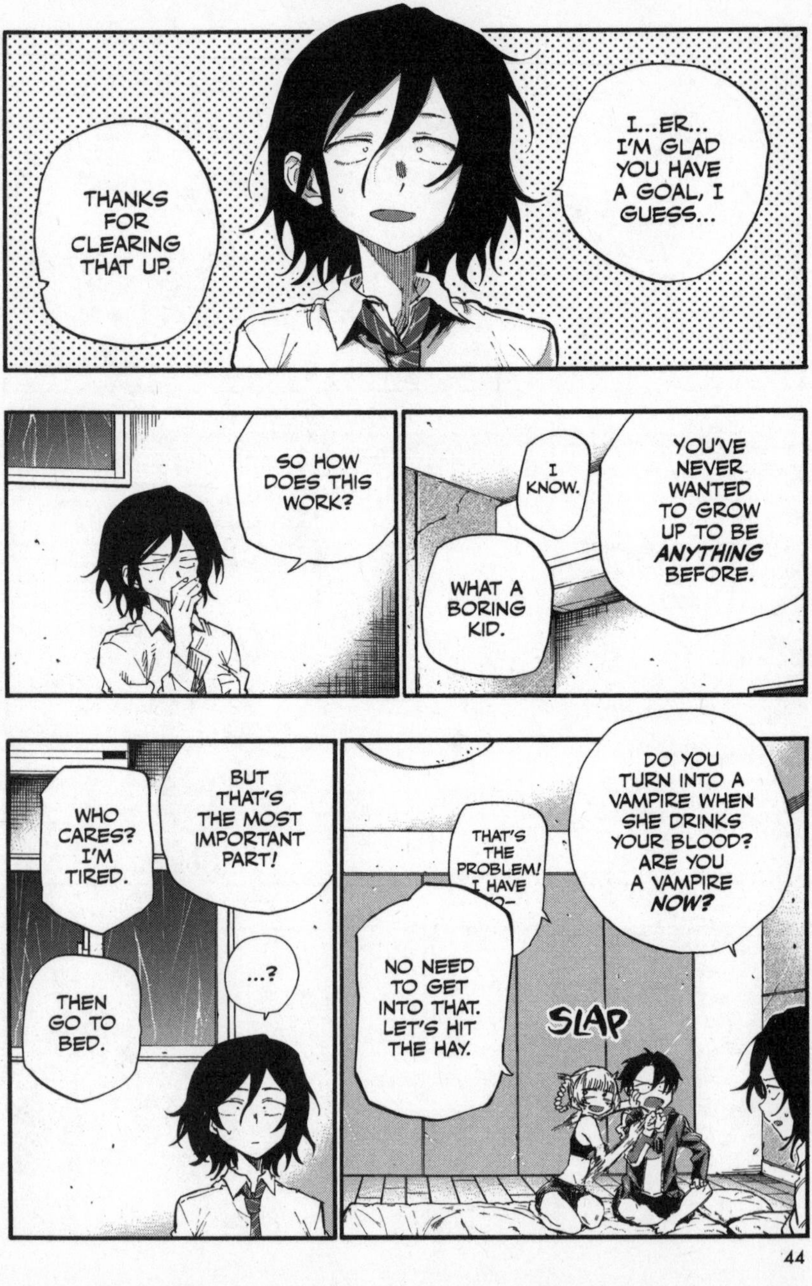
I...ER... I'M GLAD YOU HAVE A GOAL, I GUESS...
THANKS FOR CLEARING THAT UP.
YOU'VE NEVER WANTED TO GROW UP TO BE *ANYTHING* BEFORE.
I KNOW.
WHAT A BORING KID.
SO HOW DOES THIS WORK?
DO YOU TURN INTO A VAMPIRE WHEN SHE DRINKS YOUR BLOOD? ARE YOU A VAMPIRE *NOW?*
THAT'S THE PROBLEM! I HAVE
NO NEED TO GET INTO THAT. LET'S HIT THE HAY.
SLAP
BUT THAT'S THE MOST IMPORTANT PART!
WHO CARES? I'M TIRED.
...?
THEN GO TO BED.

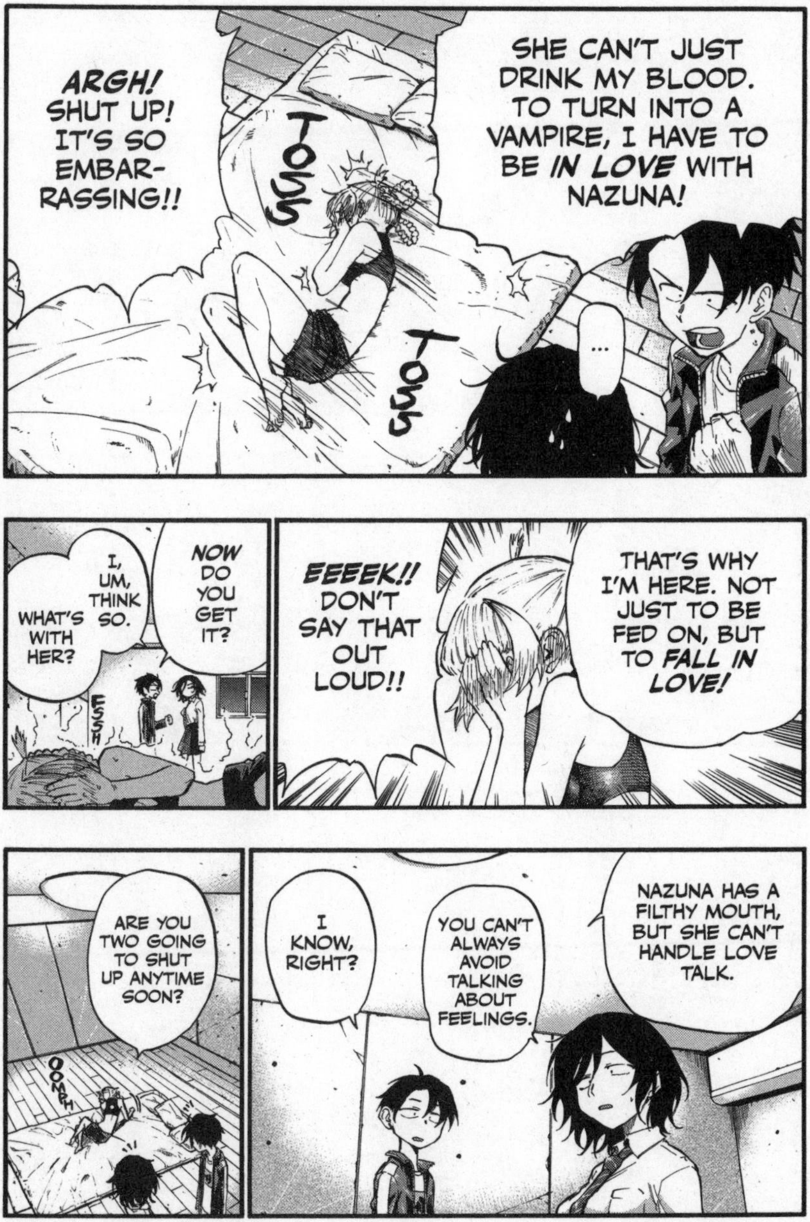
SHE CAN'T JUST DRINK MY BLOOD. TO TURN INTO A VAMPIRE, I HAVE TO BE *IN LOVE* WITH NAZUNA!
...
TOSS
TOSS
ARGH! SHUT UP! IT'S SO EMBAR-RASSING!!
THAT'S WHY I'M HERE. NOT JUST TO BE FED ON, BUT TO ***FALL IN LOVE!***
EEEEK!! DON'T SAY THAT OUT LOUD!!
NOW DO YOU GET IT?
I, UM, THINK SO.
WHAT'S WITH HER?
NAZUNA HAS A FILTHY MOUTH, BUT SHE CAN'T HANDLE LOVE TALK.
YOU CAN'T ALWAYS AVOID TALKING ABOUT FEELINGS.
I KNOW, RIGHT?
ARE YOU TWO GOING TO SHUT UP ANYTIME SOON?
OOMPH

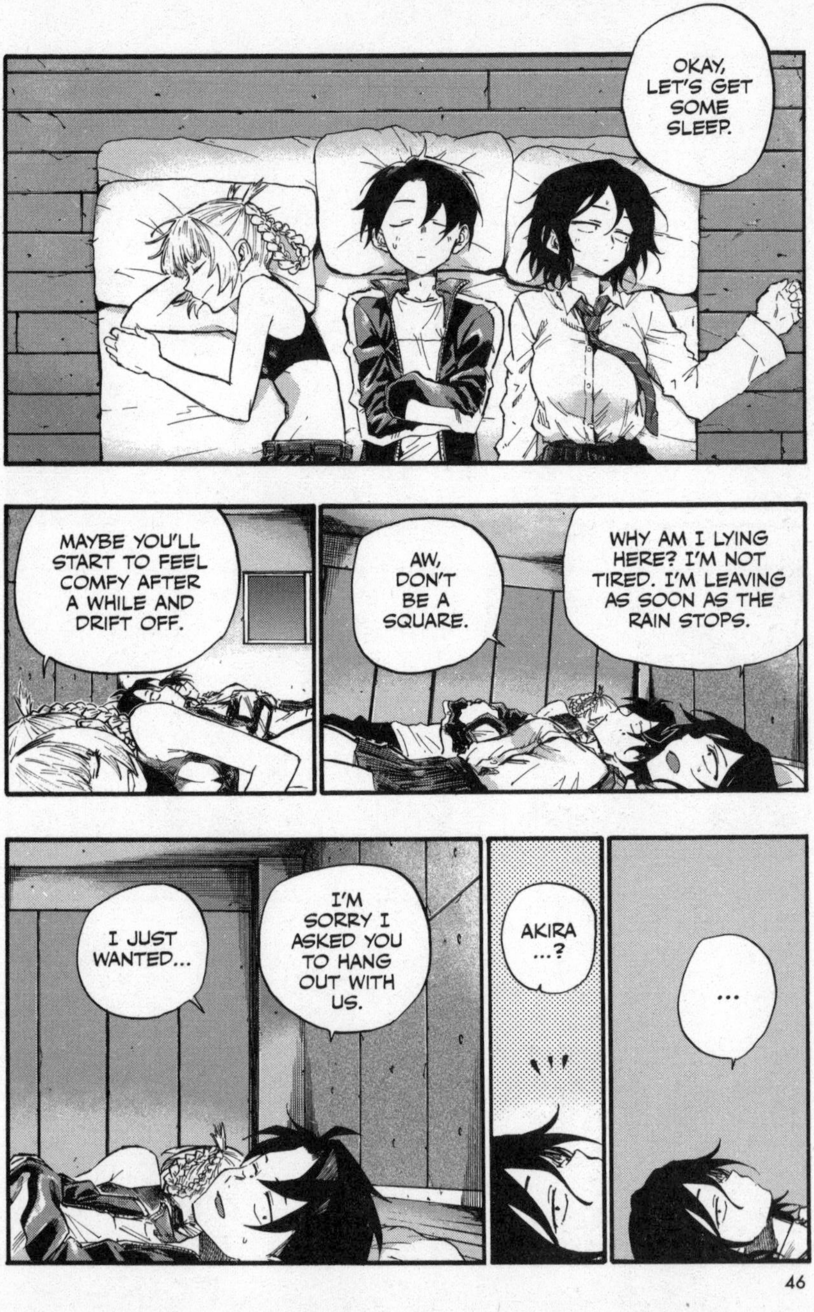
OKAY, LET'S GET SOME SLEEP.
WHY AM I LYING HERE? I'M NOT TIRED. I'M LEAVING AS SOON AS THE RAIN STOPS.
AW, DON'T BE A SQUARE.
MAYBE YOU'LL START TO FEEL COMFY AFTER A WHILE AND DRIFT OFF.
...
AKIRA ...?
I'M SORRY I ASKED YOU TO HANG OUT WITH US.
I JUST WANTED...

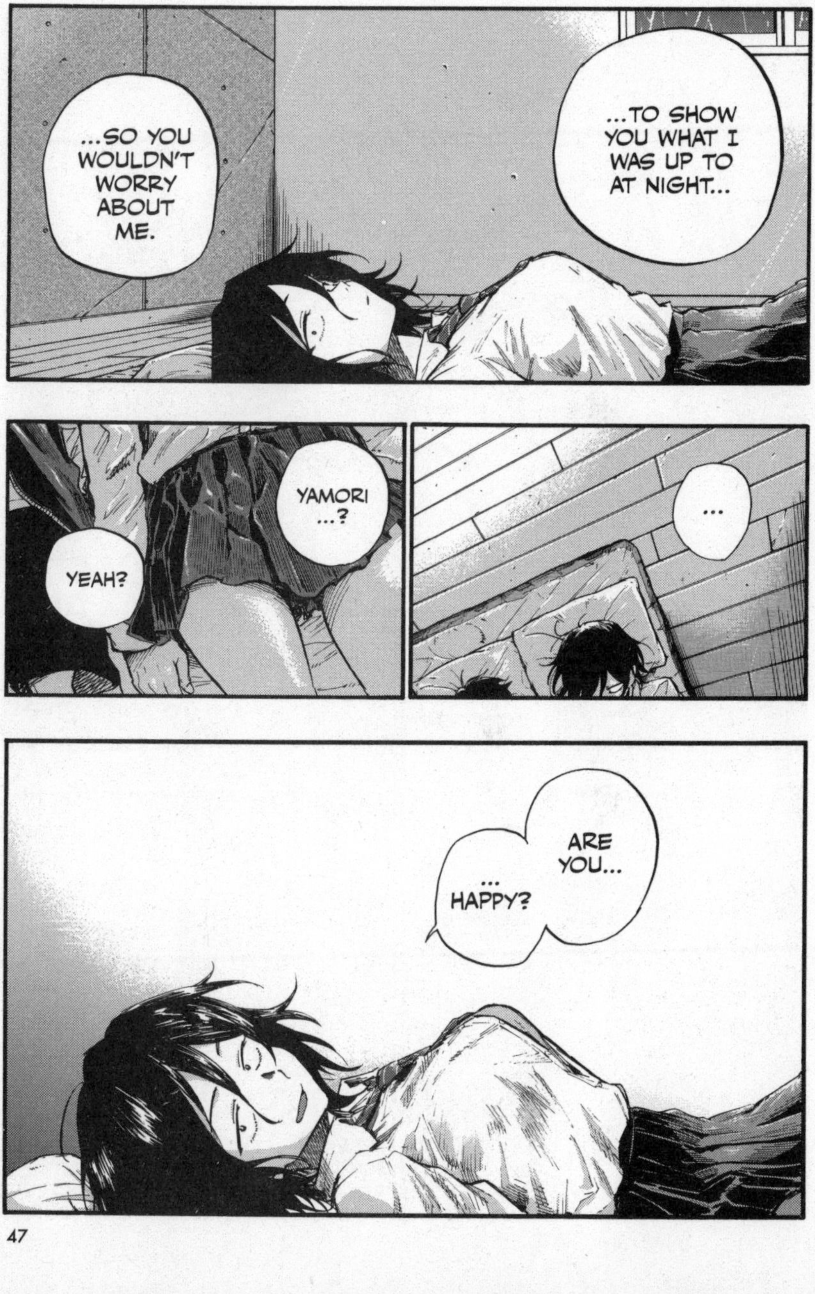
...TO SHOW YOU WHAT I WAS UP TO AT NIGHT...
...SO YOU WOULDN'T WORRY ABOUT ME.
...
YAMORI ...?
YEAH?
ARE YOU... ...HAPPY?

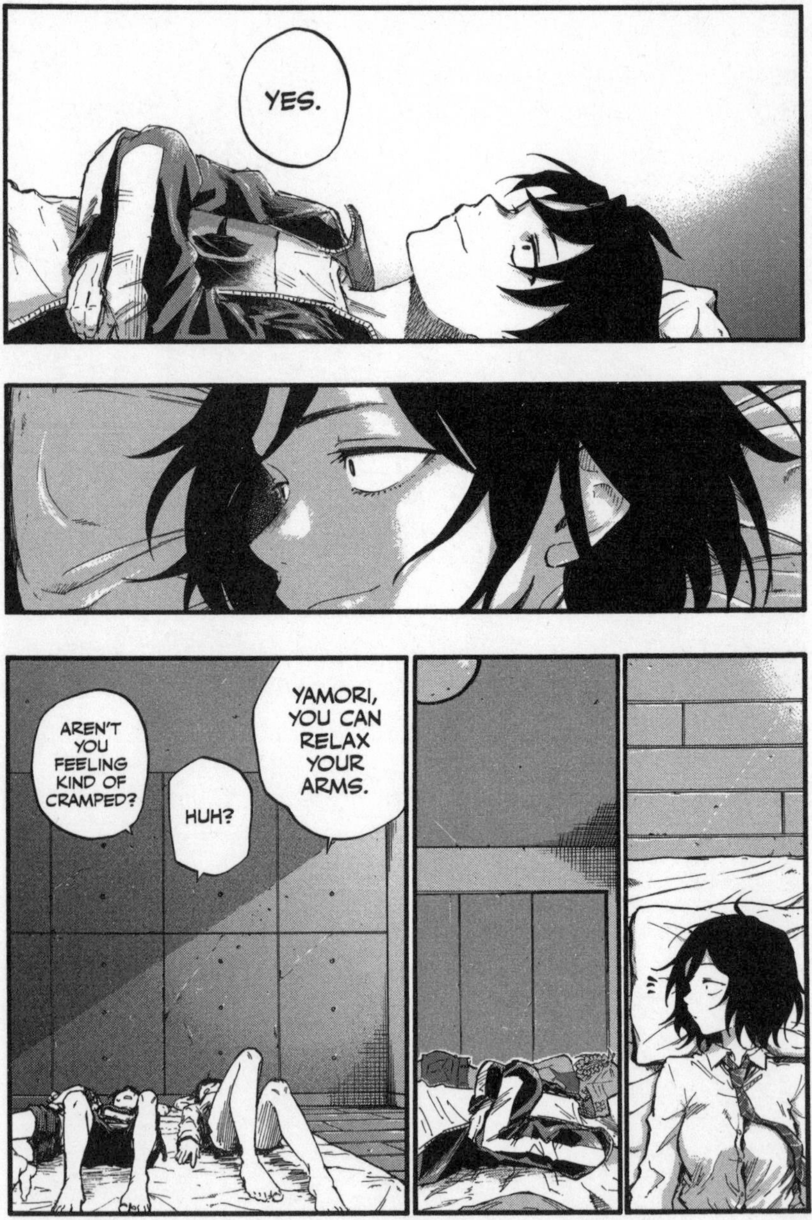
YES.
YAMORI, YOU CAN RELAX YOUR ARMS.
HUH?
AREN'T YOU FEELING KIND OF CRAMPED?

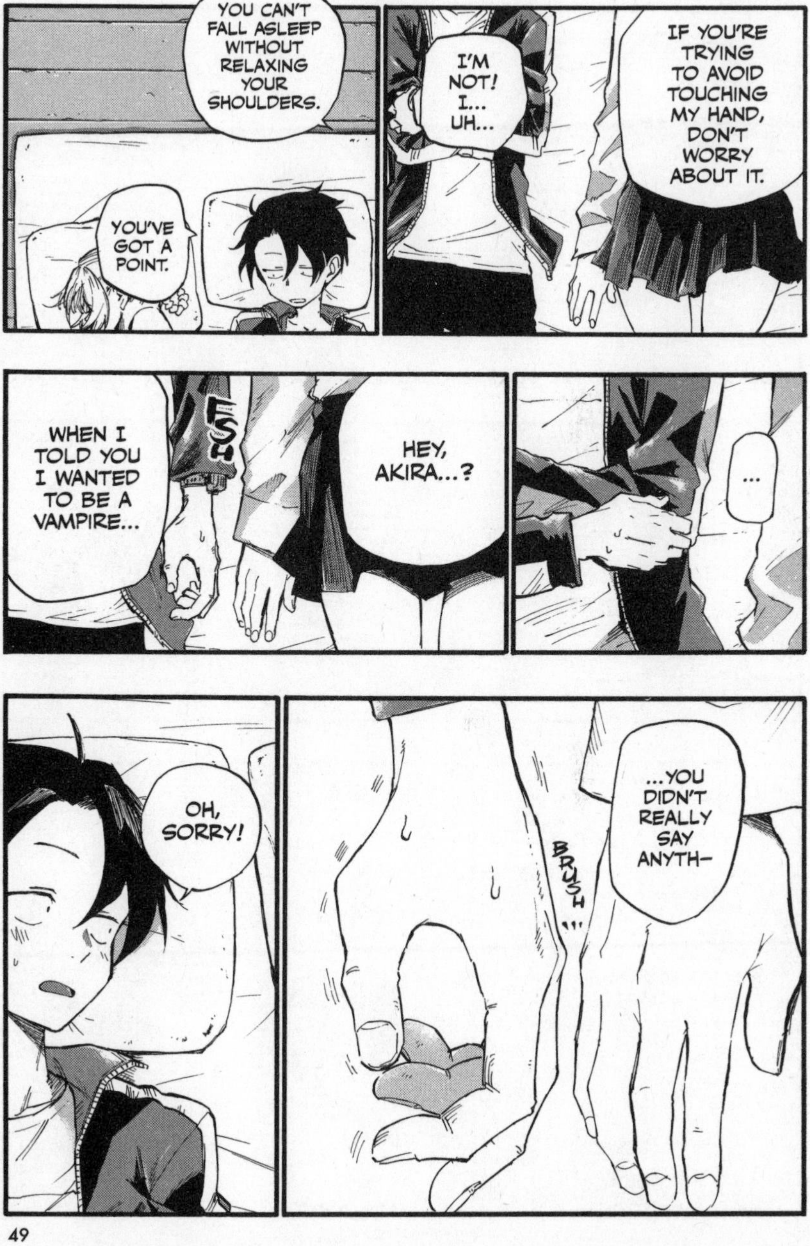
IF YOU'RE TRYING TO AVOID TOUCHING MY HAND, DON'T WORRY ABOUT IT.
I'M NOT! I... UH...
YOU CAN'T FALL ASLEEP WITHOUT RELAXING YOUR SHOULDERS.
YOU'VE GOT A POINT.
...
HEY, AKIRA...?
FSH
WHEN I TOLD YOU I WANTED TO BE A VAMPIRE...
...YOU DIDN'T REALLY SAY ANYTH-
BRUSH...
OH, SORRY!

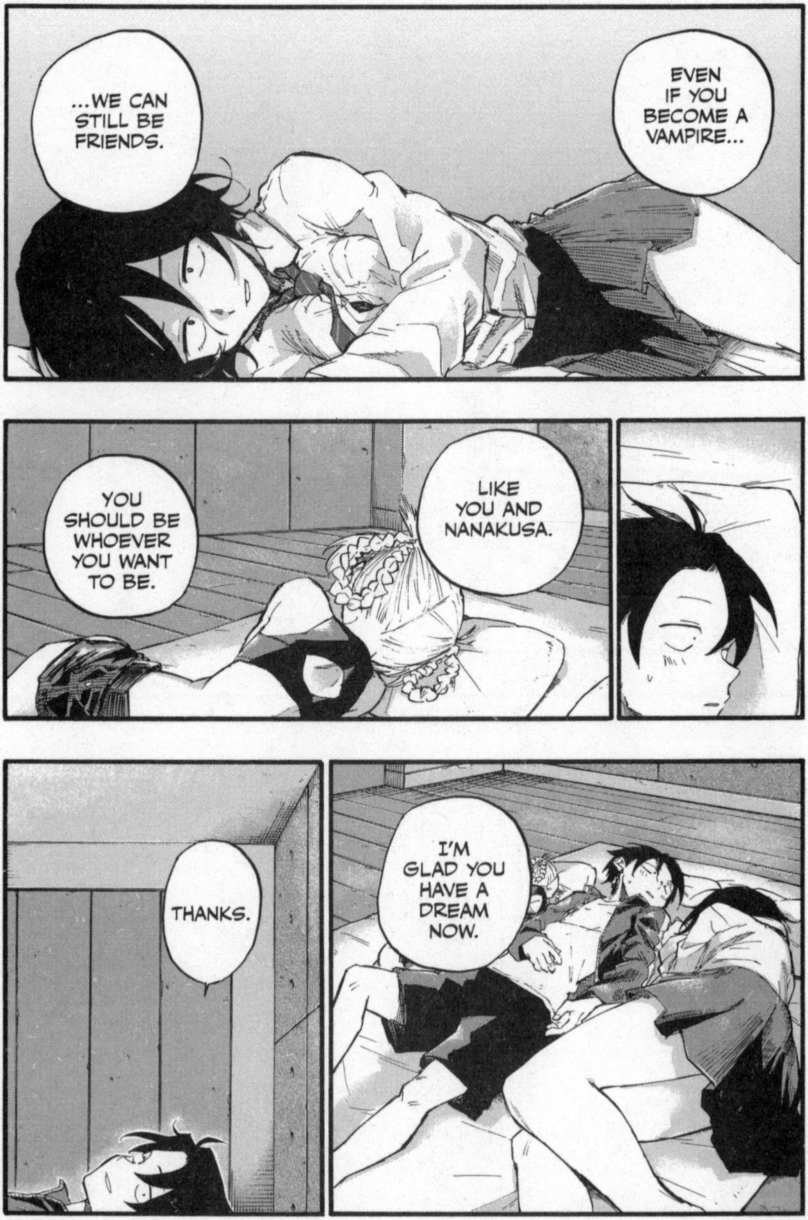
EVEN IF YOU BECOME A VAMPIRE...
...WE CAN STILL BE FRIENDS.
LIKE YOU AND NANAKUSA.
YOU SHOULD BE WHOEVER YOU WANT TO BE.
I'M GLAD YOU HAVE A DREAM NOW.
THANKS.

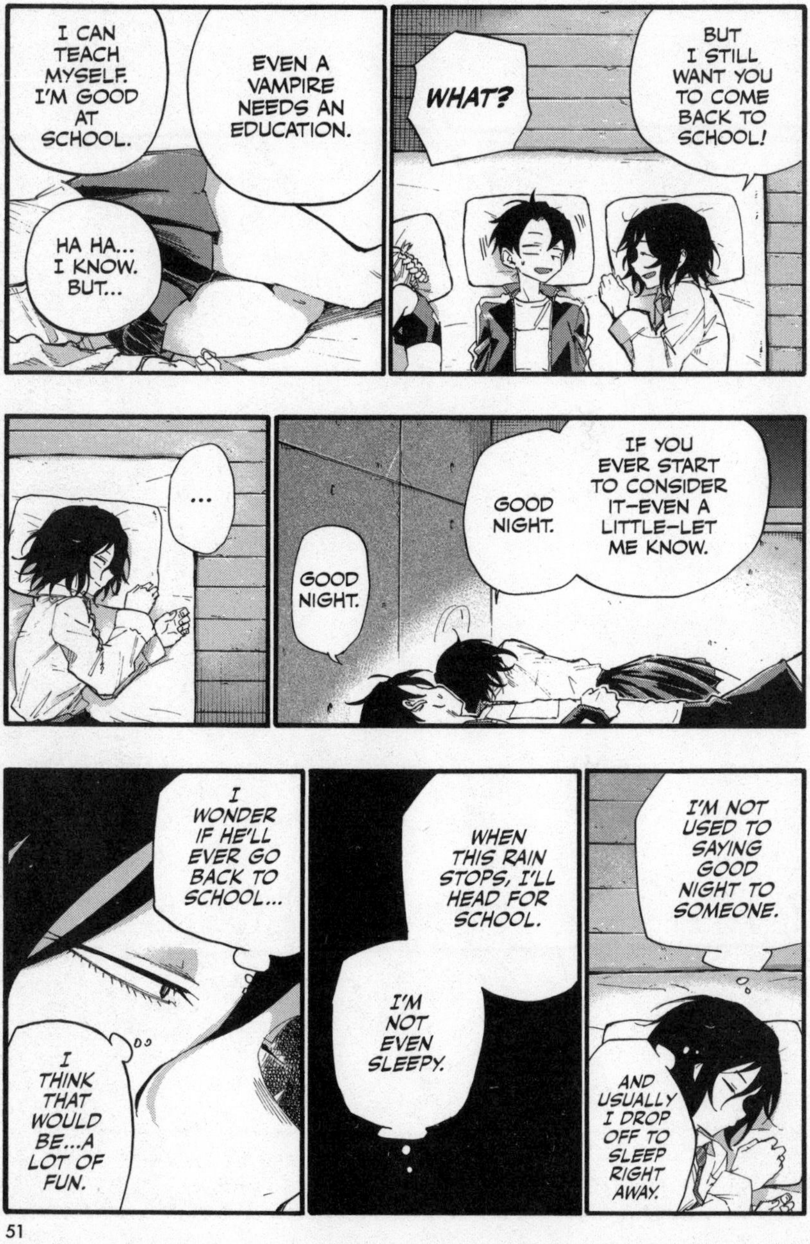
BUT I STILL WANT YOU TO COME BACK TO SCHOOL!
WHAT?
EVEN A VAMPIRE NEEDS AN EDUCATION.
I CAN TEACH MYSELF. I'M GOOD AT SCHOOL.
HA HA... I KNOW. BUT...
IF YOU EVER START TO CONSIDER IT—EVEN A LITTLE—LET ME KNOW.
GOOD NIGHT.
GOOD NIGHT.
...
I'M NOT USED TO SAYING GOOD NIGHT TO SOMEONE.
AND USUALLY I DROP OFF TO SLEEP RIGHT AWAY.
WHEN THIS RAIN STOPS, I'LL HEAD FOR SCHOOL.
I'M NOT EVEN SLEEPY.
I WONDER IF HE'LL EVER GO BACK TO SCHOOL...
I THINK THAT WOULD BE...A LOT OF FUN.

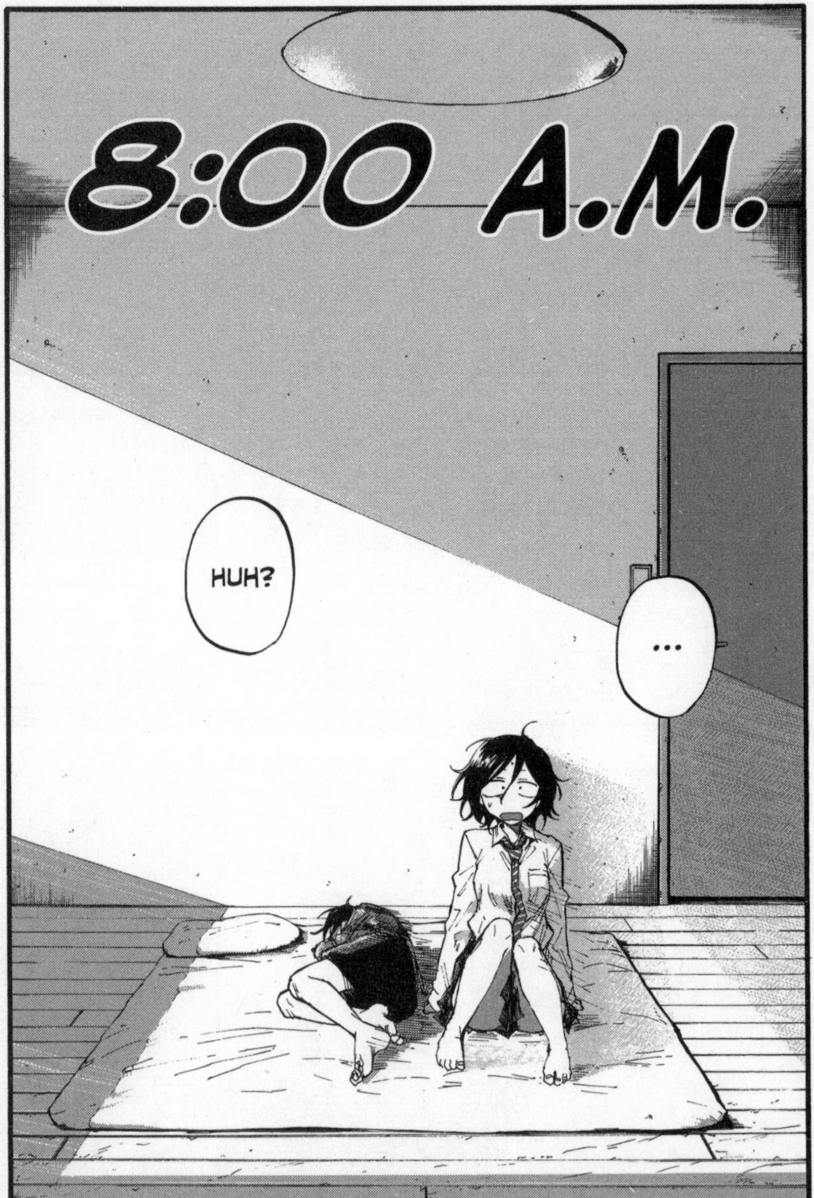
8:00 A.M.
...
HUH?

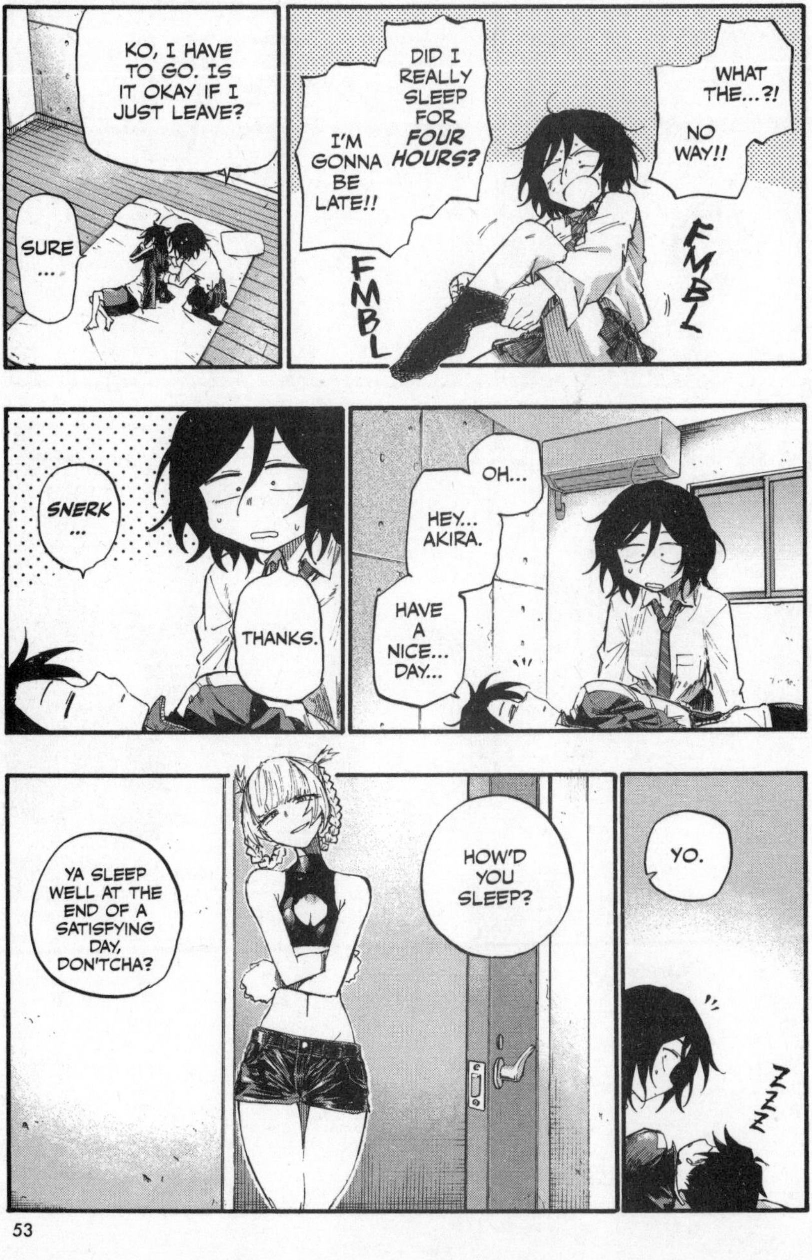
WHAT THE...?!
NO WAY!!
DID I REALLY SLEEP FOR FOUR HOURS?
I'M GONNA BE LATE!!
FMBL
FMBL
KO, I HAVE TO GO. IS IT OKAY IF I JUST LEAVE?
SURE ...
OH...
HEY... AKIRA.
HAVE A NICE... DAY...
SNERK ...
THANKS.
YO.
ZZZ
HOW'D YOU SLEEP?
YA SLEEP WELL AT THE END OF A SATISFYING DAY, DON'TCHA?

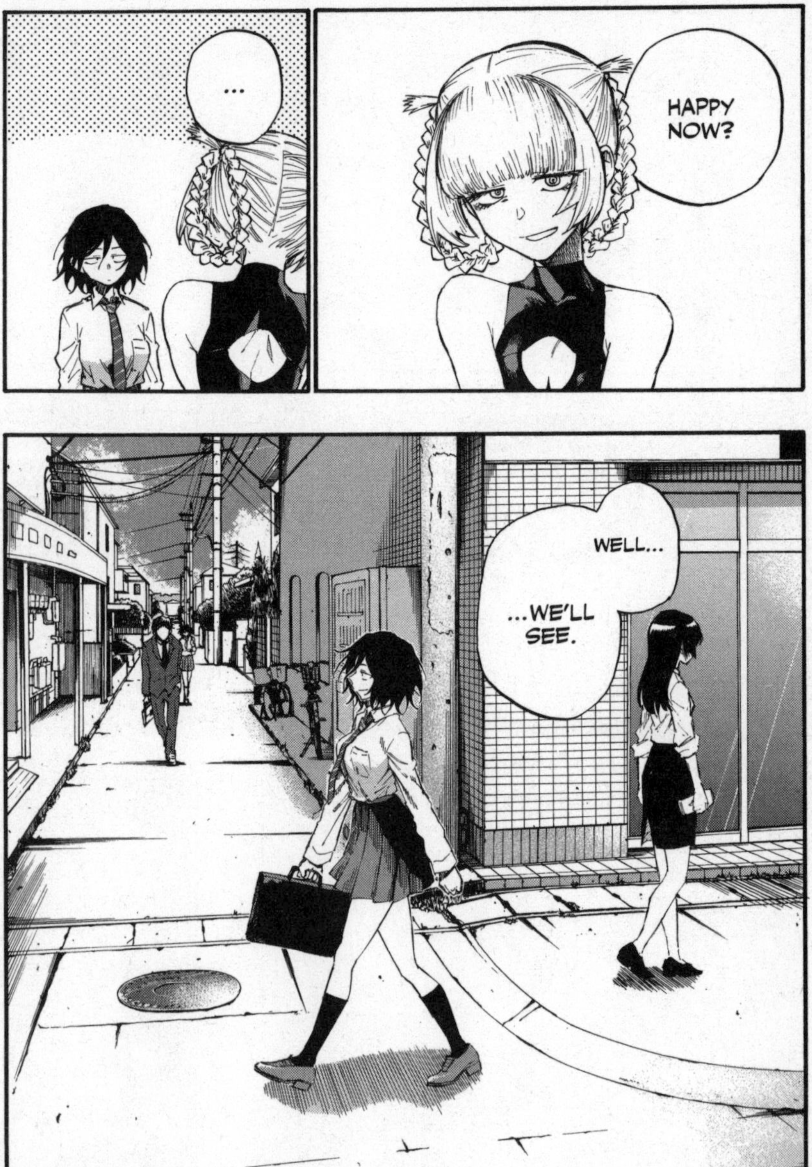
HAPPY NOW?
...
WELL...
...WE'LL SEE.

Call of the Night

Call of the Night

NIGHT 12: WELL, THAT'S A PROBLEM

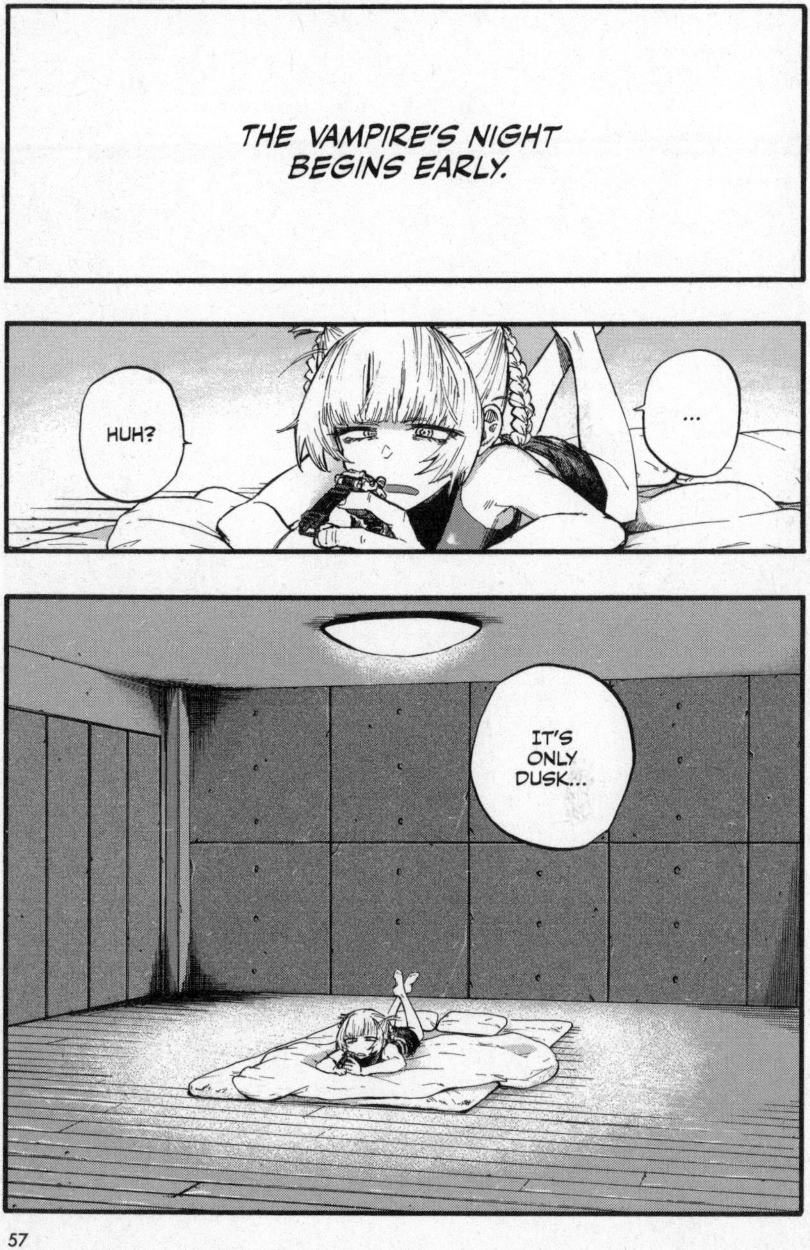
THE VAMPIRE'S NIGHT BEGINS EARLY.
...
HUH?
IT'S ONLY DUSK...

NIGHT 12:

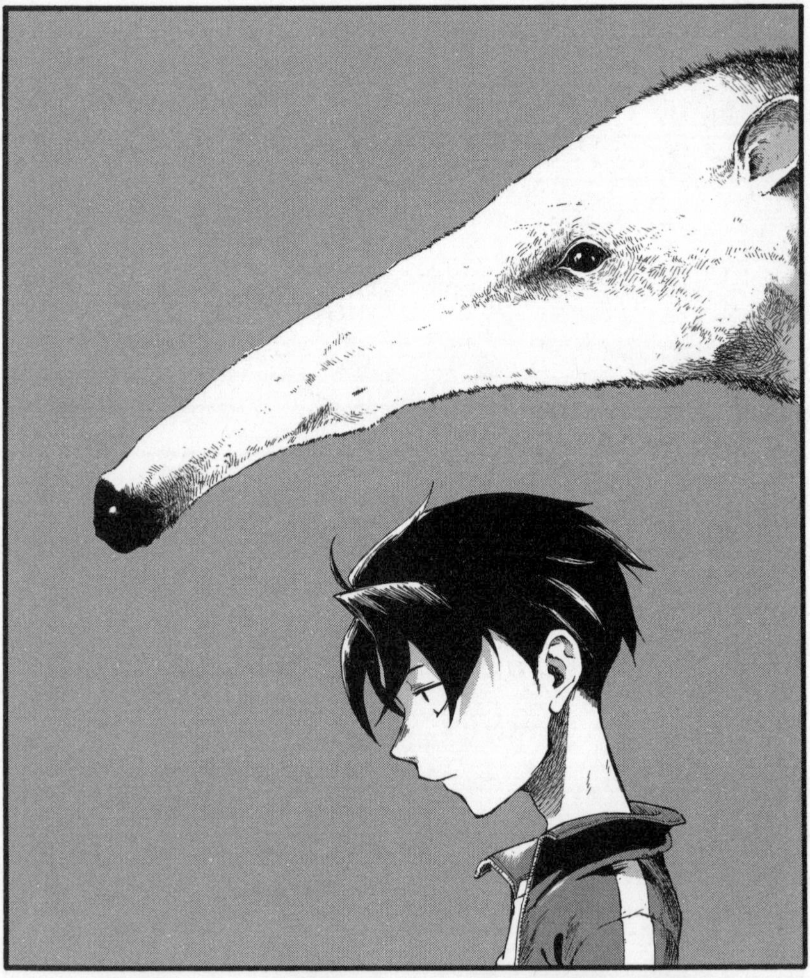

WELL, THAT'S A PROBLEM

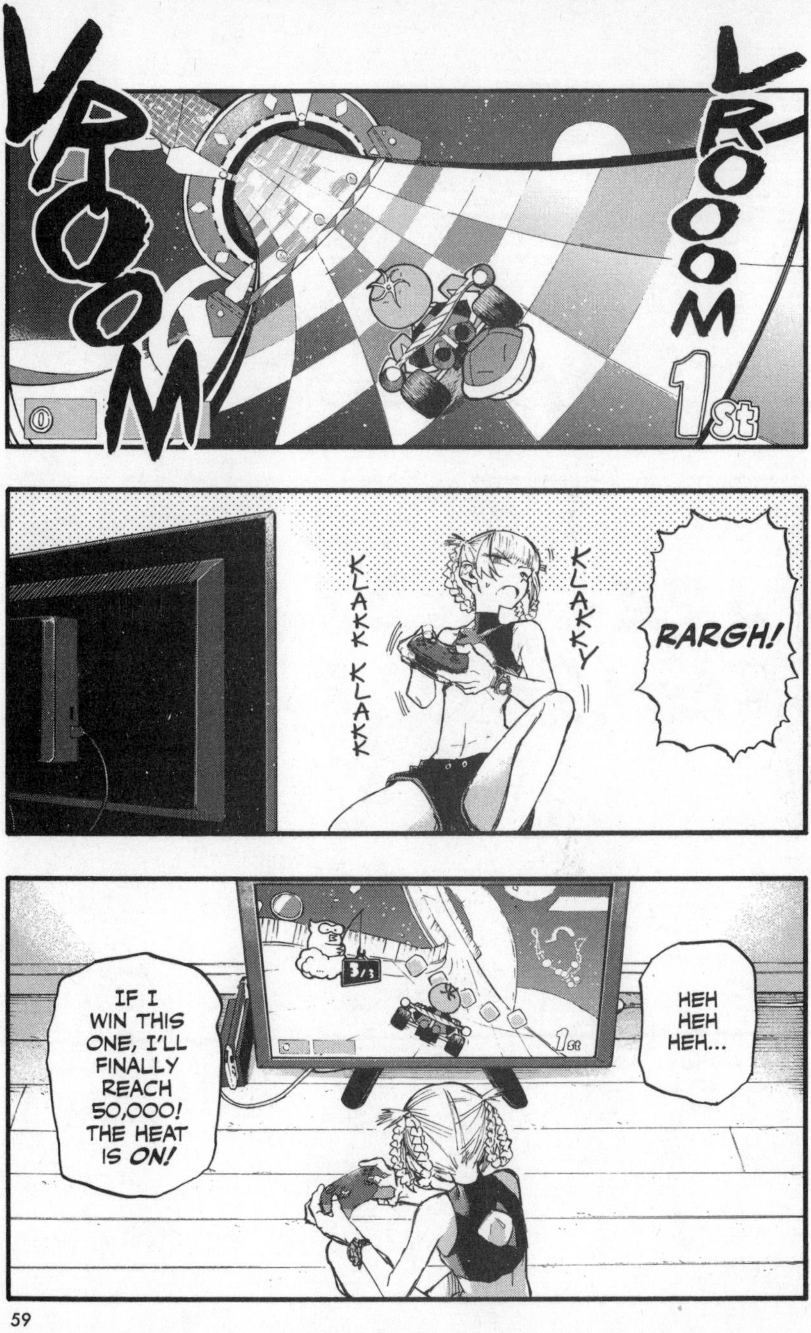
VROOOM
VROOOM
1st
RARGH!
KLAKKY
KLAKK KLAKK KLAKK
HEH HEH HEH...
IF I WIN THIS ONE, I'LL FINALLY REACH 50,000! THE HEAT IS ON!
3/3
1st

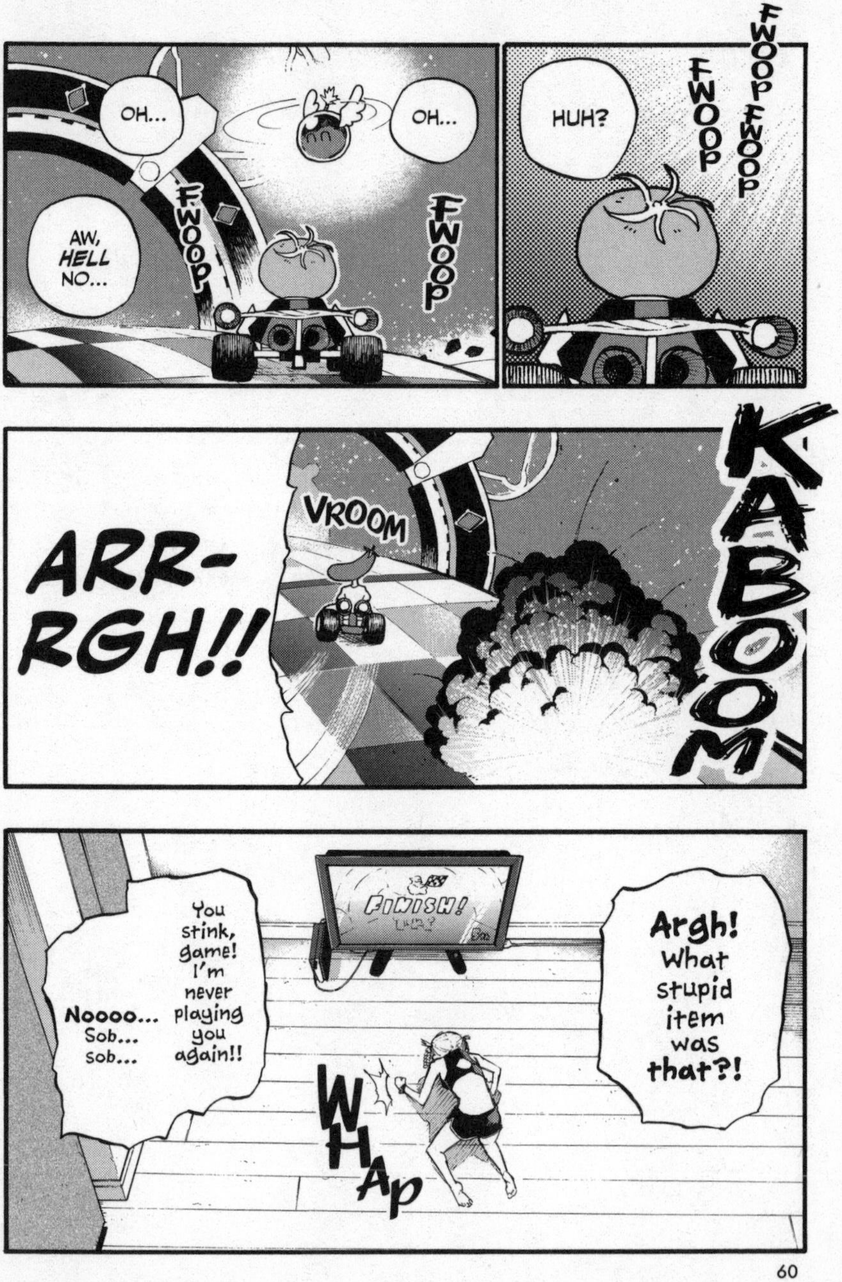
FWOOP FWOOP
FWOOP
HUH?
OH...
OH...
FWOOP
FWOOP
AW, HELL NO...
KABOOM
VROOM
ARR-RGH!!
Argh! What stupid item was that?!
FINISH!
WHAp
You stink, game! I'm never playing you again!!
Noooo... Sob... sob...

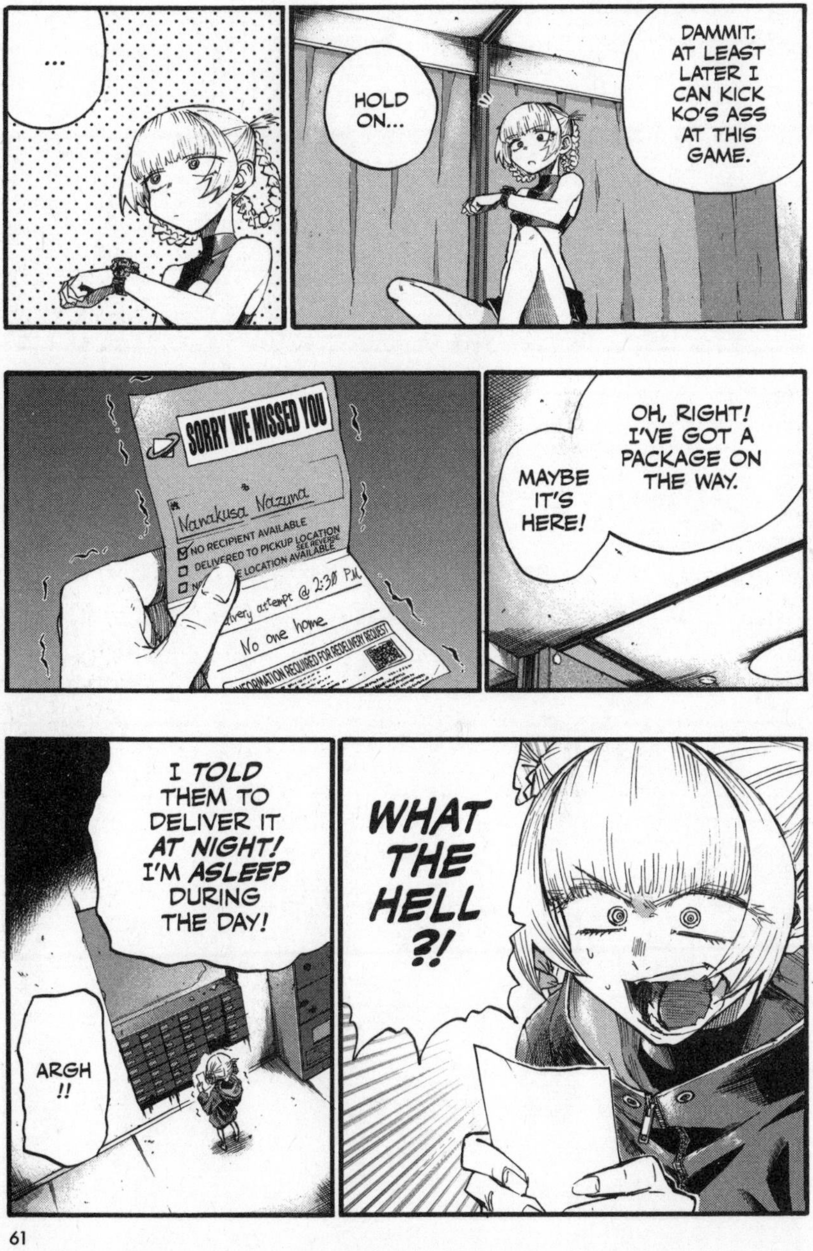

DAMMIT. AT LEAST LATER I CAN KICK KO'S ASS AT THIS GAME.
HOLD ON...
...
OH, RIGHT! I'VE GOT A PACKAGE ON THE WAY.
MAYBE IT'S HERE!
SORRY WE MISSED YOU
Nanakusa Nazuna
NO RECIPIENT AVAILABLE
DELIVERED TO PICKUP LOCATION
SEE REVERSE
No one home
WHAT THE HELL ?!
I TOLD THEM TO DELIVER IT AT NIGHT! I'M ASLEEP DURING THE DAY!
ARGH !!

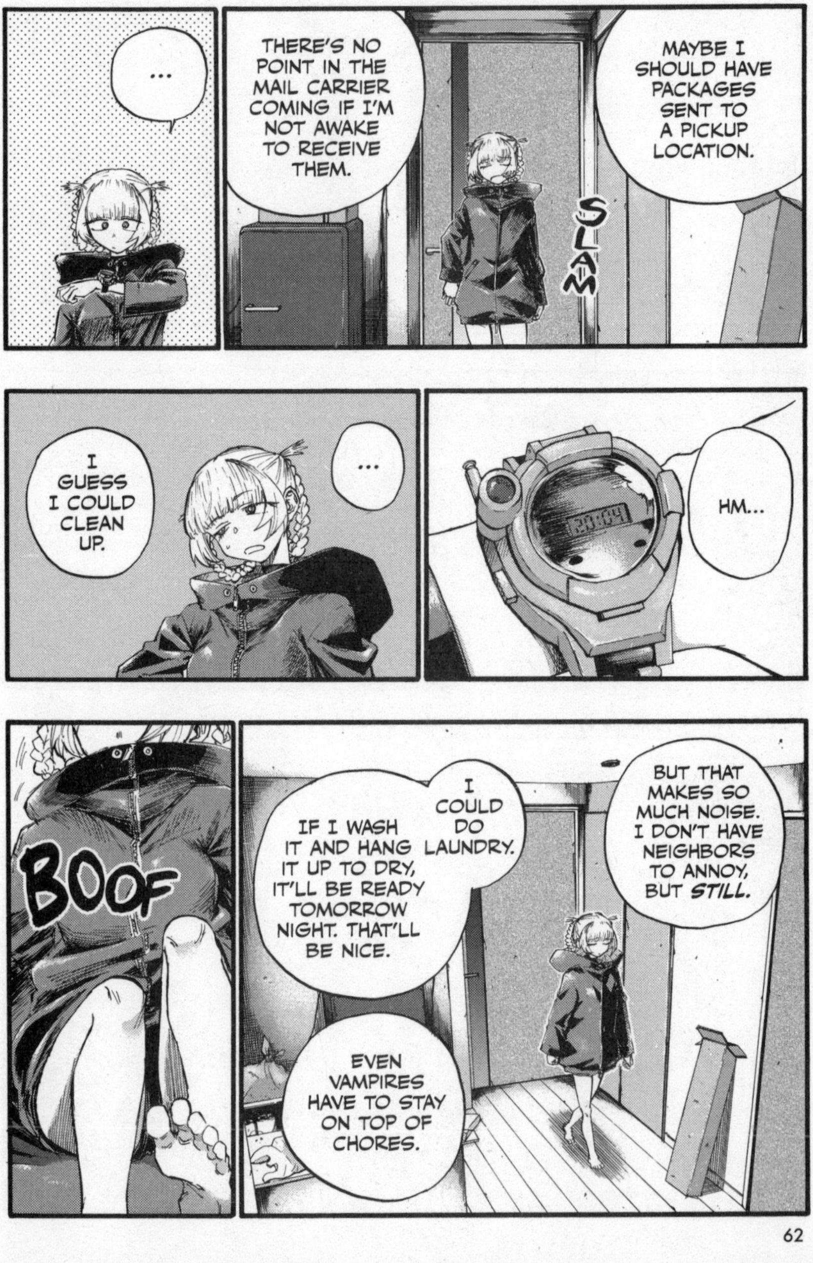

MAYBE I SHOULD HAVE PACKAGES SENT TO A PICKUP LOCATION.
THERE'S NO POINT IN THE MAIL CARRIER COMING IF I'M NOT AWAKE TO RECEIVE THEM.
SLAM
...
HM...
...
I GUESS I COULD CLEAN UP.
BUT THAT MAKES SO MUCH NOISE. I DON'T HAVE NEIGHBORS TO ANNOY, BUT ***STILL***.
I COULD DO LAUNDRY.
IF I WASH IT AND HANG IT UP TO DRY, IT'LL BE READY TOMORROW NIGHT. THAT'LL BE NICE.
EVEN VAMPIRES HAVE TO STAY ON TOP OF CHORES.
BOOF

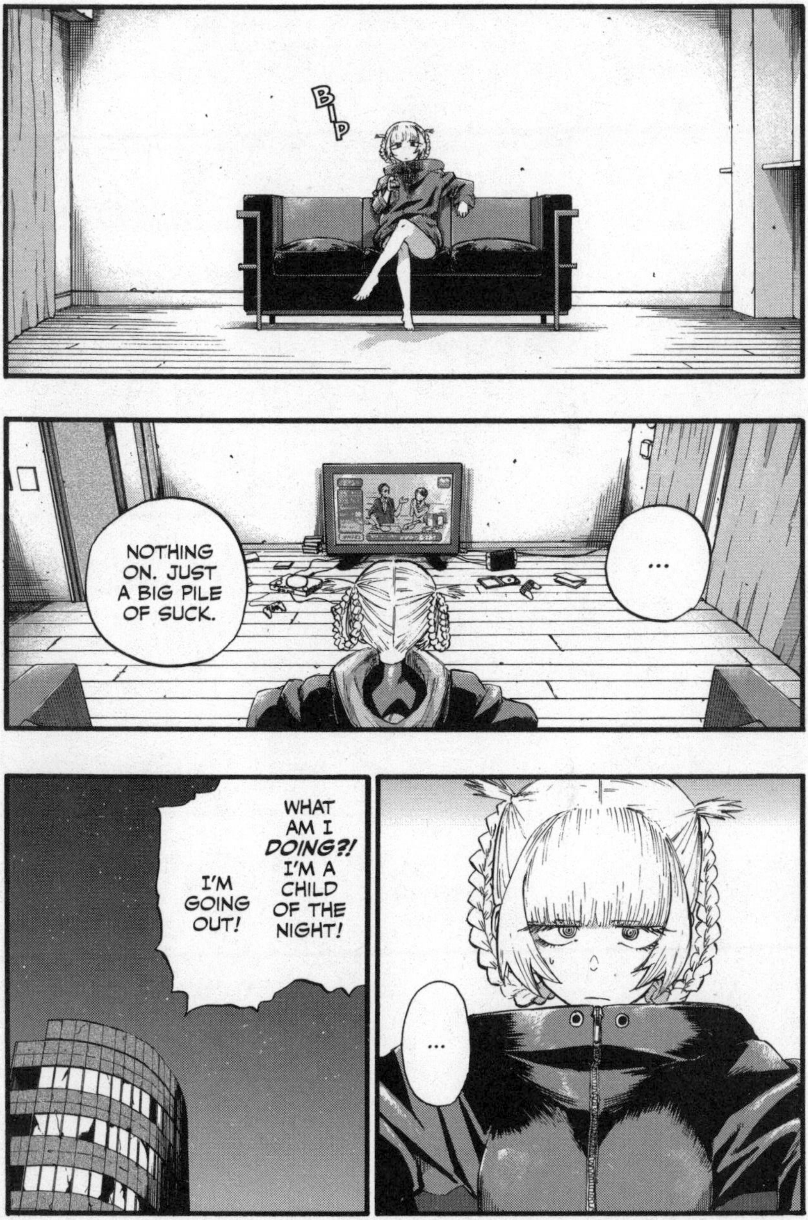
BIP
...
NOTHING ON. JUST A BIG PILE OF SUCK.
...
WHAT AM I DOING?! I'M A CHILD OF THE NIGHT!
I'M GOING OUT!

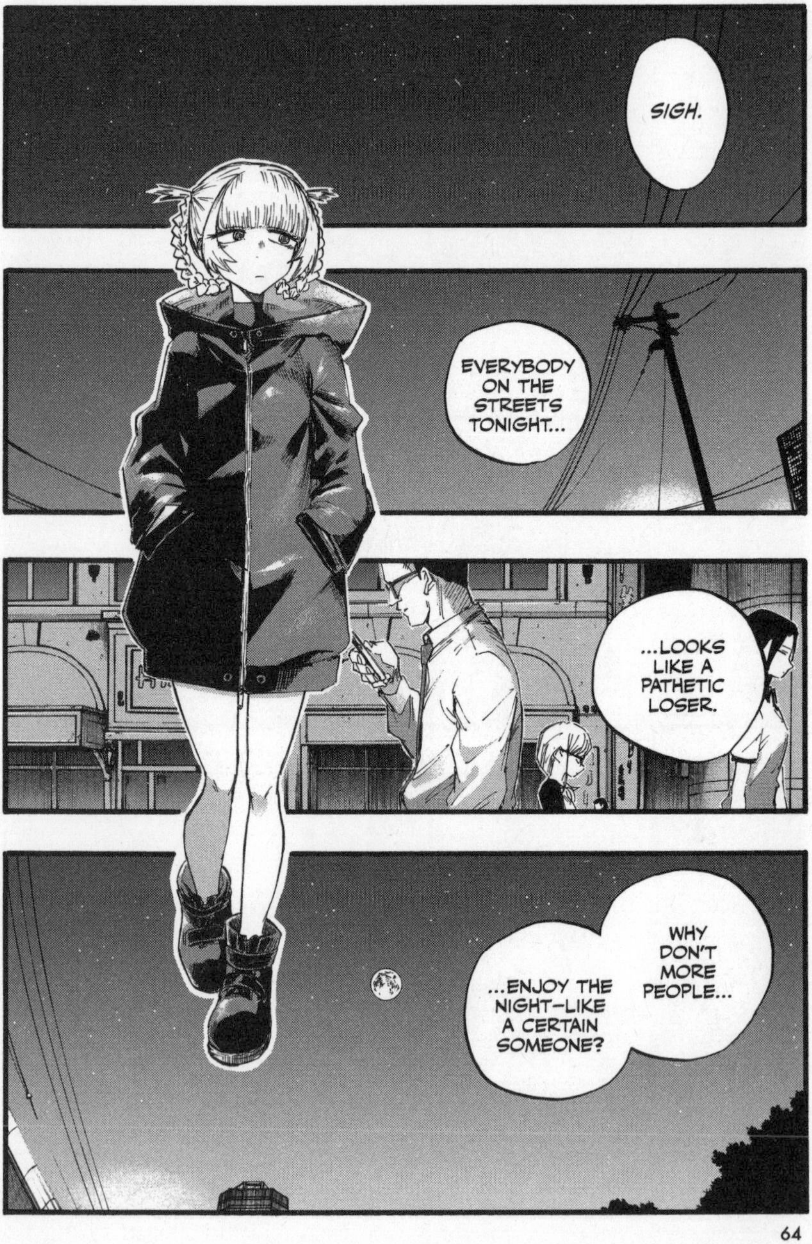
SIGH.
EVERYBODY ON THE STREETS TONIGHT...
...LOOKS LIKE A PATHETIC LOSER.
WHY DON'T MORE PEOPLE...
...ENJOY THE NIGHT—LIKE A CERTAIN SOMEONE?

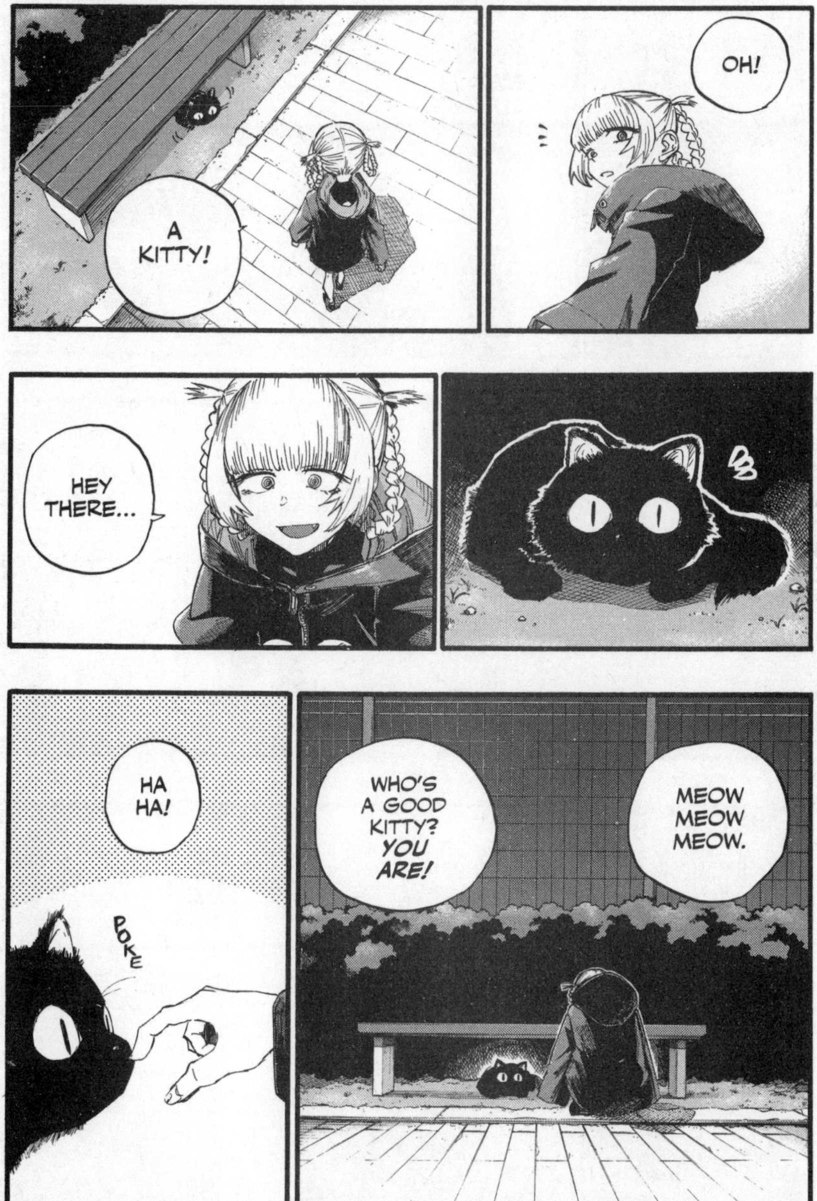
OH!
A KITTY!
HEY THERE...
MEOW MEOW MEOW.
WHO'S A GOOD KITTY? YOU ARE!
HA HA!
POKE

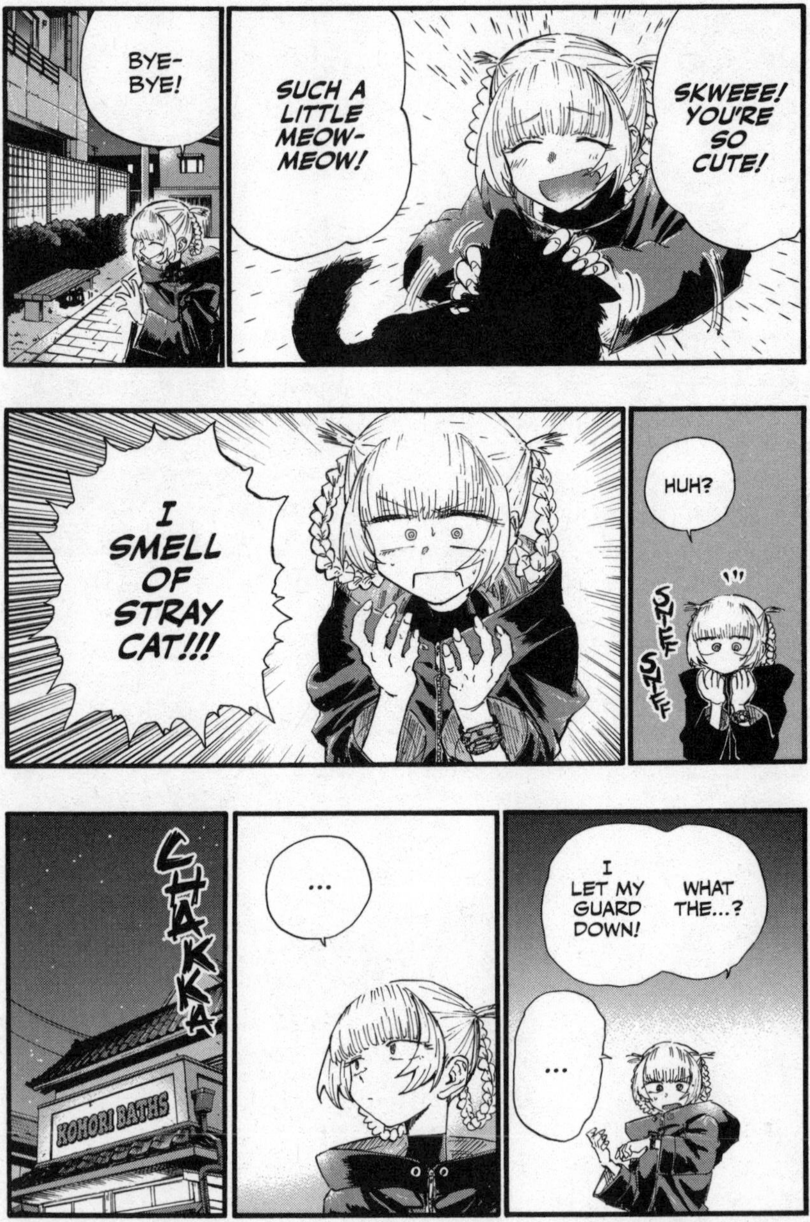
SKWEEE! YOU'RE SO CUTE!
SUCH A LITTLE MEOW-MEOW!
BYE-BYE!
HUH?
SNIFF SNIFF
I SMELL OF STRAY CAT!!!
WHAT THE...?
I LET MY GUARD DOWN!
...
...
CHAKKA
KOHORI BATHS

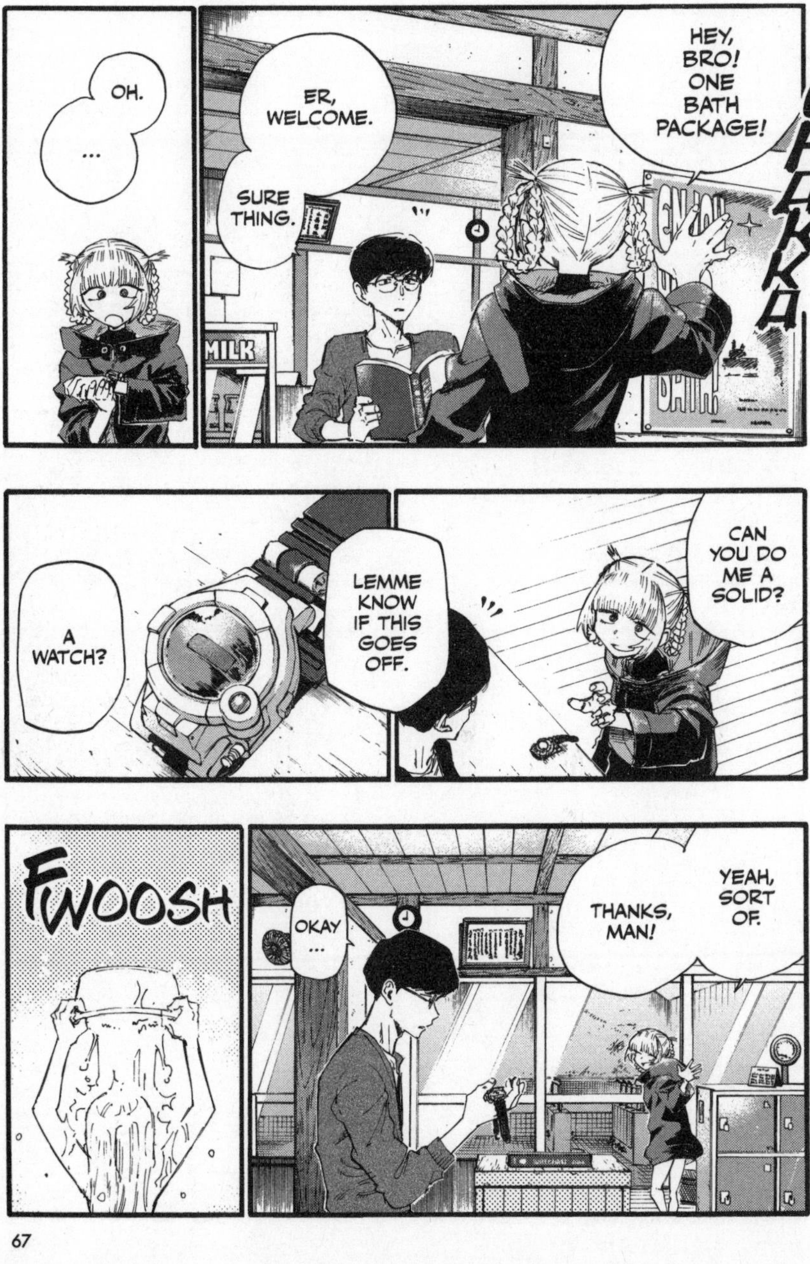
HEY, BRO! ONE BATH PACKAGE!
CHAKA
ER, WELCOME.
SURE THING.
OH.
...
CAN YOU DO ME A SOLID?
LEMME KNOW IF THIS GOES OFF.
A WATCH?
YEAH, SORT OF.
THANKS, MAN!
OKAY ...
FWOOSH

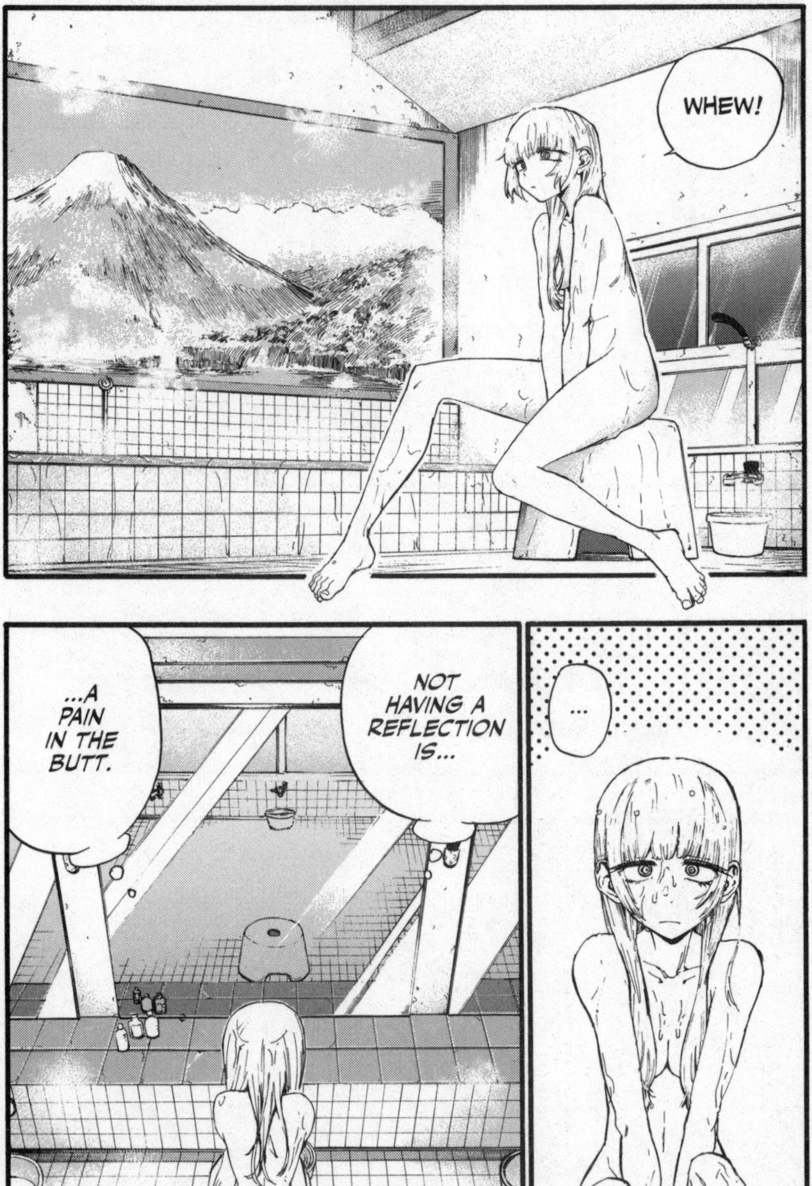
WHEW!
...
NOT HAVING A REFLECTION IS...
...A PAIN IN THE BUTT.

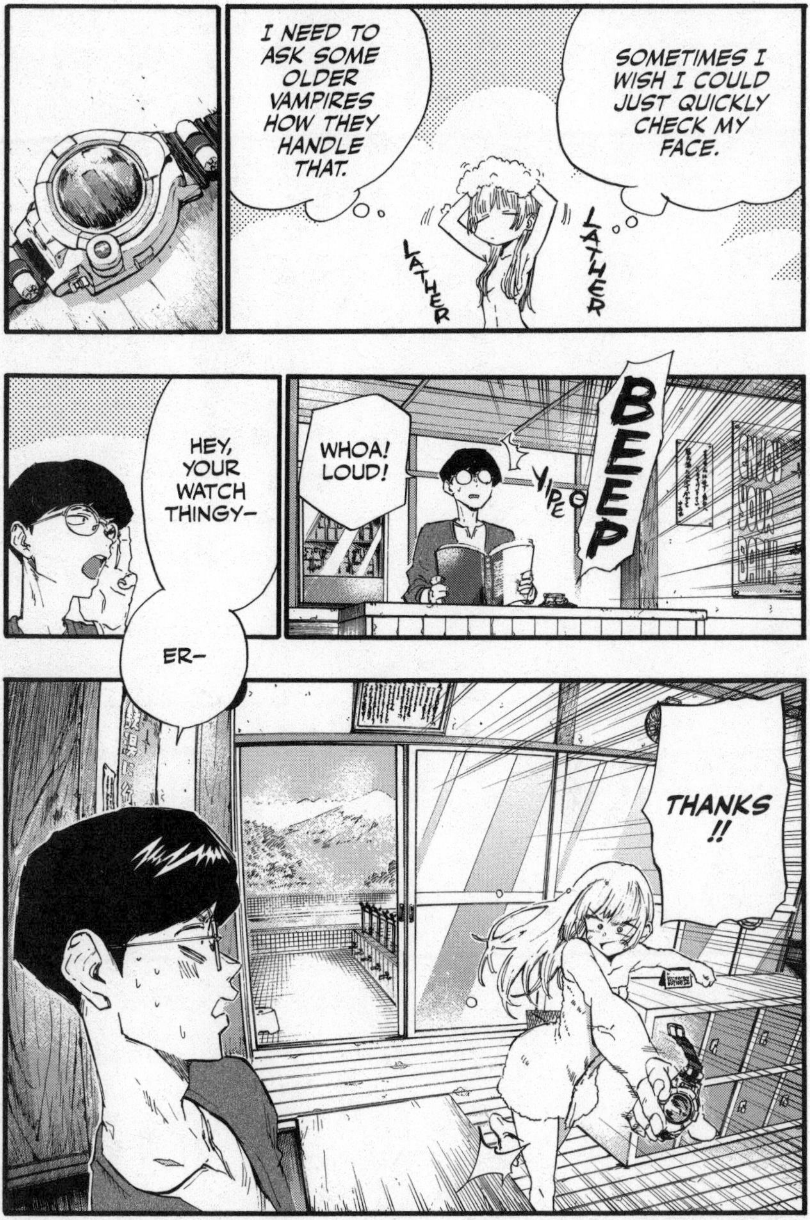
SOMETIMES I WISH I COULD JUST QUICKLY CHECK MY FACE.
I NEED TO ASK SOME OLDER VAMPIRES HOW THEY HANDLE THAT.
LATHER
LATHER
BEEP
YIPE
WHOA! LOUD!
HEY, YOUR WATCH THINGY—
ER—
THANKS!!

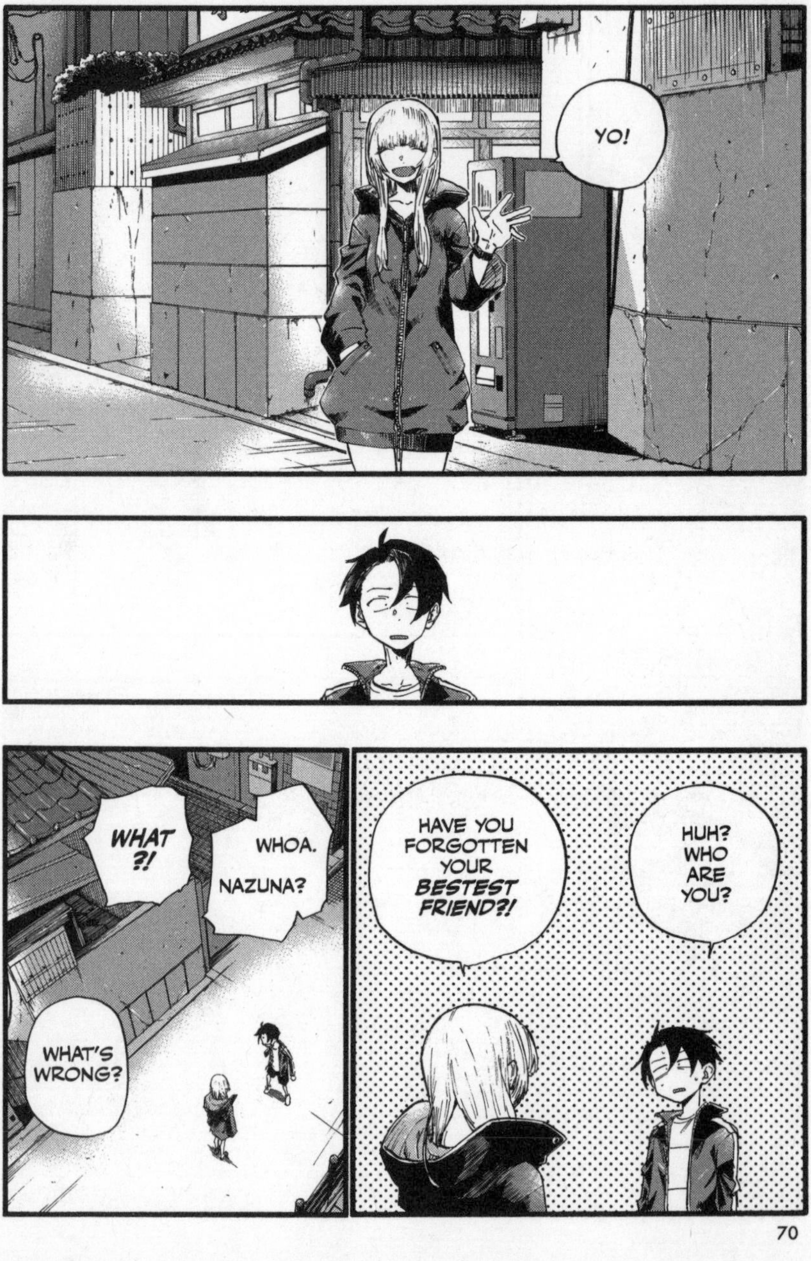
YO!
HUH? WHO ARE YOU?
HAVE YOU FORGOTTEN YOUR *BESTEST* FRIEND?!
WHOA. NAZUNA?
WHAT ?!
WHAT'S WRONG?

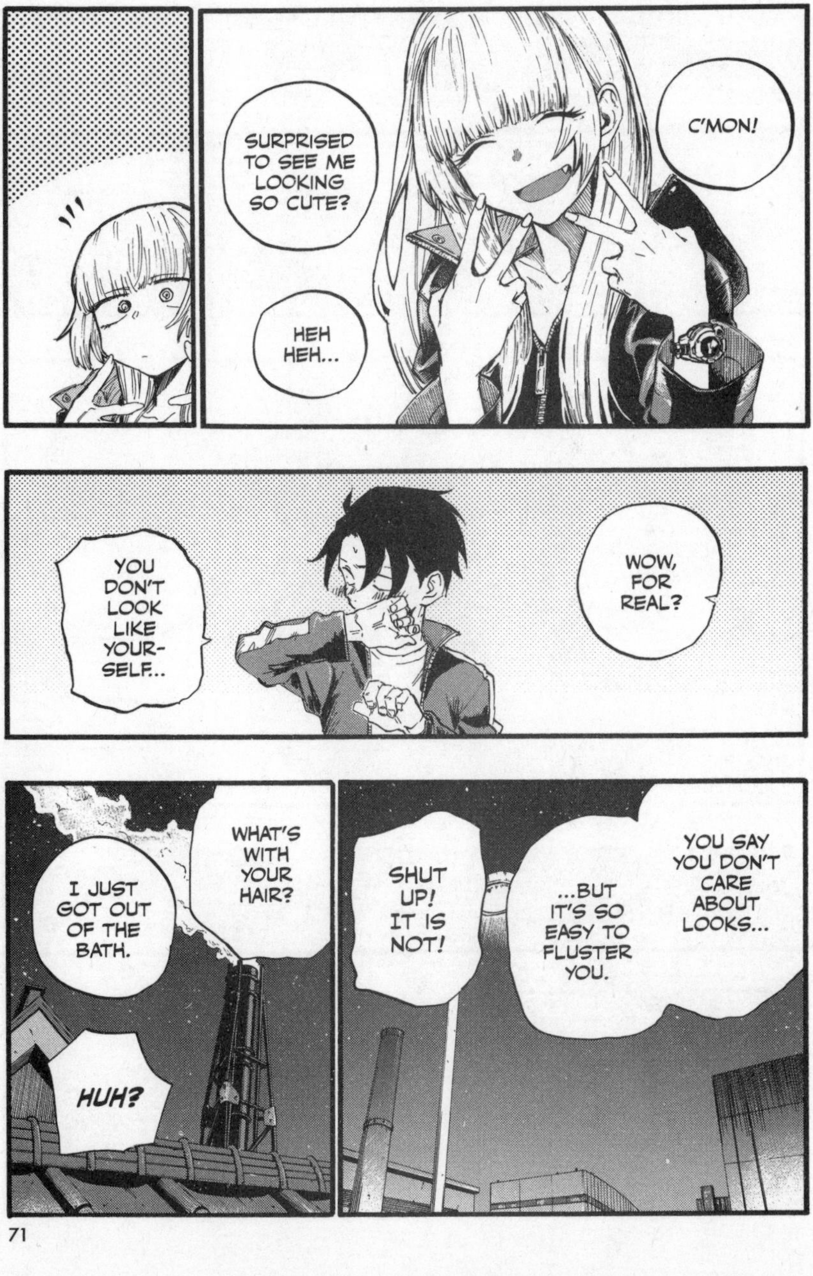
C'MON!
SURPRISED TO SEE ME LOOKING SO CUTE?
HEH HEH...
WOW, FOR REAL?
YOU DON'T LOOK LIKE YOUR-SELF...
YOU SAY YOU DON'T CARE ABOUT LOOKS...
...BUT IT'S SO EASY TO FLUSTER YOU.
SHUT UP! IT IS NOT!
WHAT'S WITH YOUR HAIR?
I JUST GOT OUT OF THE BATH.
HUH?

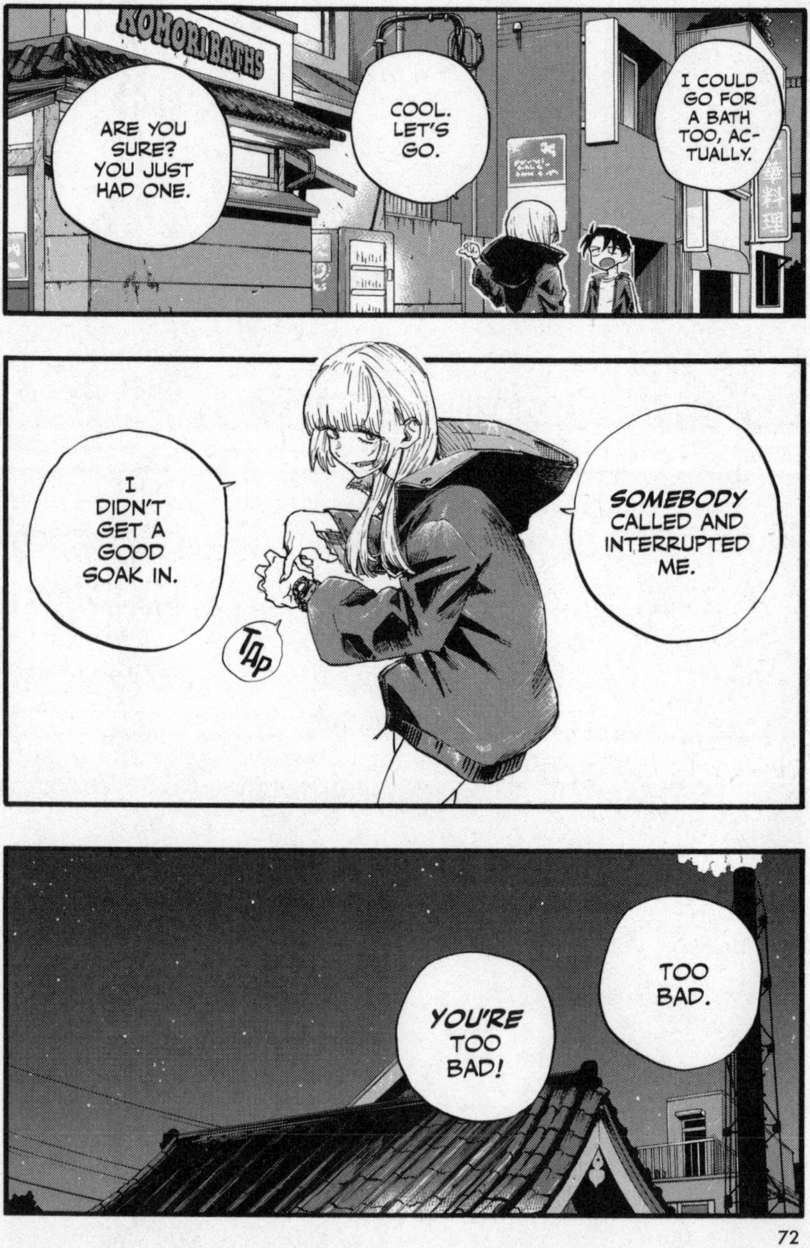
KOMORI BATHS
I COULD GO FOR A BATH TOO, ACTUALLY.
COOL. LET'S GO.
ARE YOU SURE? YOU JUST HAD ONE.
SOMEBODY CALLED AND INTERRUPTED ME.
I DIDN'T GET A GOOD SOAK IN.
TAP
TOO BAD.
YOU'RE TOO BAD!

Call of the Night

Call of the Night

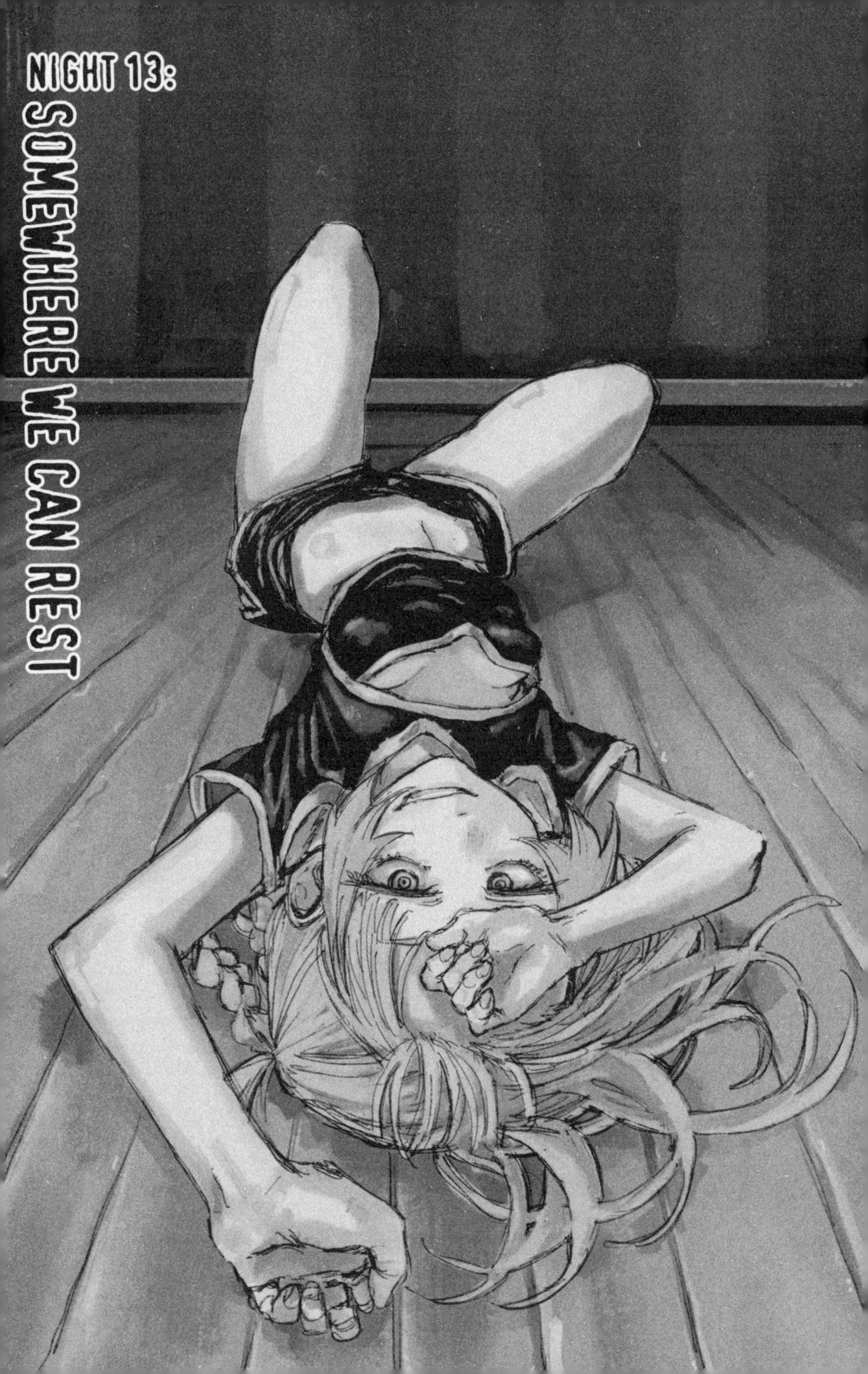
NIGHT 13:
SOMEWHERE WE CAN REST

Call of the Night

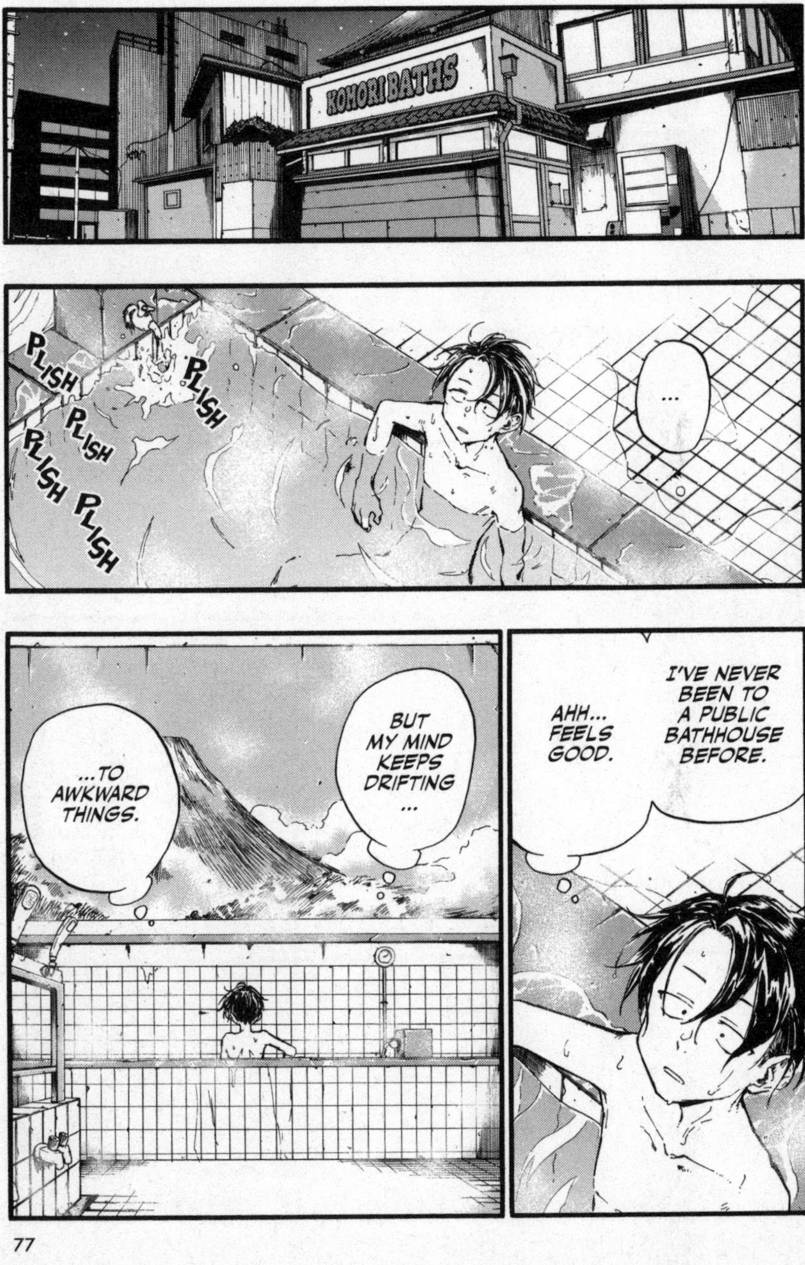
KOMORI BATHS
...
PLISH
PLISH
PLISH
PLISH
PLISH
PLISH
I'VE NEVER BEEN TO A PUBLIC BATHHOUSE BEFORE.
AHH... FEELS GOOD.
BUT MY MIND KEEPS DRIFTING ...
...TO AWKWARD THINGS.

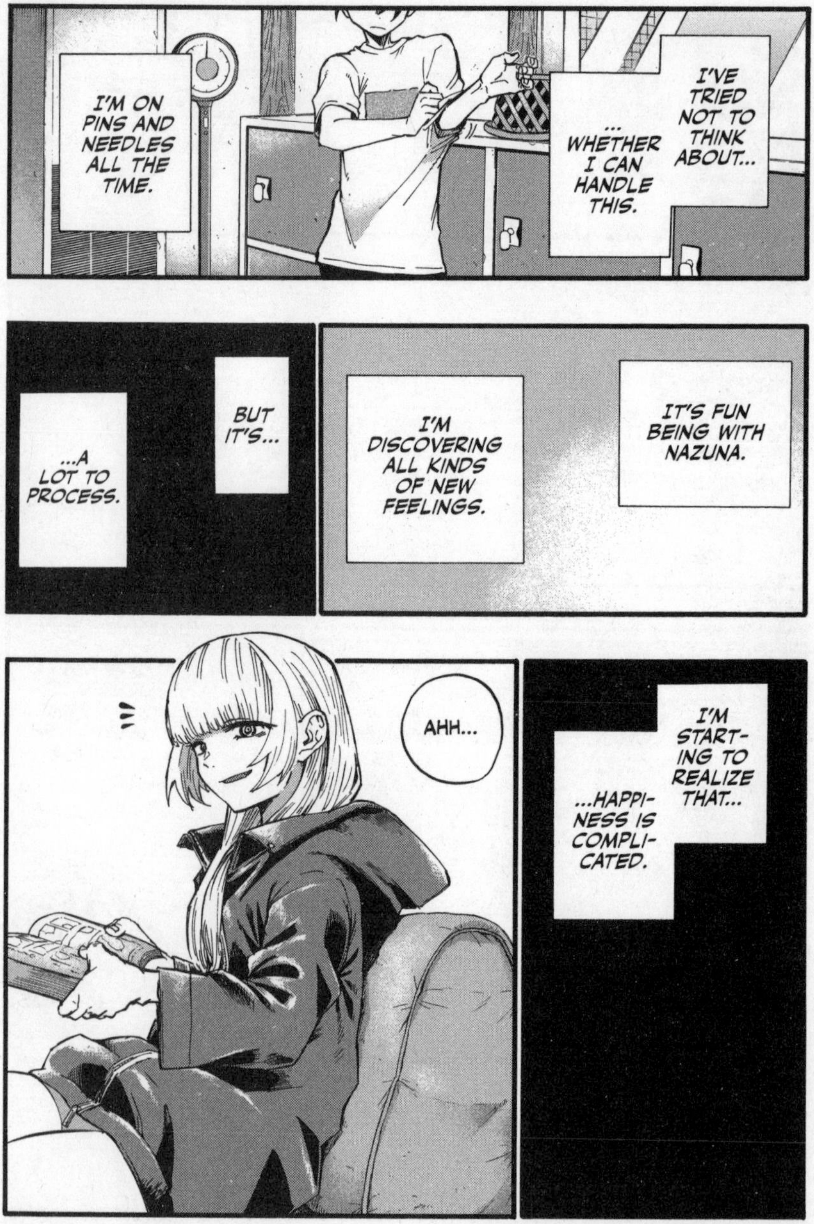
I'VE TRIED NOT TO THINK ABOUT...
...WHETHER I CAN HANDLE THIS.
I'M ON PINS AND NEEDLES ALL THE TIME.
IT'S FUN BEING WITH NAZUNA.
I'M DISCOVERING ALL KINDS OF NEW FEELINGS.
BUT IT'S...
...A LOT TO PROCESS.
I'M STARTING TO REALIZE THAT...
...HAPPINESS IS COMPLICATED.
AHH...

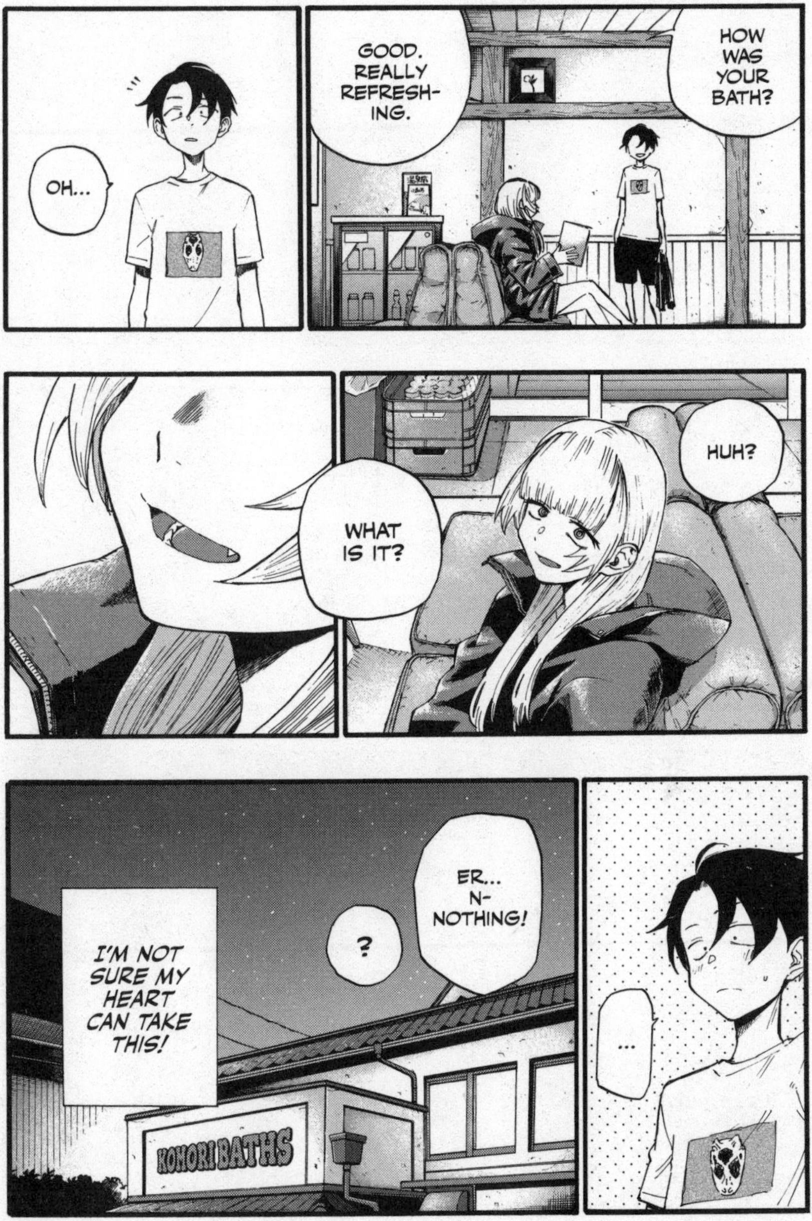
HOW WAS YOUR BATH?
GOOD. REALLY REFRESH-ING.
OH...
HUH?
WHAT IS IT?
...
ER... N-NOTHING!
?
I'M NOT SURE MY HEART CAN TAKE THIS!
KONORI BATHS

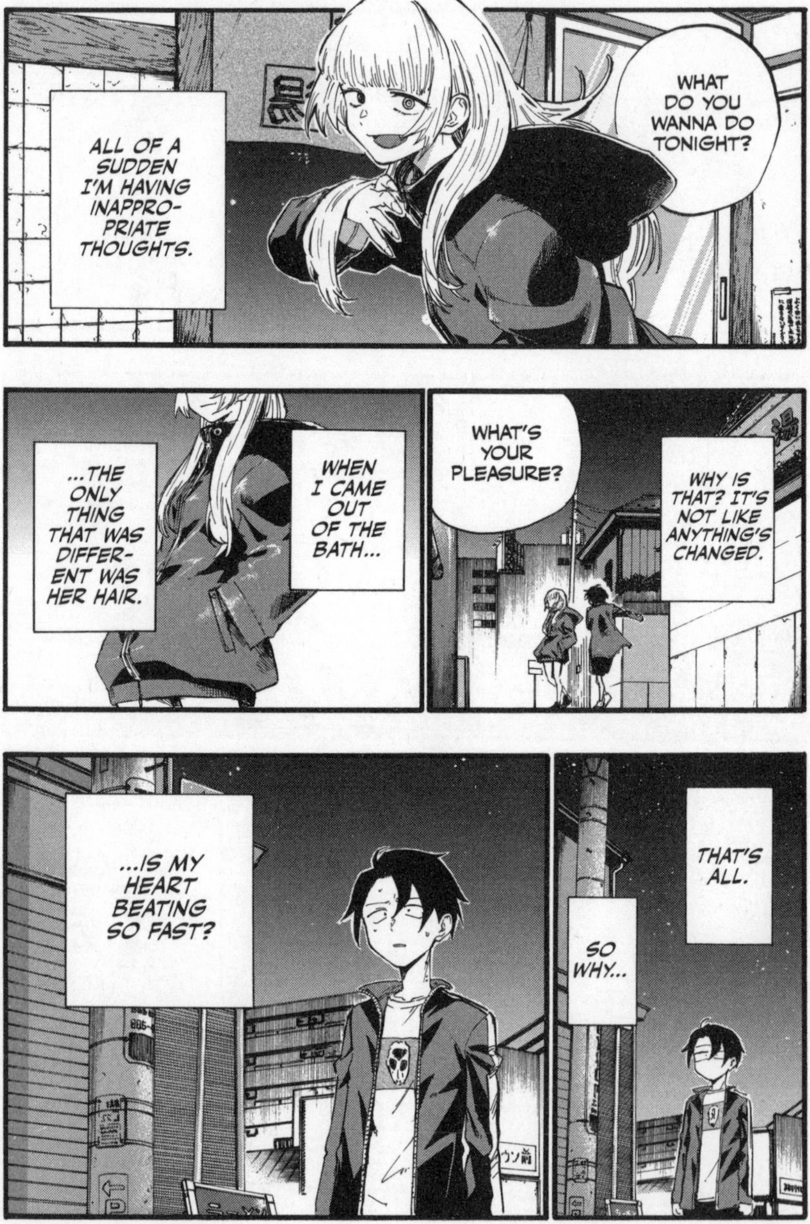
WHAT DO YOU WANNA DO TONIGHT?
ALL OF A SUDDEN I'M HAVING INAPPROPRIATE THOUGHTS.
WHAT'S YOUR PLEASURE?
WHY IS THAT? IT'S NOT LIKE ANYTHING'S CHANGED.
WHEN I CAME OUT OF THE BATH...
...THE ONLY THING THAT WAS DIFFERENT WAS HER HAIR.
THAT'S ALL.
SO WHY...
...IS MY HEART BEATING SO FAST?

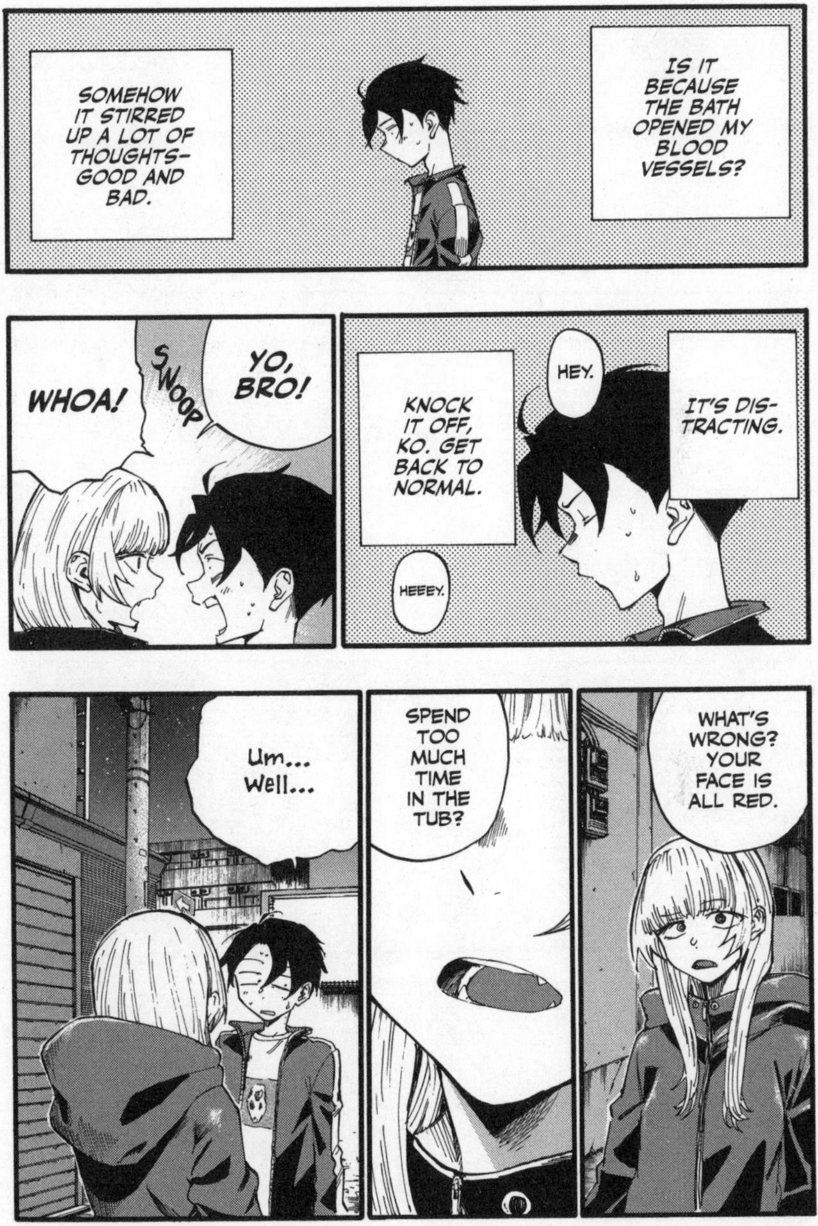
IS IT BECAUSE THE BATH OPENED MY BLOOD VESSELS?
SOMEHOW IT STIRRED UP A LOT OF THOUGHTS- GOOD AND BAD.
IT'S DIS-TRACTING.
HEY.
KNOCK IT OFF, KO. GET BACK TO NORMAL.
HEEEY.
YO, BRO!
SWOOP
WHOA!
WHAT'S WRONG? YOUR FACE IS ALL RED.
SPEND TOO MUCH TIME IN THE TUB?
Um... Well...

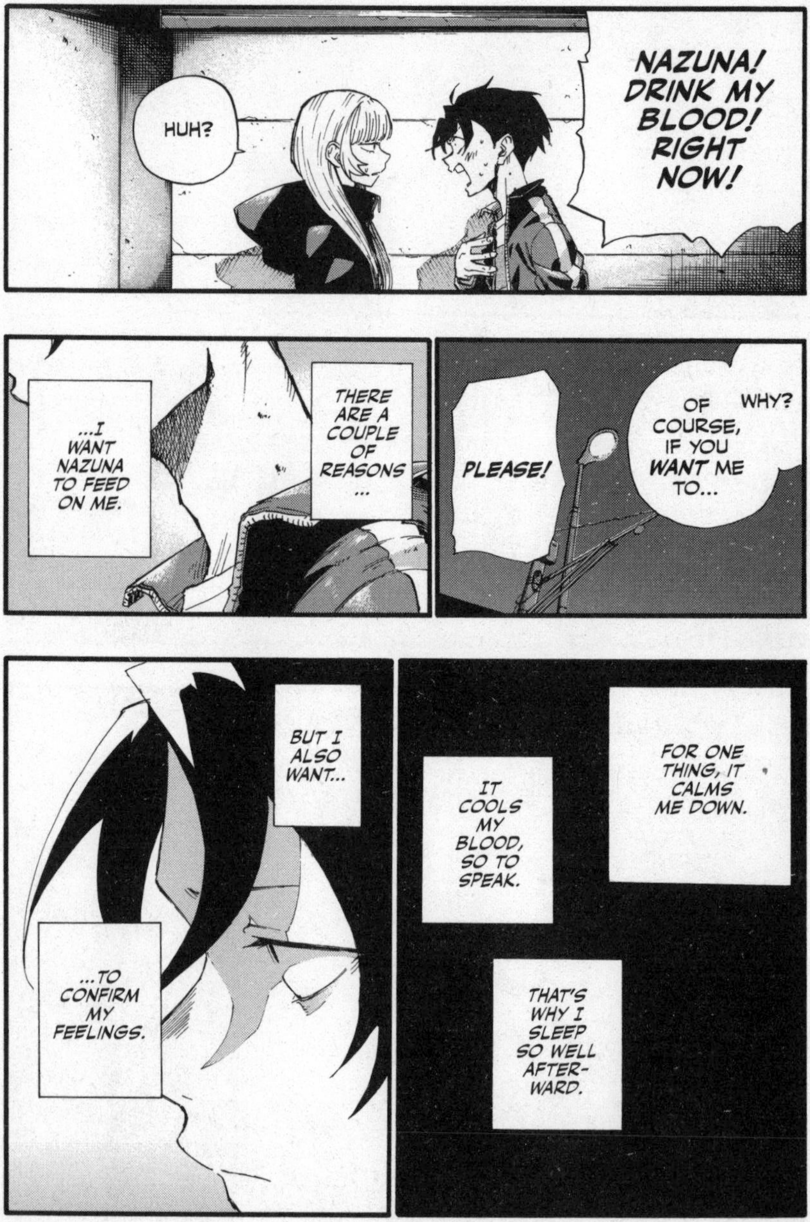
NAZUNA! DRINK MY BLOOD! RIGHT NOW!
HUH?
WHY?
OF COURSE, IF YOU WANT ME TO...
PLEASE!
THERE ARE A COUPLE OF REASONS...
...I WANT NAZUNA TO FEED ON ME.
FOR ONE THING, IT CALMS ME DOWN.
IT COOLS MY BLOOD, SO TO SPEAK.
THAT'S WHY I SLEEP SO WELL AFTER-WARD.
BUT I ALSO WANT...
...TO CONFIRM MY FEELINGS.

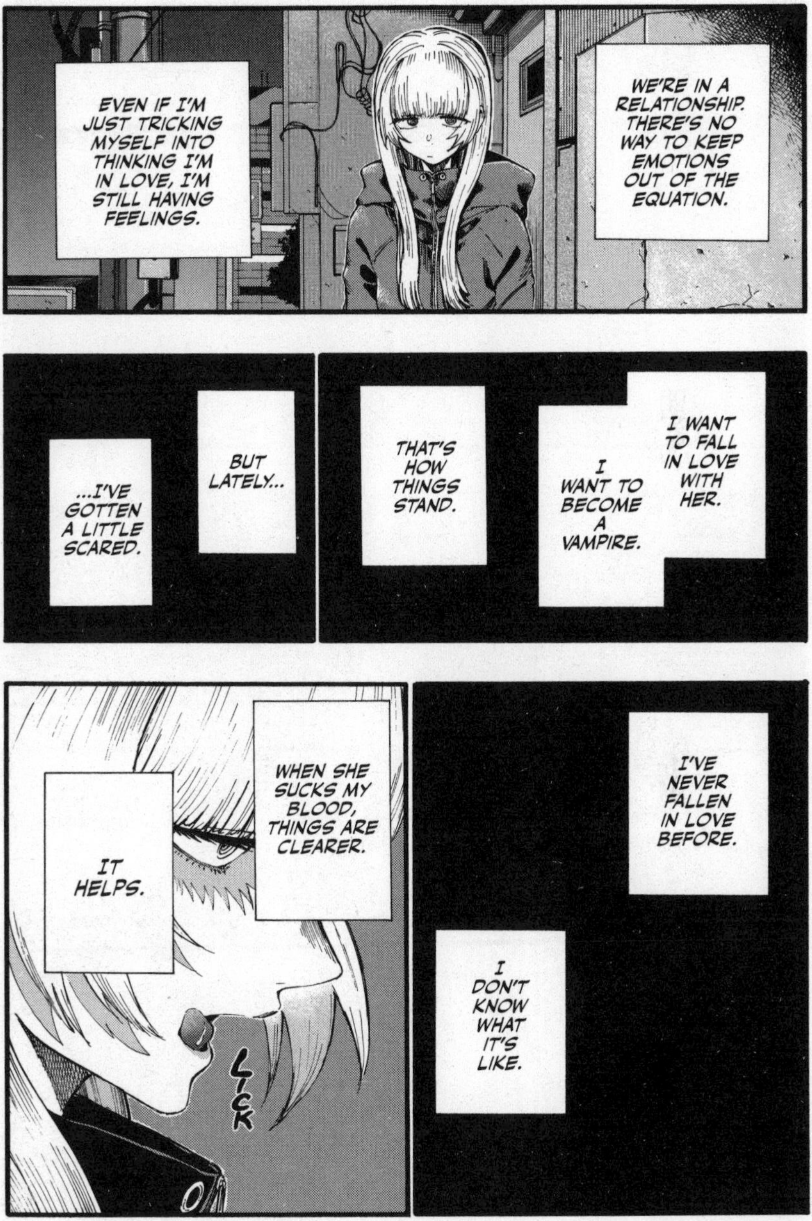
WE'RE IN A RELATIONSHIP. THERE'S NO WAY TO KEEP EMOTIONS OUT OF THE EQUATION.
EVEN IF I'M JUST TRICKING MYSELF INTO THINKING I'M IN LOVE, I'M STILL HAVING FEELINGS.
I WANT TO FALL IN LOVE WITH HER.
I WANT TO BECOME A VAMPIRE.
THAT'S HOW THINGS STAND.
BUT LATELY...
...I'VE GOTTEN A LITTLE SCARED.
I'VE NEVER FALLEN IN LOVE BEFORE.
I DON'T KNOW WHAT IT'S LIKE.
WHEN SHE SUCKS MY BLOOD, THINGS ARE CLEARER.
IT HELPS.
LICK

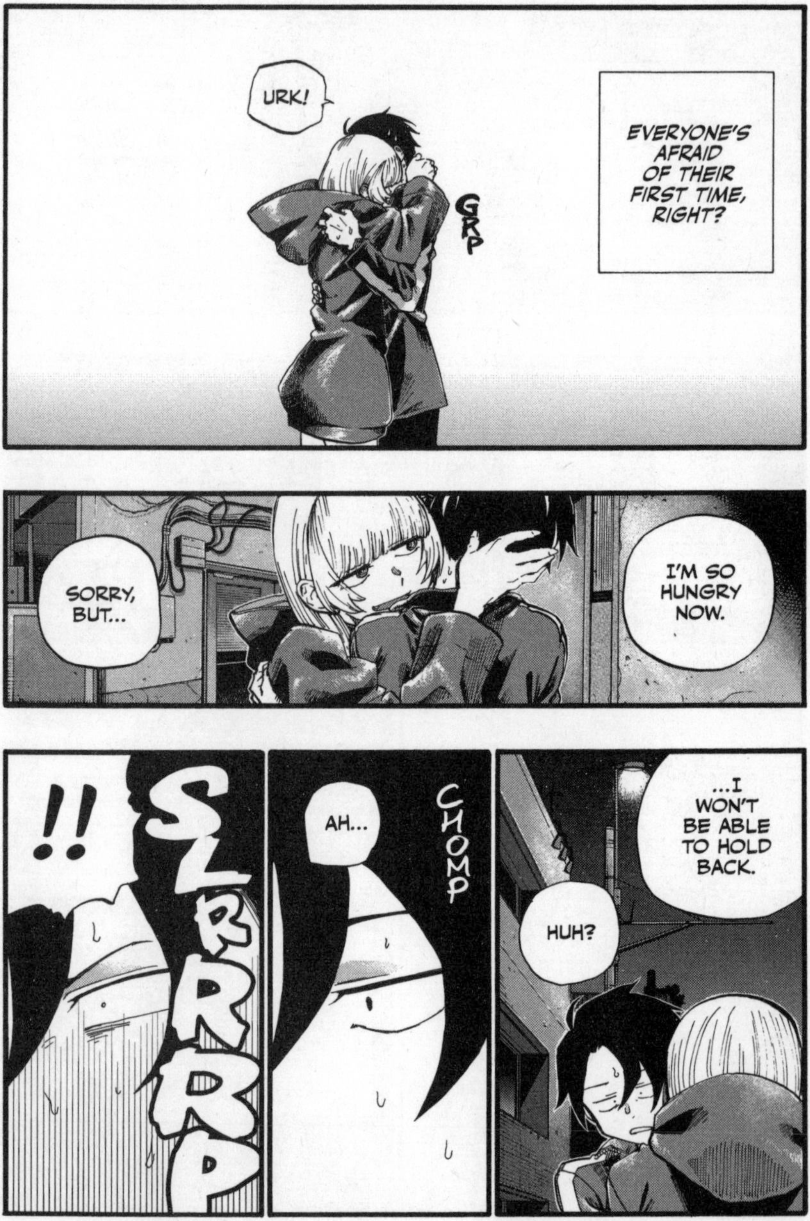
EVERYONE'S AFRAID OF THEIR FIRST TIME, RIGHT?
URK!
GRP
I'M SO HUNGRY NOW.
SORRY, BUT...
...I WON'T BE ABLE TO HOLD BACK.
HUH?
CHOMP
AH...
SLRRP
!!

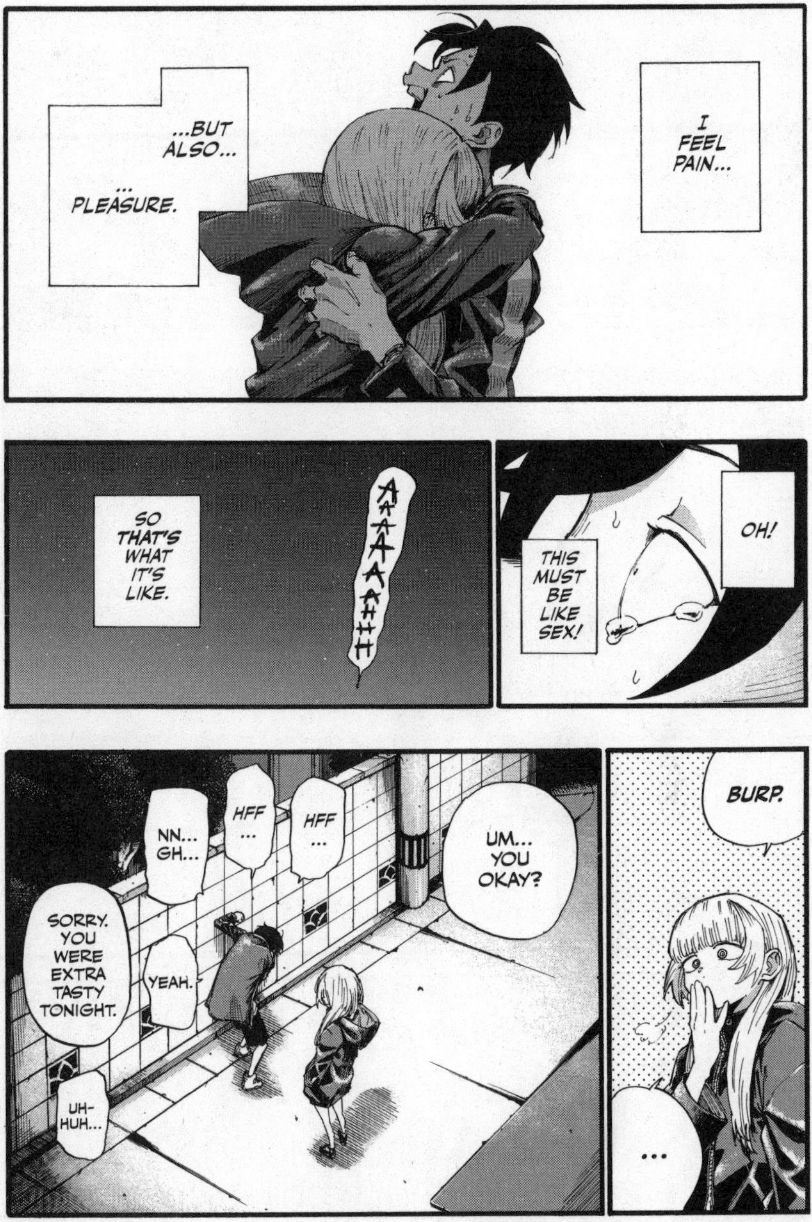

I FEEL PAIN...
...BUT ALSO...
... PLEASURE.
OH!
THIS MUST BE LIKE SEX!
AAAAAHHH
SO THAT'S WHAT IT'S LIKE.
BURP.
...
UM... YOU OKAY?
HFF ...
HFF ...
NN... GH...
SORRY. YOU WERE EXTRA TASTY TONIGHT.
YEAH.
UH-HUH...

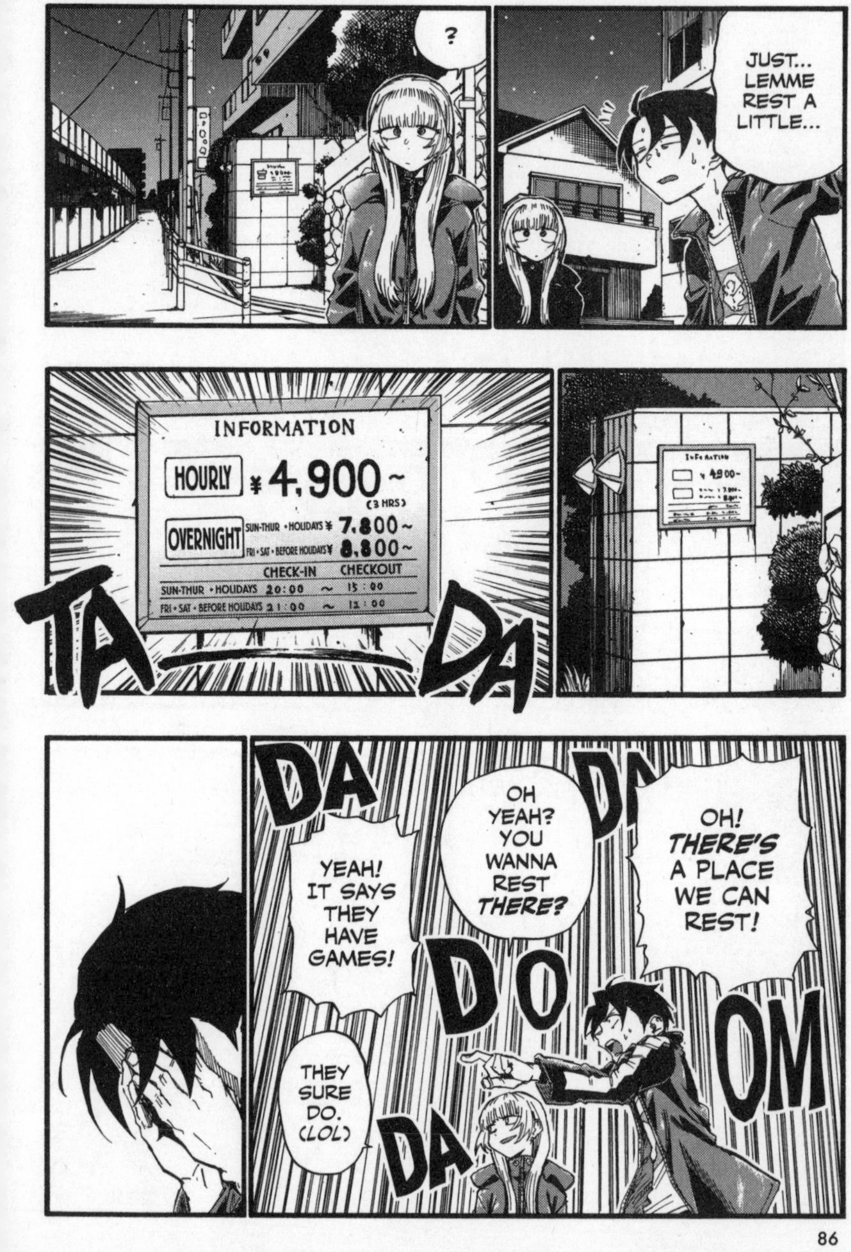
JUST... LEMME REST A LITTLE...
?
INFORMATION
HOURLY ¥4,900~
(3 HRS)
OVERNIGHT SUN-THUR • HOLIDAYS ¥ 7,800~
FRI • SAT • BEFORE HOLIDAYS ¥ 8,800~
CHECK-IN CHECKOUT
SUN-THUR • HOLIDAYS 20:00 ~ 15:00
FRI • SAT • BEFORE HOLIDAYS 21:00 ~ 12:00
TA—DA
OH! THERE'S A PLACE WE CAN REST!
DA
OH YEAH? YOU WANNA REST THERE?
DA
YEAH! IT SAYS THEY HAVE GAMES!
DO
OM
THEY SURE DO. (LOL)
DA

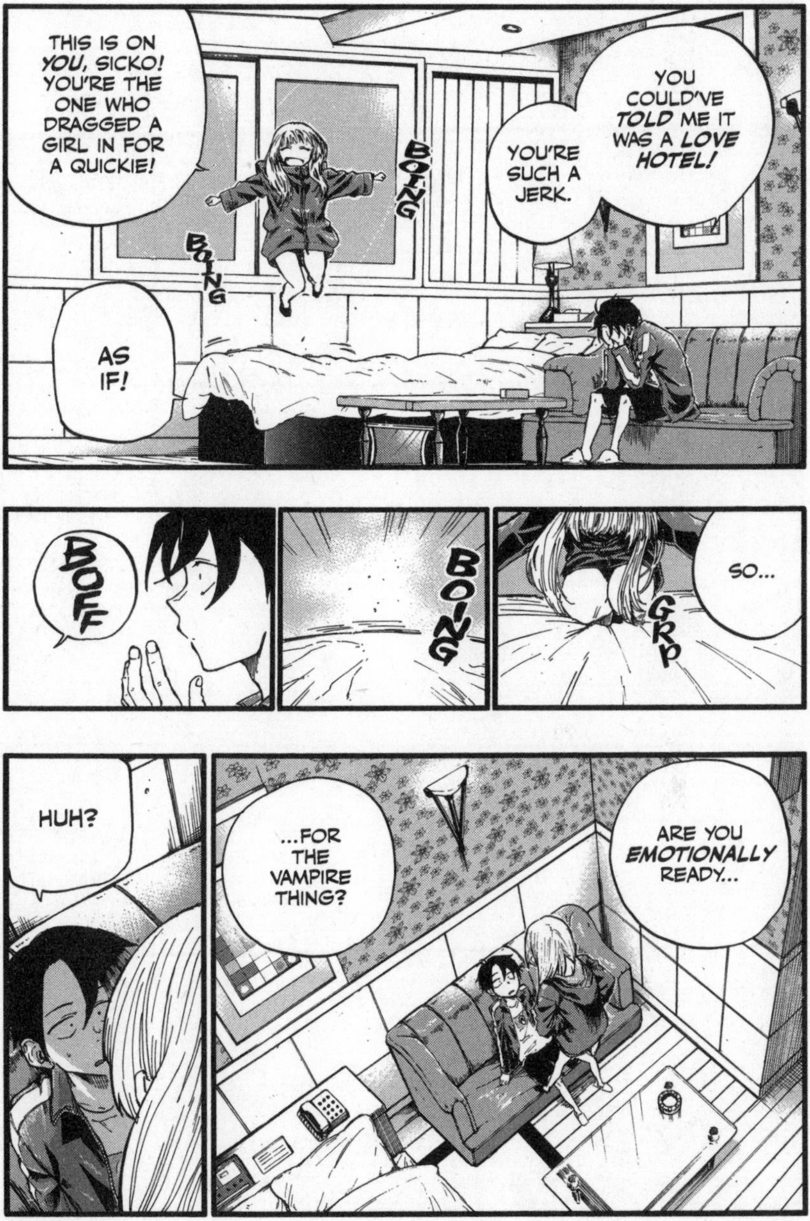
YOU COULD'VE *TOLD* ME IT WAS A *LOVE HOTEL!*
YOU'RE SUCH A JERK.
THIS IS ON *YOU*, SICKO! YOU'RE THE ONE WHO DRAGGED A GIRL IN FOR A QUICKIE!
BOING
BOING
AS IF!
SO...
GRP
BOING
BOFF
ARE YOU *EMOTIONALLY* READY...
...FOR THE VAMPIRE THING?
HUH?

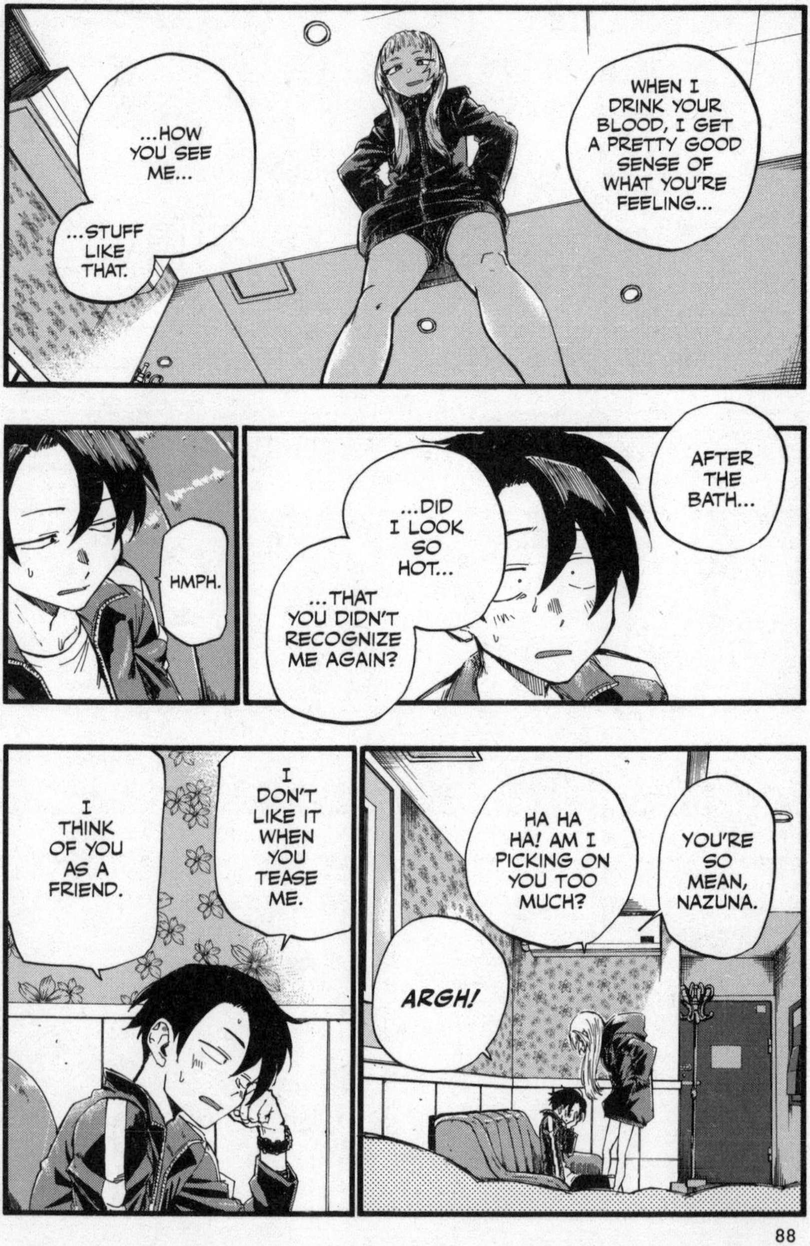
WHEN I DRINK YOUR BLOOD, I GET A PRETTY GOOD SENSE OF WHAT YOU'RE FEELING...
...HOW YOU SEE ME...
...STUFF LIKE THAT.
AFTER THE BATH...
...DID I LOOK SO HOT...
...THAT YOU DIDN'T RECOGNIZE ME AGAIN?
HMPH.
YOU'RE SO MEAN, NAZUNA.
HA HA HA! AM I PICKING ON YOU TOO MUCH?
ARGH!
I DON'T LIKE IT WHEN YOU TEASE ME.
I THINK OF YOU AS A FRIEND.

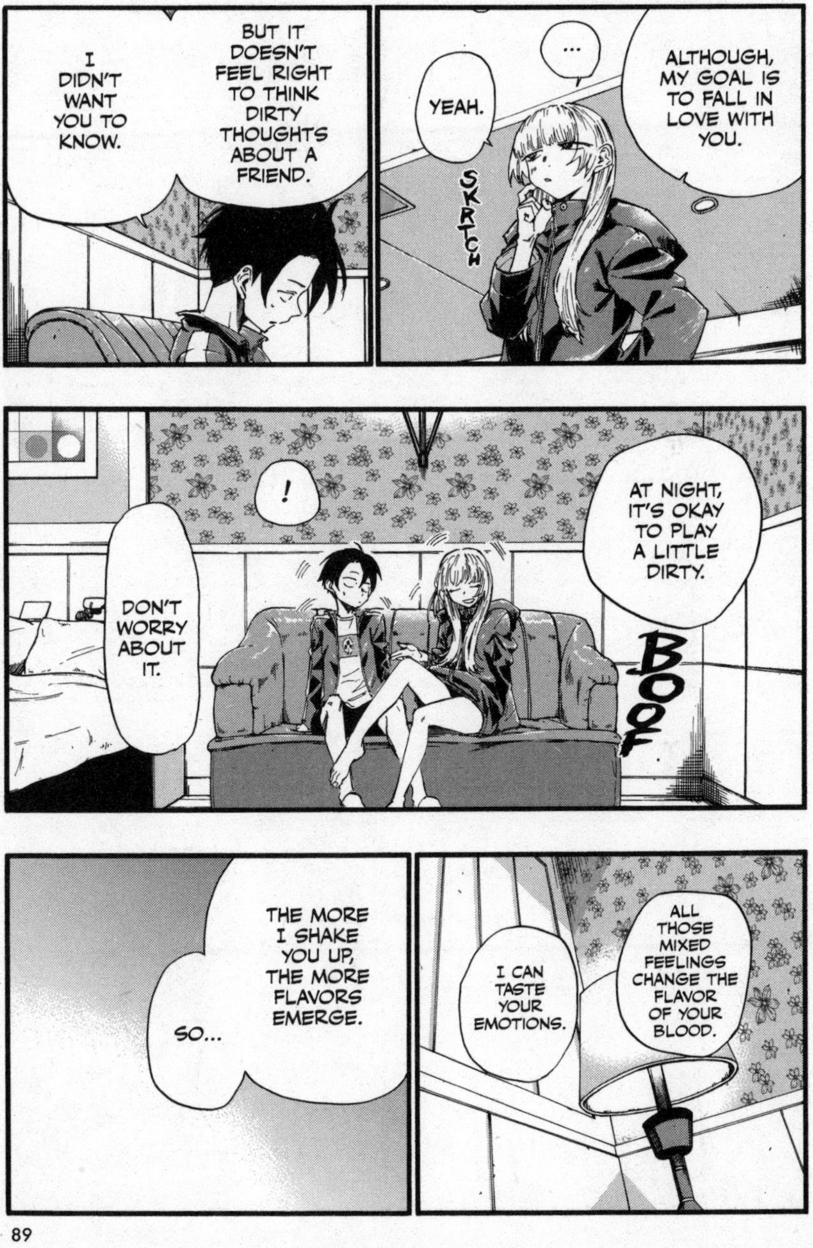
ALTHOUGH, MY GOAL IS TO FALL IN LOVE WITH YOU.
...
YEAH.
SKRTCH
BUT IT DOESN'T FEEL RIGHT TO THINK DIRTY THOUGHTS ABOUT A FRIEND.
I DIDN'T WANT YOU TO KNOW.
AT NIGHT, IT'S OKAY TO PLAY A LITTLE DIRTY.
BOOF
!
DON'T WORRY ABOUT IT.
ALL THOSE MIXED FEELINGS CHANGE THE FLAVOR OF YOUR BLOOD.
I CAN TASTE YOUR EMOTIONS.
THE MORE I SHAKE YOU UP, THE MORE FLAVORS EMERGE.
SO...

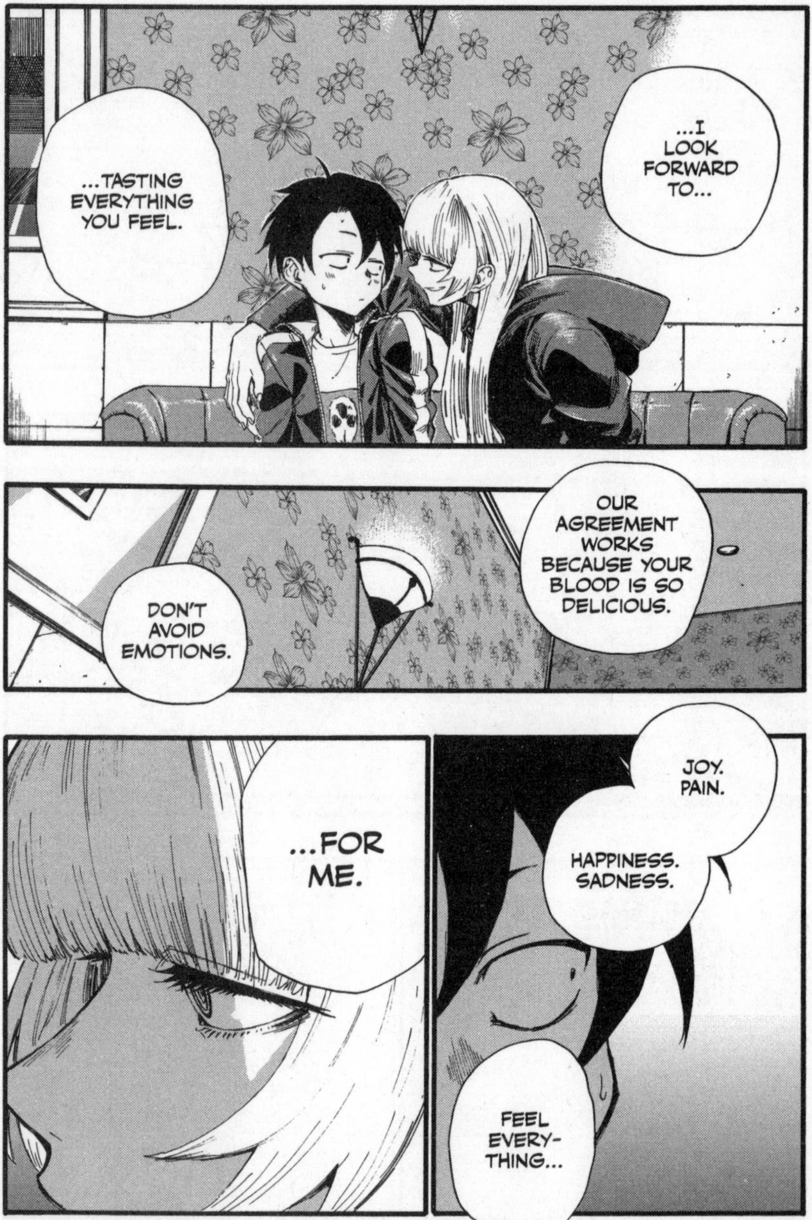
...I LOOK FORWARD TO...
...TASTING EVERYTHING YOU FEEL.
OUR AGREEMENT WORKS BECAUSE YOUR BLOOD IS SO DELICIOUS.
DON'T AVOID EMOTIONS.
JOY. PAIN.
HAPPINESS. SADNESS.
FEEL EVERY-THING...
...FOR ME.

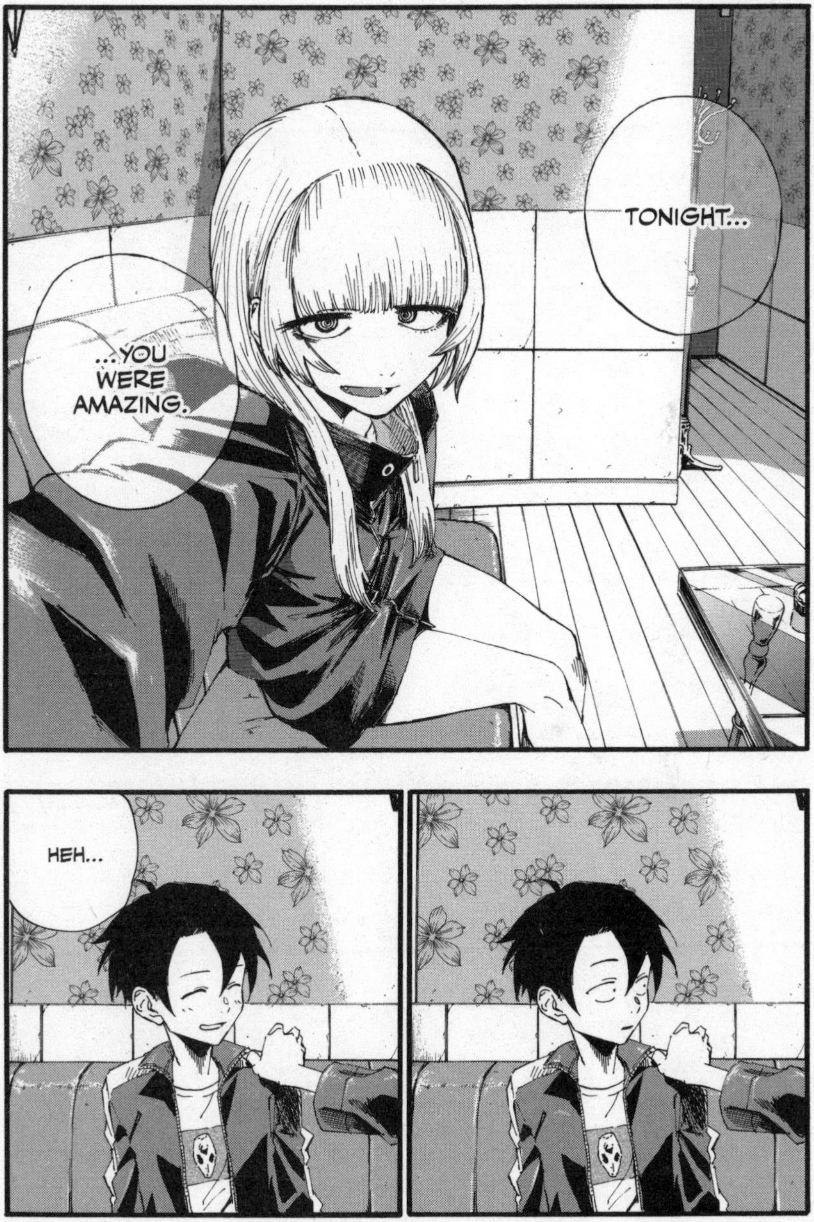
TONIGHT...
...YOU WERE AMAZING.
HEH...

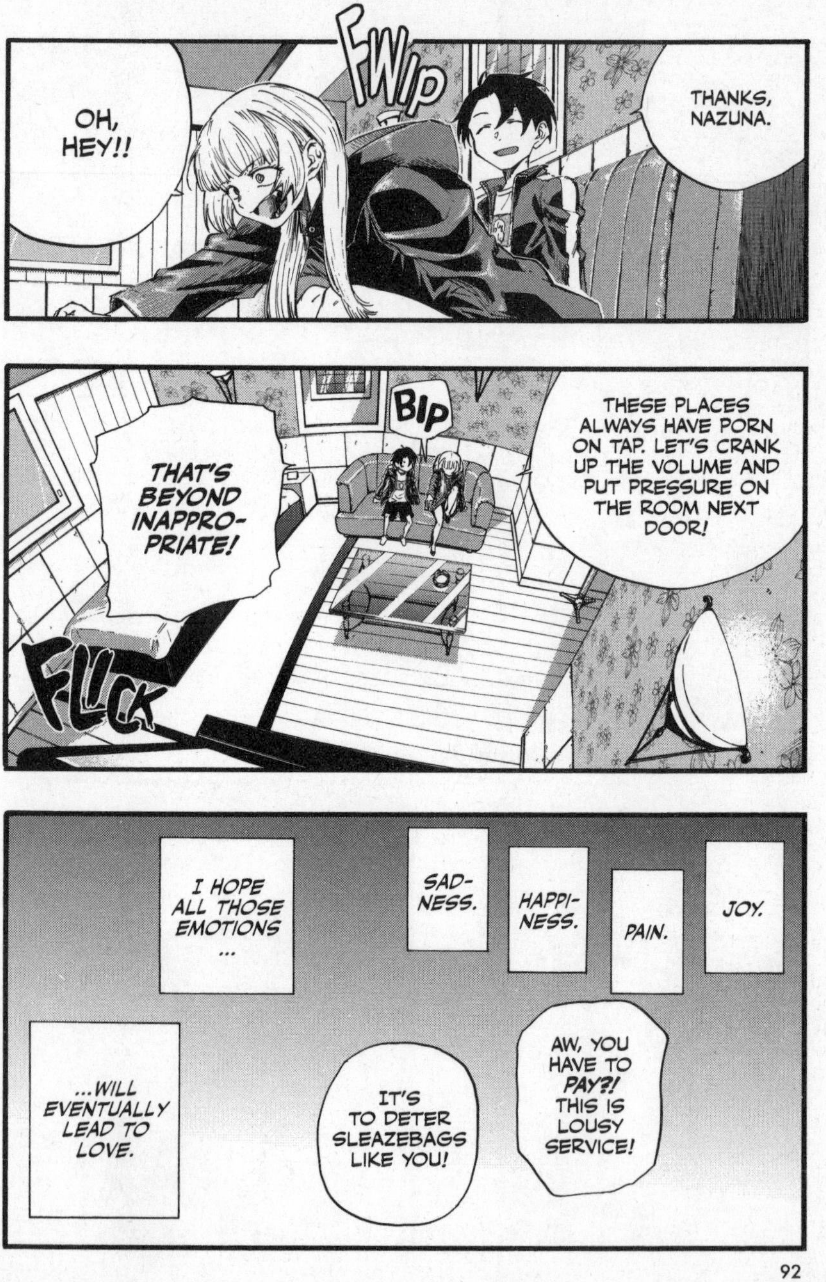
THANKS, NAZUNA.
FWIP
OH, HEY!!
THESE PLACES ALWAYS HAVE PORN ON TAP. LET'S CRANK UP THE VOLUME AND PUT PRESSURE ON THE ROOM NEXT DOOR!
BIP
THAT'S BEYOND INAPPROPRIATE!
FLICK
JOY.
PAIN.
HAPPINESS.
SADNESS.
I HOPE ALL THOSE EMOTIONS...
AW, YOU HAVE TO PAY?! THIS IS LOUSY SERVICE!
IT'S TO DETER SLEAZEBAGS LIKE YOU!
...WILL EVENTUALLY LEAD TO LOVE.

Call of the Night

Call of the Night

NIGHT 14: ONE OF THE BEAUTIFUL PEOPLE

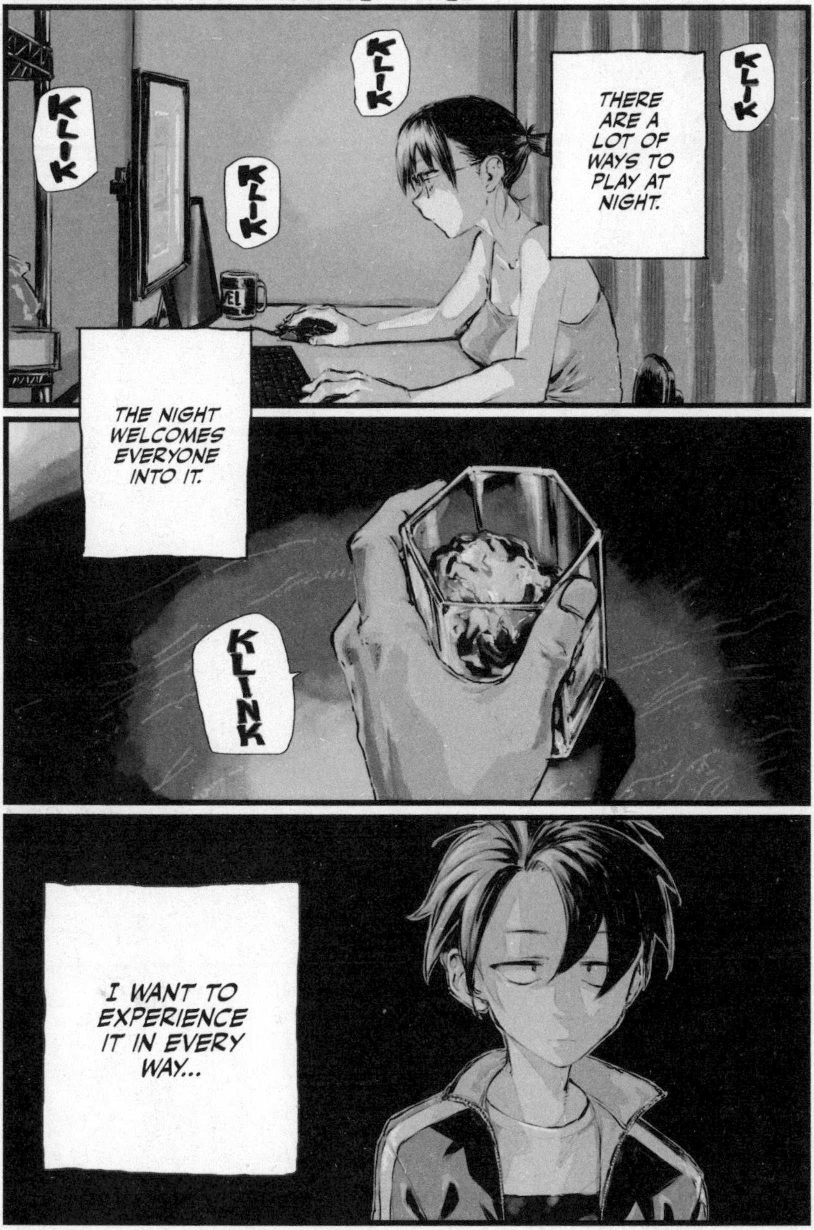
KLIK
THERE ARE A LOT OF WAYS TO PLAY AT NIGHT.
KLIK
KLIK
KLIK
THE NIGHT WELCOMES EVERYONE INTO IT.
KLINK
I WANT TO EXPERIENCE IT IN EVERY WAY...

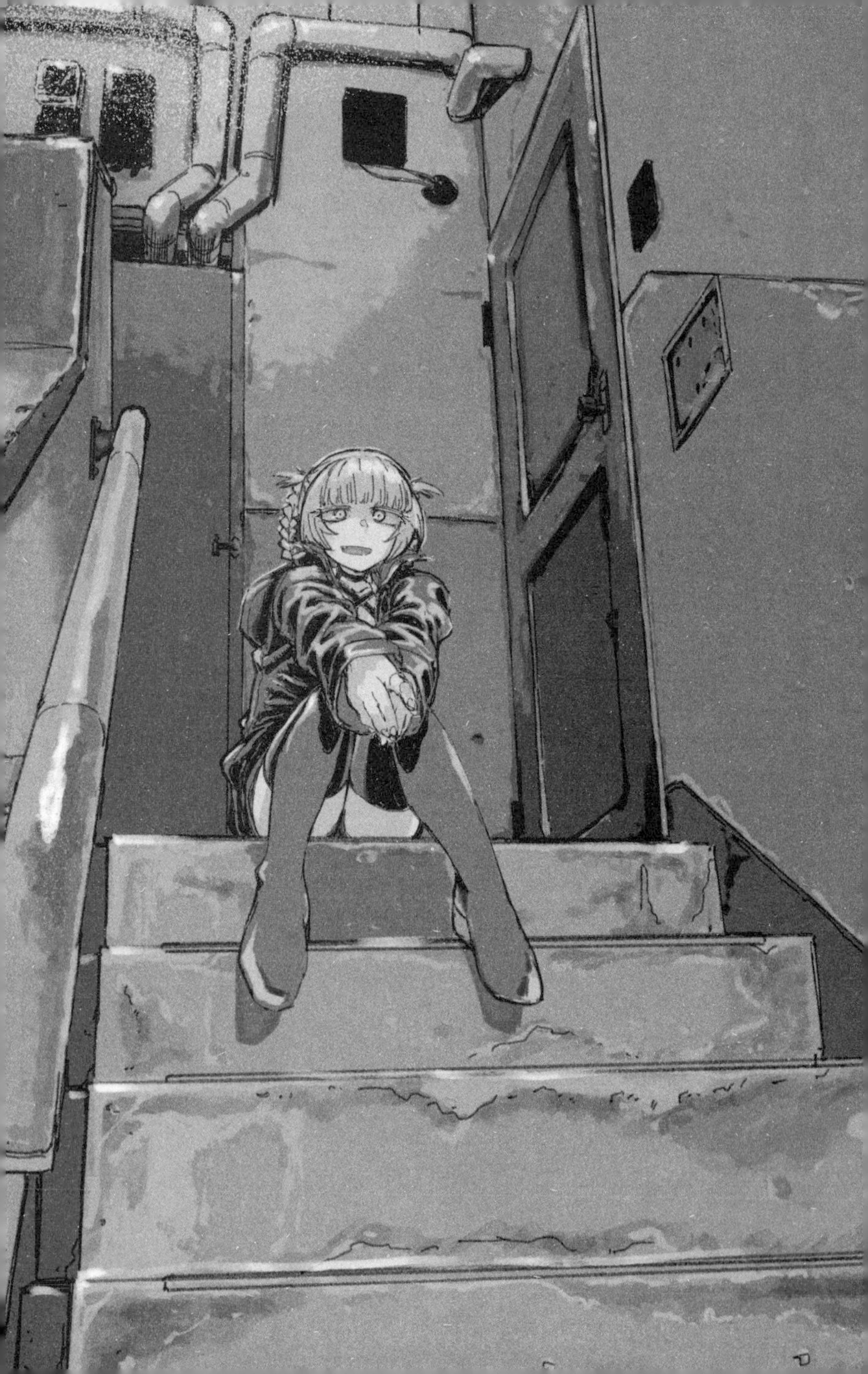

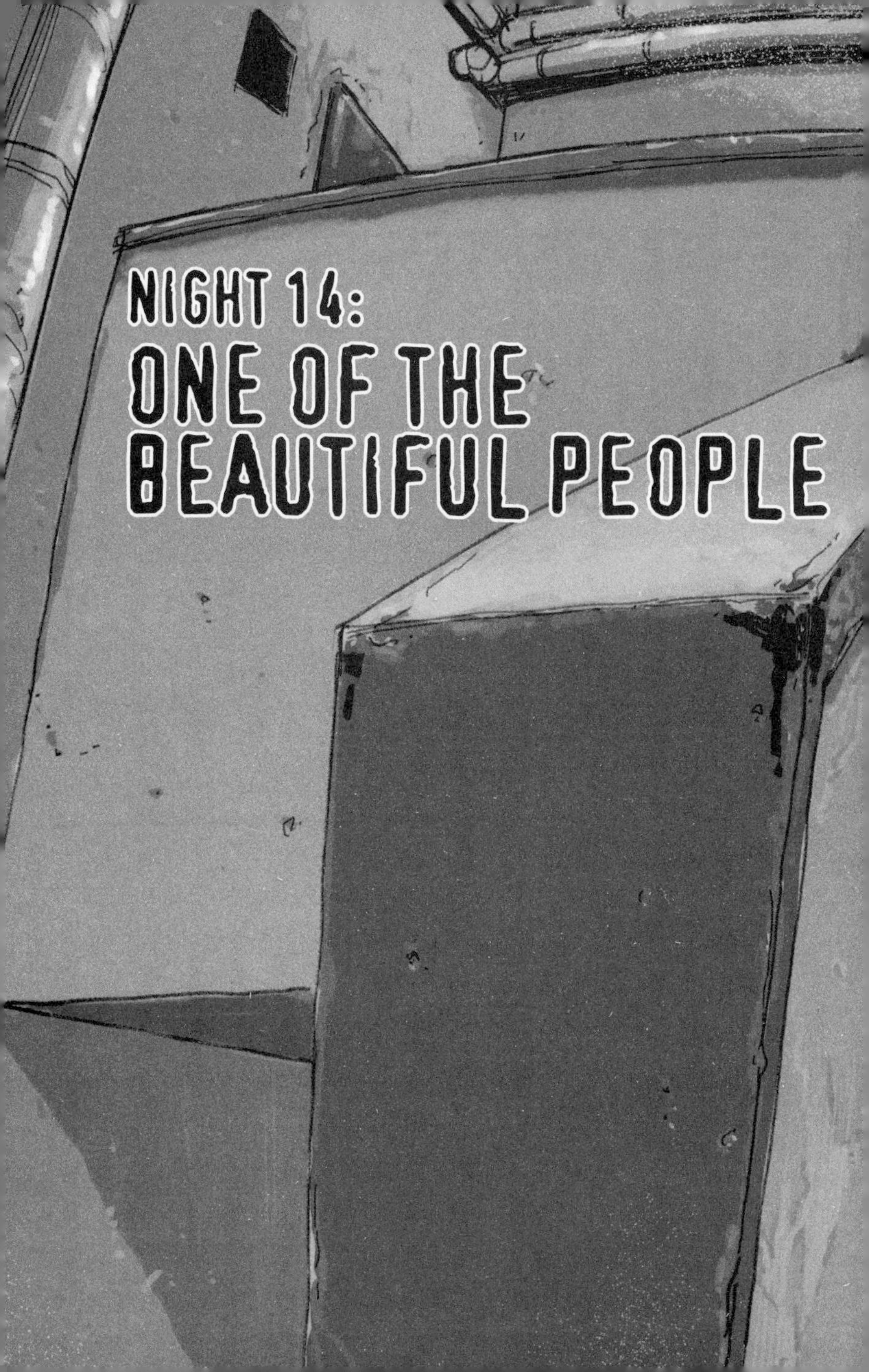
NIGHT 14:
ONE OF THE
BEAUTIFUL PEOPLE

Call of the Night

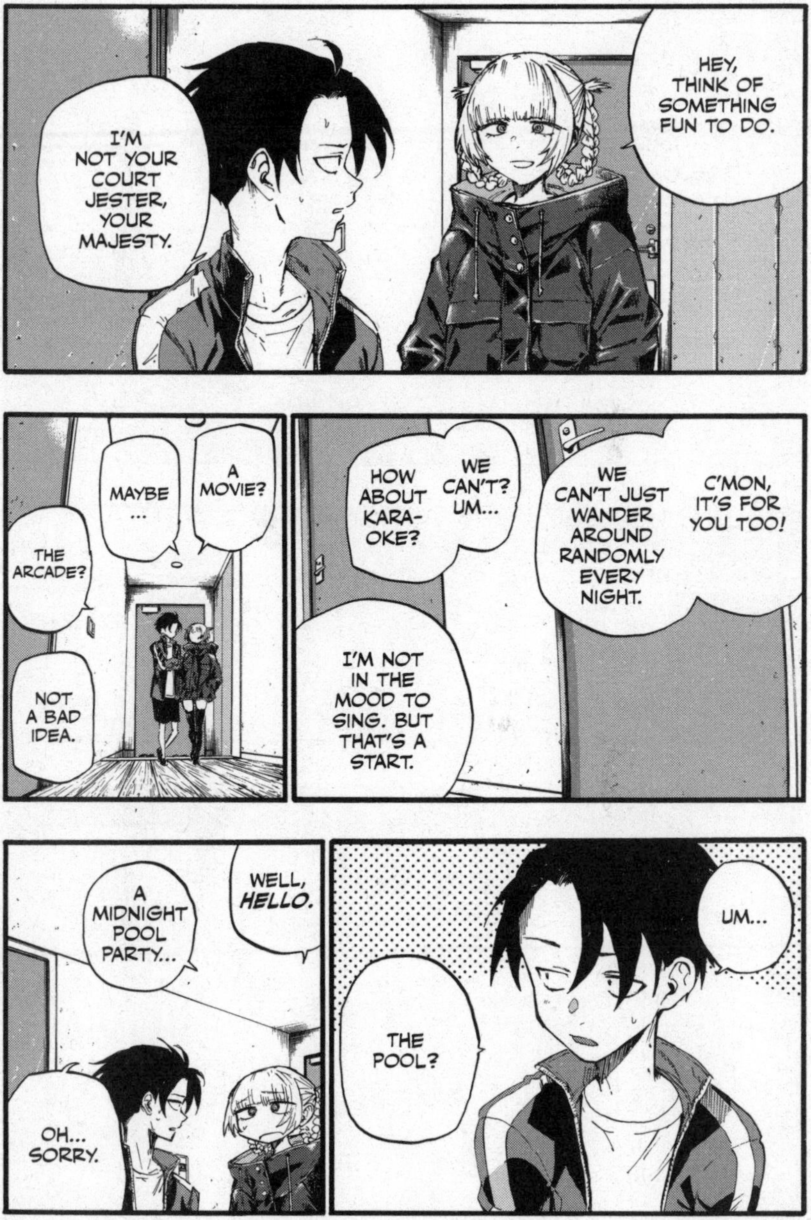
HEY, THINK OF SOMETHING FUN TO DO.
I'M NOT YOUR COURT JESTER, YOUR MAJESTY.
C'MON, IT'S FOR YOU TOO!
WE CAN'T JUST WANDER AROUND RANDOMLY EVERY NIGHT.
WE CAN'T? UM...
HOW ABOUT KARA-OKE?
I'M NOT IN THE MOOD TO SING. BUT THAT'S A START.
A MOVIE?
MAYBE ...
THE ARCADE?
NOT A BAD IDEA.
UM...
THE POOL?
WELL, *HELLO.*
A MIDNIGHT POOL PARTY...
OH... SORRY.

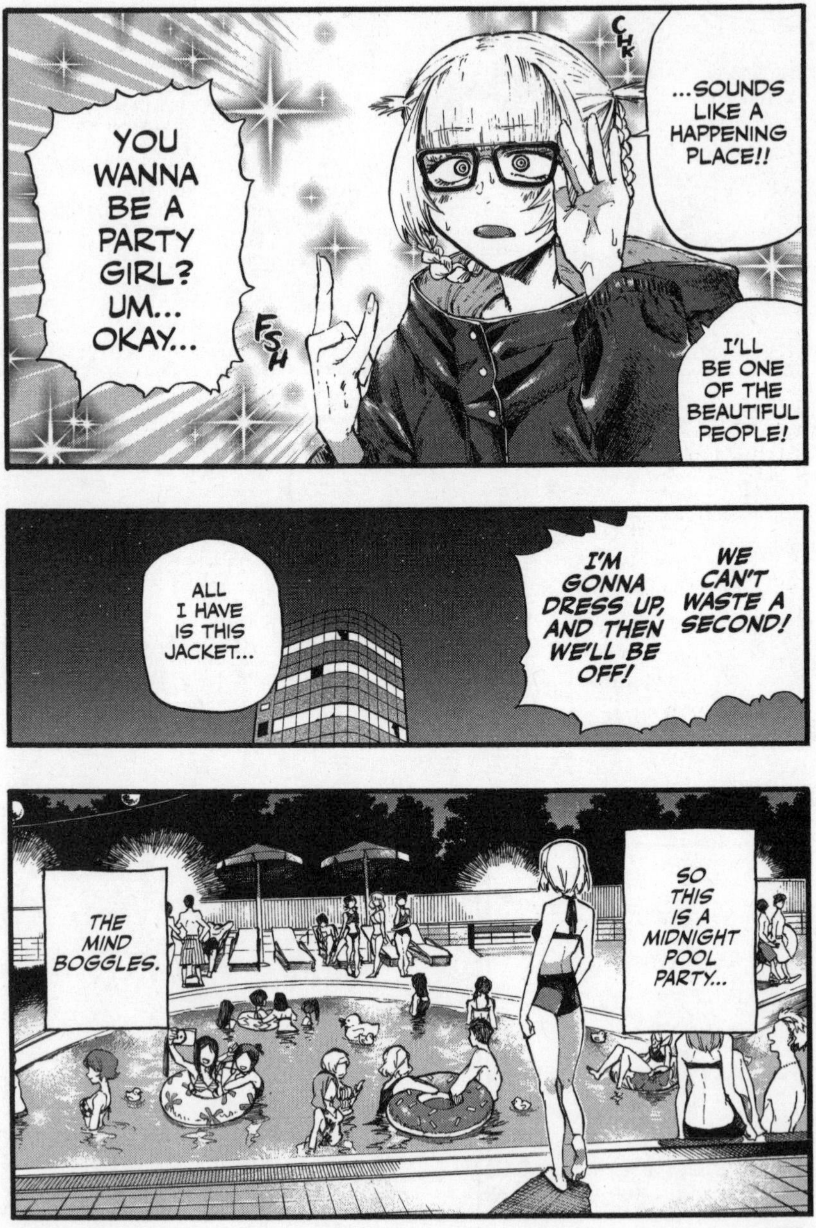
CHK
...SOUNDS LIKE A HAPPENING PLACE!!
I'LL BE ONE OF THE BEAUTIFUL PEOPLE!
FSH
YOU WANNA BE A PARTY GIRL? UM... OKAY...
WE CAN'T WASTE A SECOND!
I'M GONNA DRESS UP, AND THEN WE'LL BE OFF!
ALL I HAVE IS THIS JACKET...
SO THIS IS A MIDNIGHT POOL PARTY...
THE MIND BOGGLES.

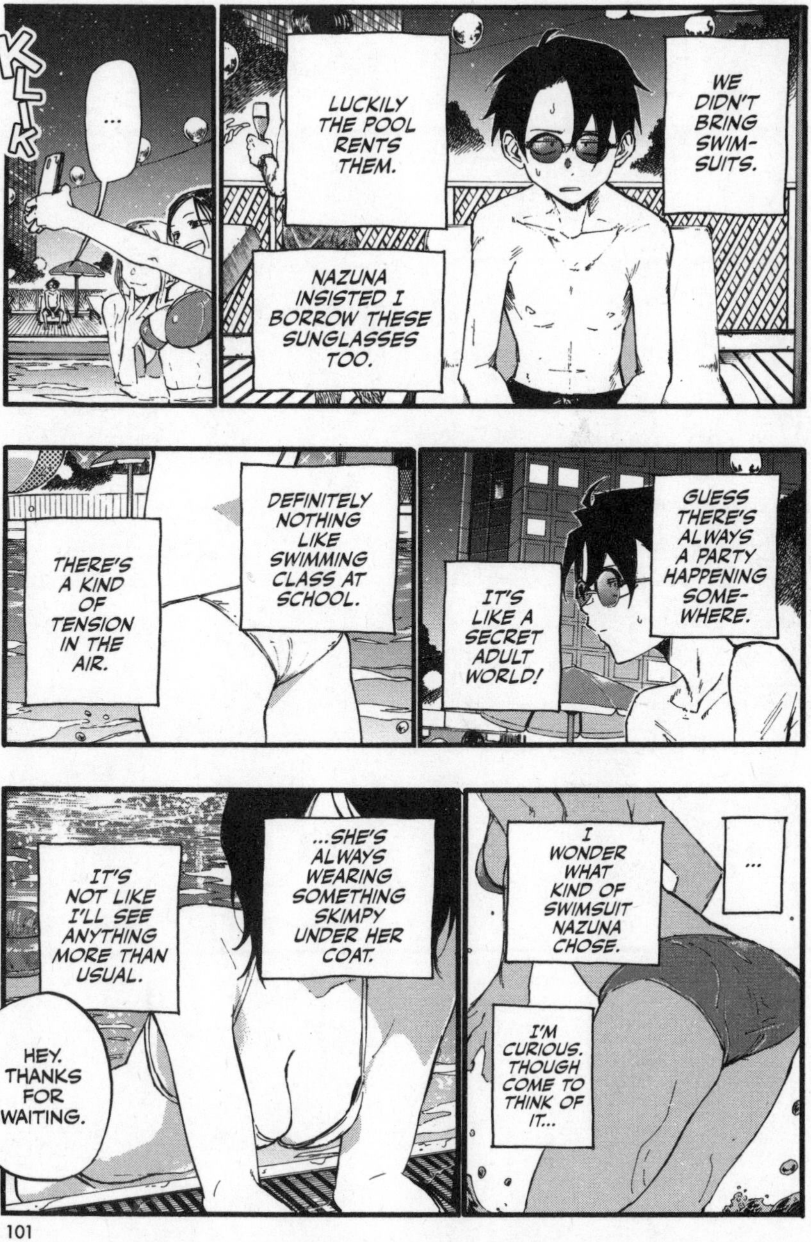
WE DIDN'T BRING SWIM-SUITS.
LUCKILY THE POOL RENTS THEM.
NAZUNA INSISTED I BORROW THESE SUNGLASSES TOO.
KLIK
...
GUESS THERE'S ALWAYS A PARTY HAPPENING SOME-WHERE.
IT'S LIKE A SECRET ADULT WORLD!
DEFINITELY NOTHING LIKE SWIMMING CLASS AT SCHOOL.
THERE'S A KIND OF TENSION IN THE AIR.
...
I WONDER WHAT KIND OF SWIMSUIT NAZUNA CHOSE.
I'M CURIOUS. THOUGH COME TO THINK OF IT...
...SHE'S ALWAYS WEARING SOMETHING SKIMPY UNDER HER COAT.
IT'S NOT LIKE I'LL SEE ANYTHING MORE THAN USUAL.
HEY. THANKS FOR WAITING.

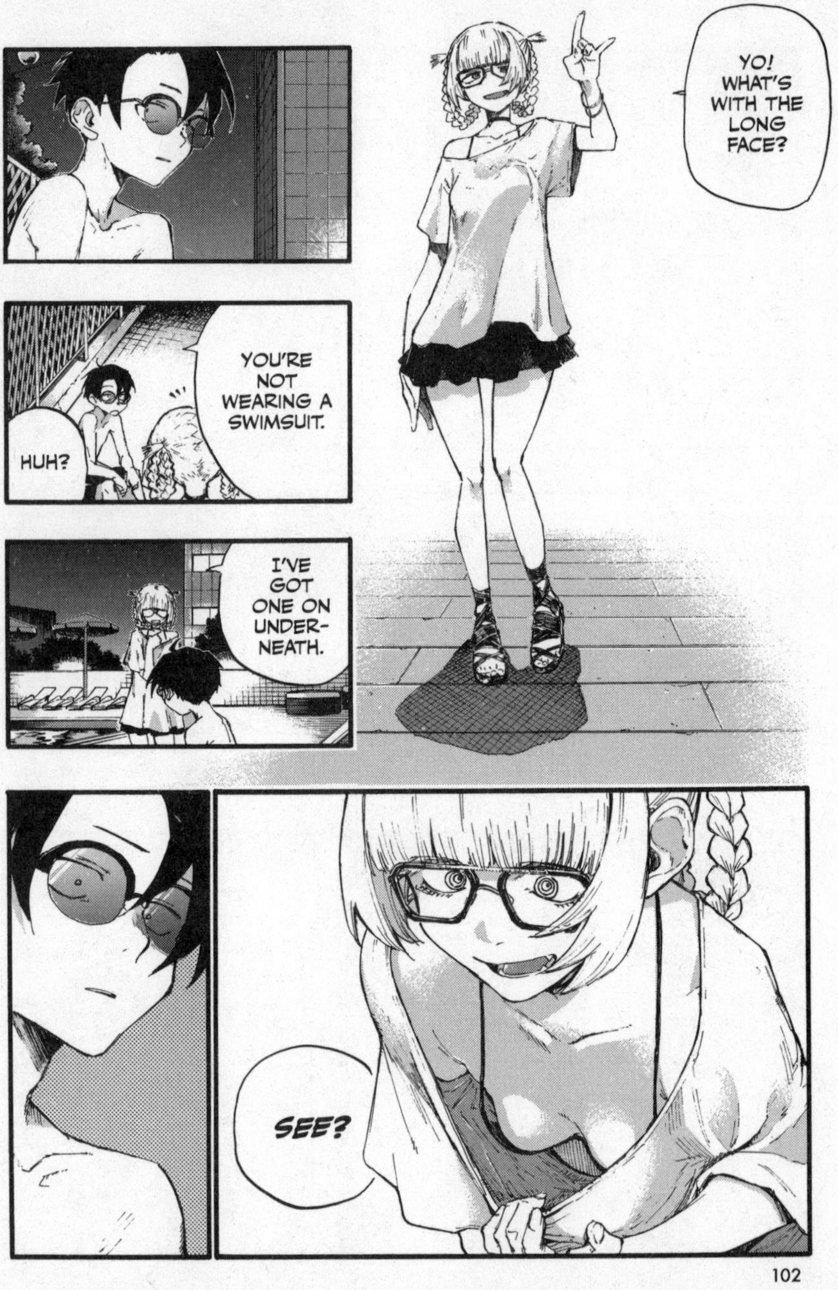
YO! WHAT'S WITH THE LONG FACE?
YOU'RE NOT WEARING A SWIMSUIT.
HUH?
I'VE GOT ONE ON UNDER-NEATH.
SEE?

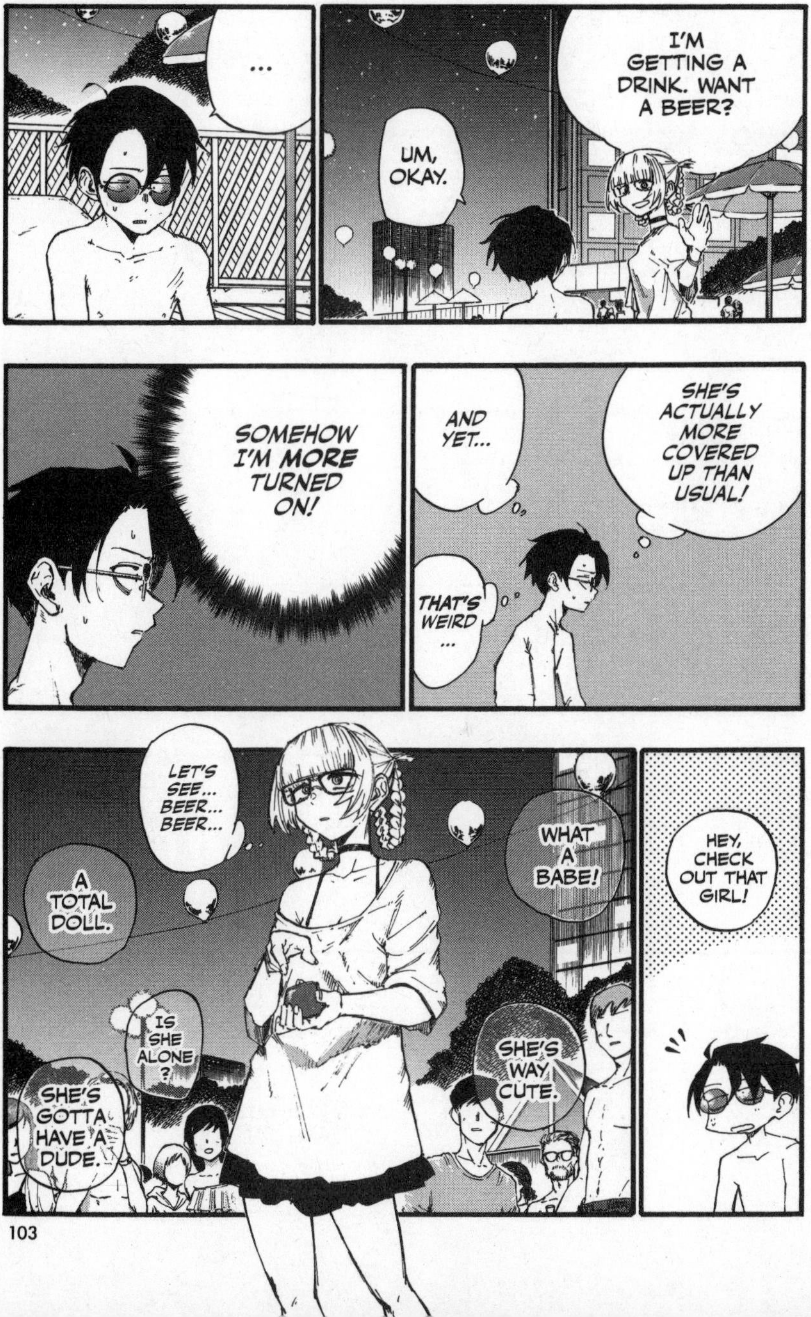
I'M GETTING A DRINK. WANT A BEER?
UM, OKAY.
...
SHE'S ACTUALLY MORE COVERED UP THAN USUAL!
AND YET...
THAT'S WEIRD ...
SOMEHOW I'M MORE TURNED ON!
HEY, CHECK OUT THAT GIRL!
WHAT A BABE!
LET'S SEE... BEER... BEER...
A TOTAL DOLL.
SHE'S WAY CUTE.
IS SHE ALONE?
SHE'S GOTTA HAVE A DUDE.

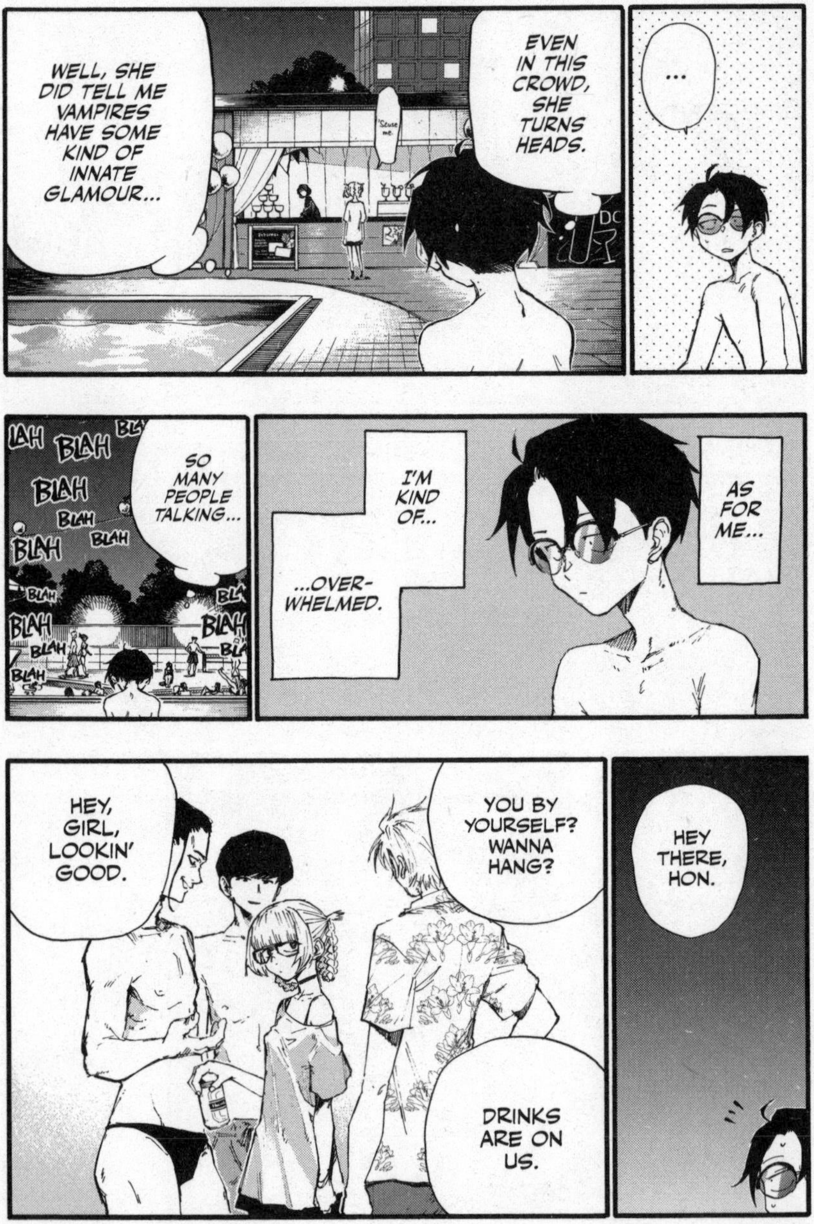
...
EVEN IN THIS CROWD, SHE TURNS HEADS.
'Scuse me.
WELL, SHE DID TELL ME VAMPIRES HAVE SOME KIND OF INNATE GLAMOUR...
AS FOR ME...
I'M KIND OF...
...OVER-WHELMED.
SO MANY PEOPLE TALKING...
BLAH
BLAH
BLAH
BLAH
BLAH
BLAH
BLAH
BLAH
BLAH
BLAH
HEY THERE, HON.
YOU BY YOURSELF? WANNA HANG?
HEY, GIRL, LOOKIN' GOOD.
DRINKS ARE ON US.

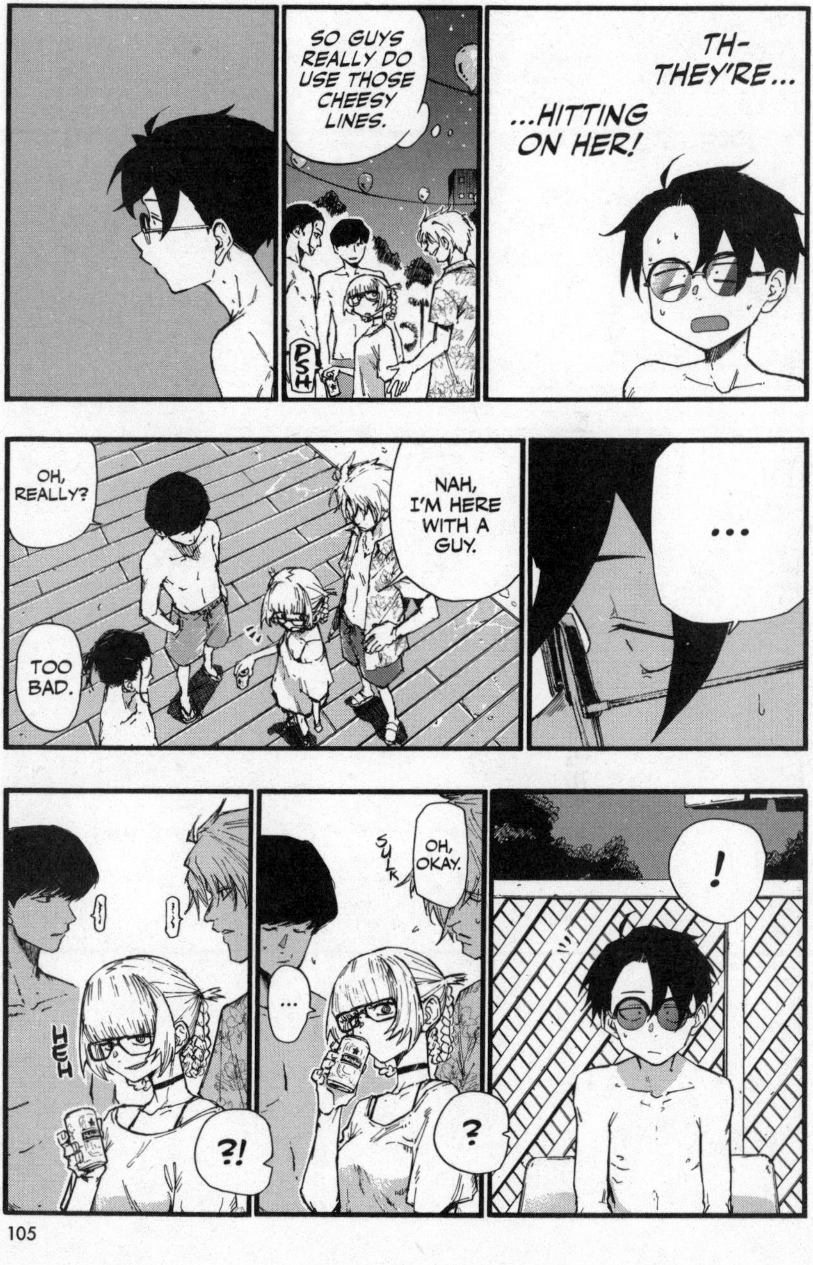
TH- THEY'RE...
...HITTING ON HER!
SO GUYS REALLY DO USE THOSE CHEESY LINES.
PSH
...
NAH, I'M HERE WITH A GUY.
OH, REALLY?
TOO BAD.
!
OH, OKAY.
SULK
...
?
HEH
?!

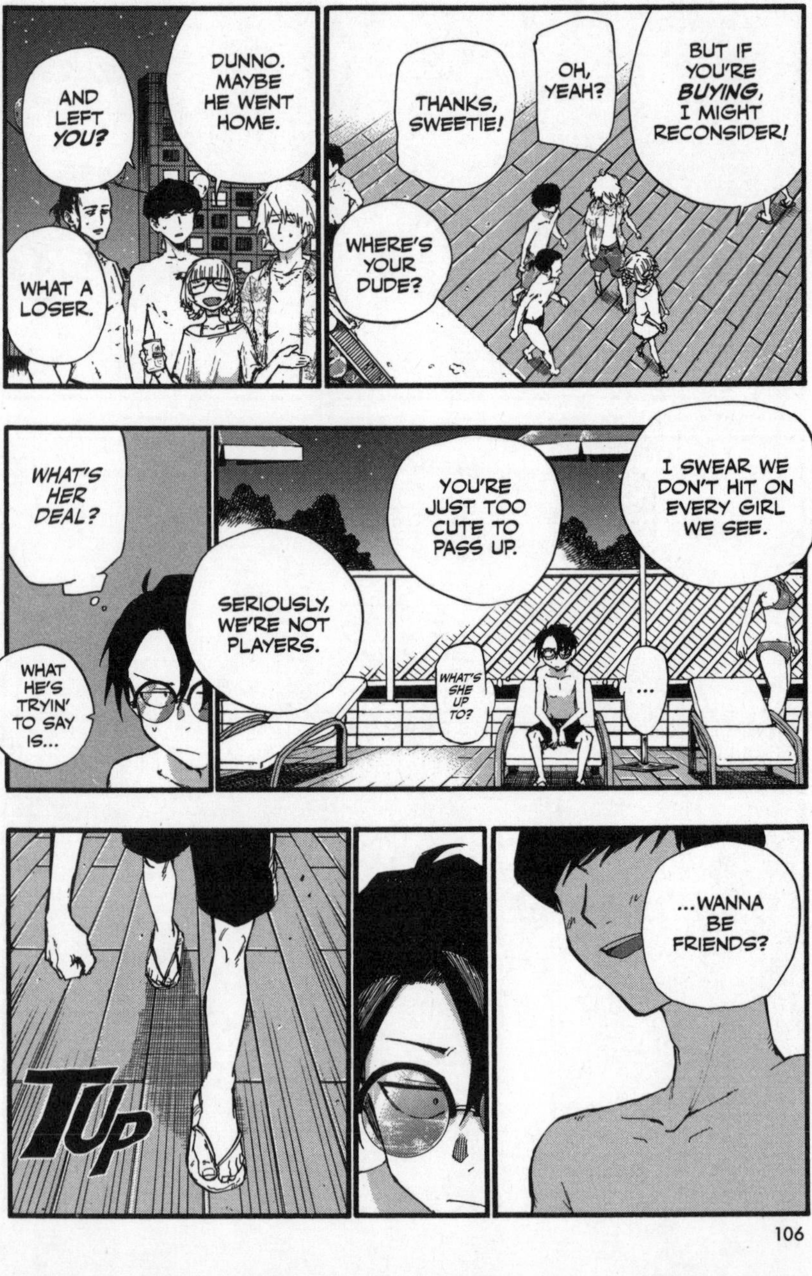
BUT IF YOU'RE *BUYING*, I MIGHT RECONSIDER!
OH, YEAH?
THANKS, SWEETIE!
WHERE'S YOUR DUDE?
DUNNO. MAYBE HE WENT HOME.
AND LEFT *YOU?*
WHAT A LOSER.
I SWEAR WE DON'T HIT ON EVERY GIRL WE SEE.
YOU'RE JUST TOO CUTE TO PASS UP.
...
WHAT'S SHE UP TO?
SERIOUSLY, WE'RE NOT PLAYERS.
WHAT'S HER DEAL?
WHAT HE'S TRYIN' TO SAY IS...
...WANNA BE FRIENDS?
TUP

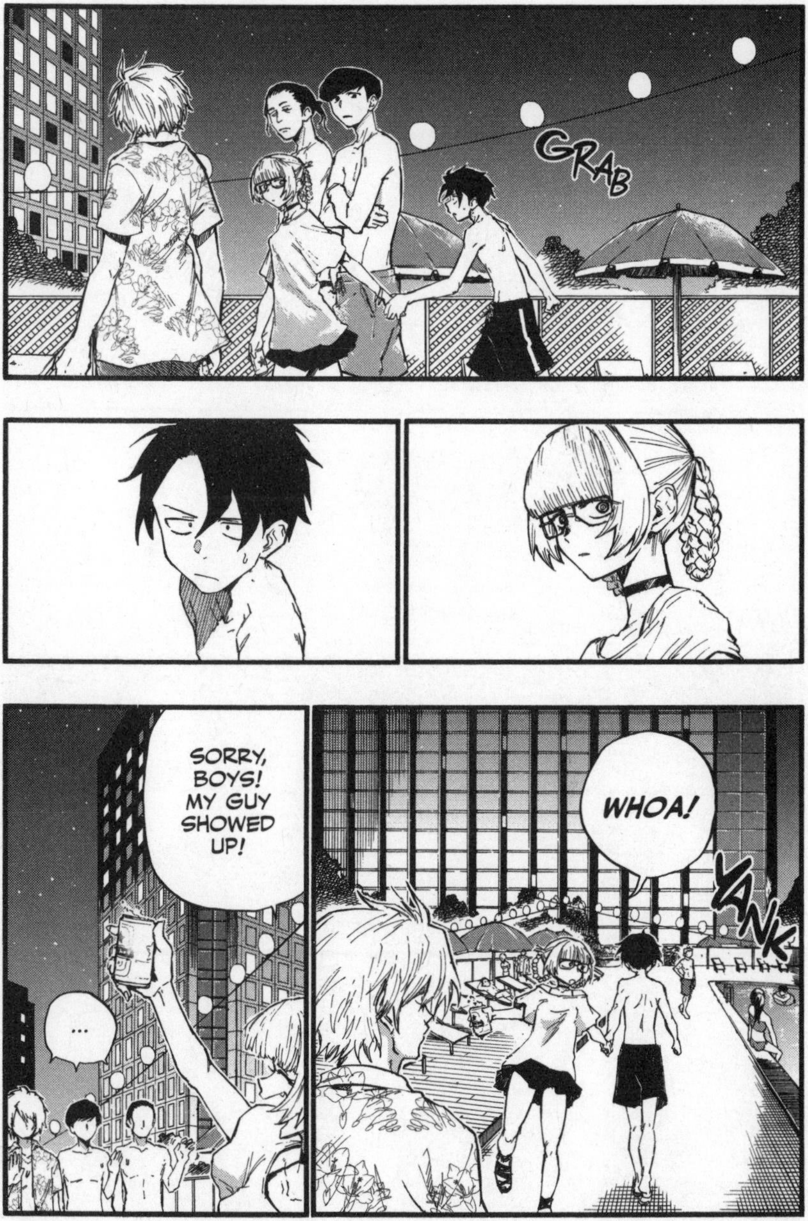
GRAB
WHOA!
YANK
SORRY, BOYS! MY GUY SHOWED UP!
...

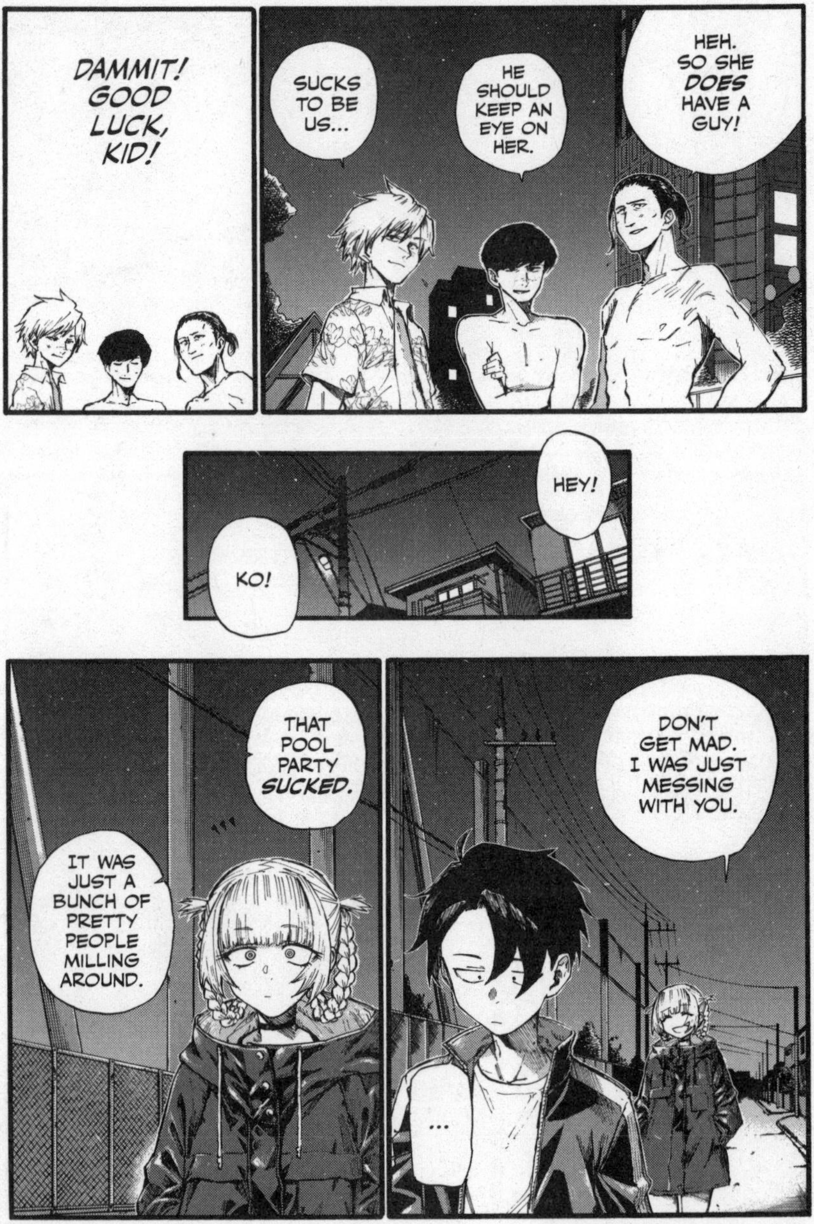
HEH. SO SHE DOES HAVE A GUY!
HE SHOULD KEEP AN EYE ON HER.
SUCKS TO BE US...
DAMMIT! GOOD LUCK, KID!
HEY!
KO!
DON'T GET MAD. I WAS JUST MESSING WITH YOU.
...
THAT POOL PARTY SUCKED.
IT WAS JUST A BUNCH OF PRETTY PEOPLE MILLING AROUND.

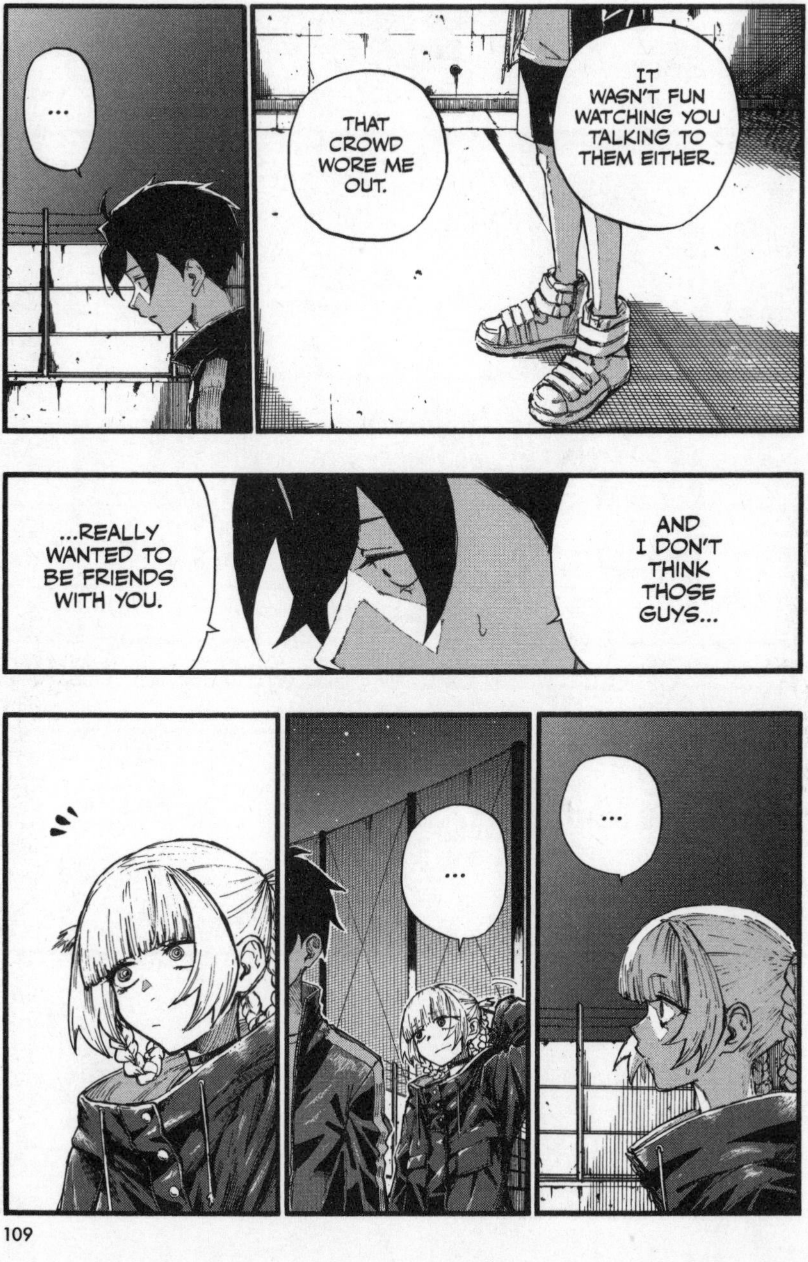
IT WASN'T FUN WATCHING YOU TALKING TO THEM EITHER.
THAT CROWD WORE ME OUT.
...
AND I DON'T THINK THOSE GUYS...
...REALLY WANTED TO BE FRIENDS WITH YOU.
...
...

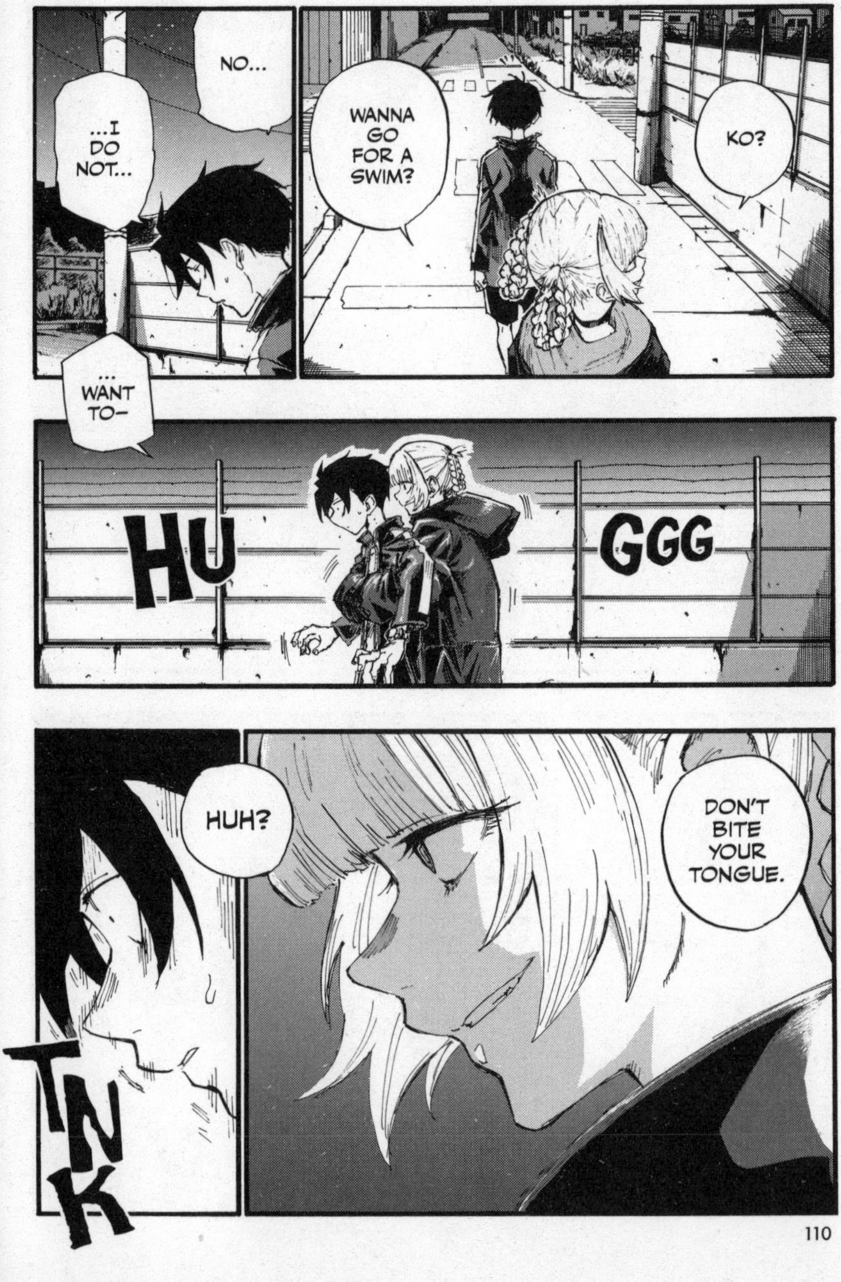
KO?
WANNA GO FOR A SWIM?
NO...
...I DO NOT...
...WANT TO-
HU GGG
DON'T BITE YOUR TONGUE.
HUH?
TNK

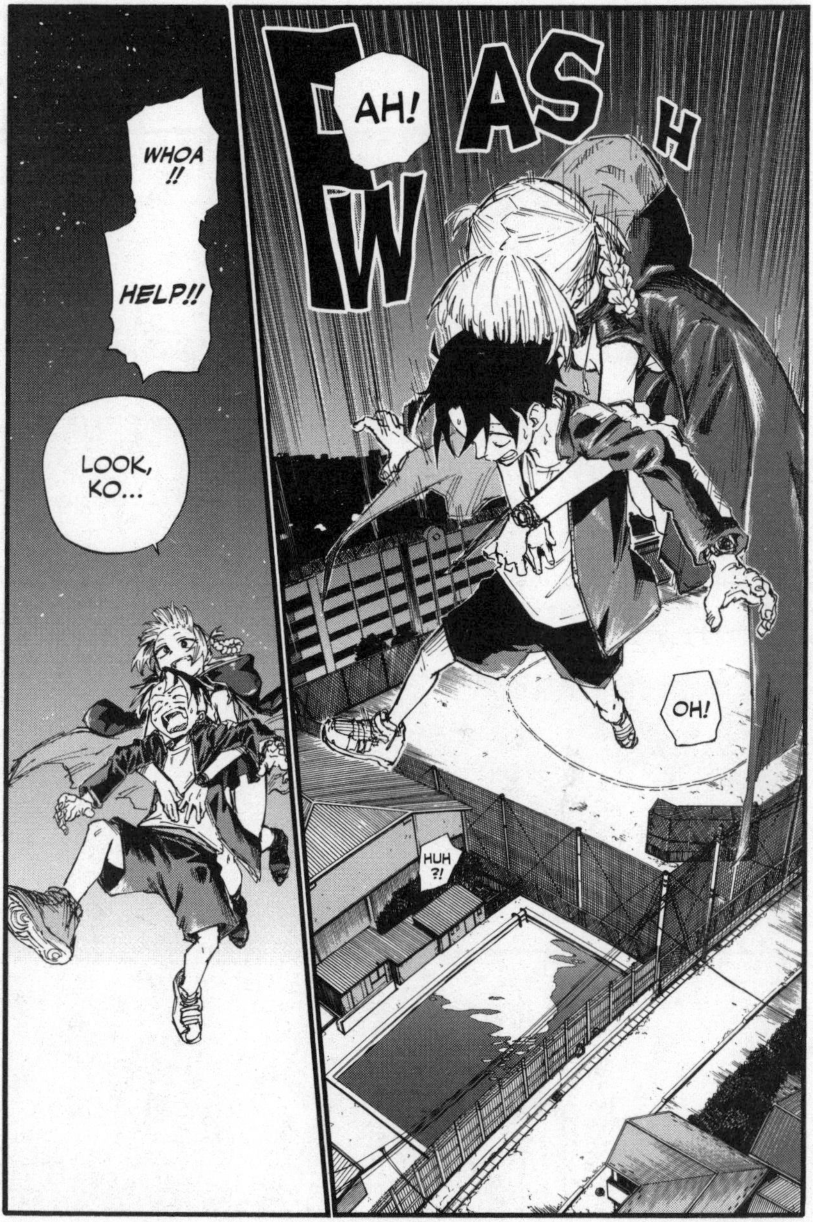

FWASH
AH!
OH!
HUH ?!
WHOA !!
HELP!!
LOOK, KO...

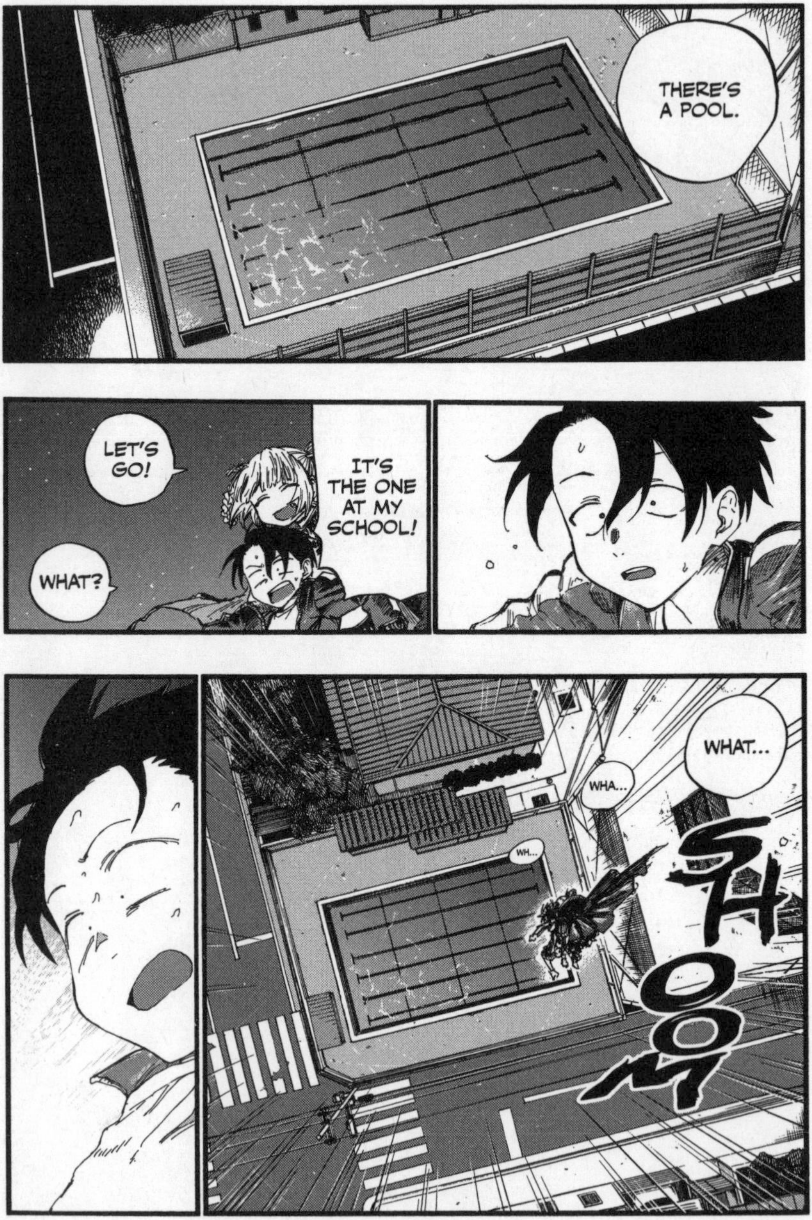
THERE'S A POOL.
IT'S THE ONE AT MY SCHOOL!
LET'S GO!
WHAT?
WHAT...
WHA...
WH...
SHOOM

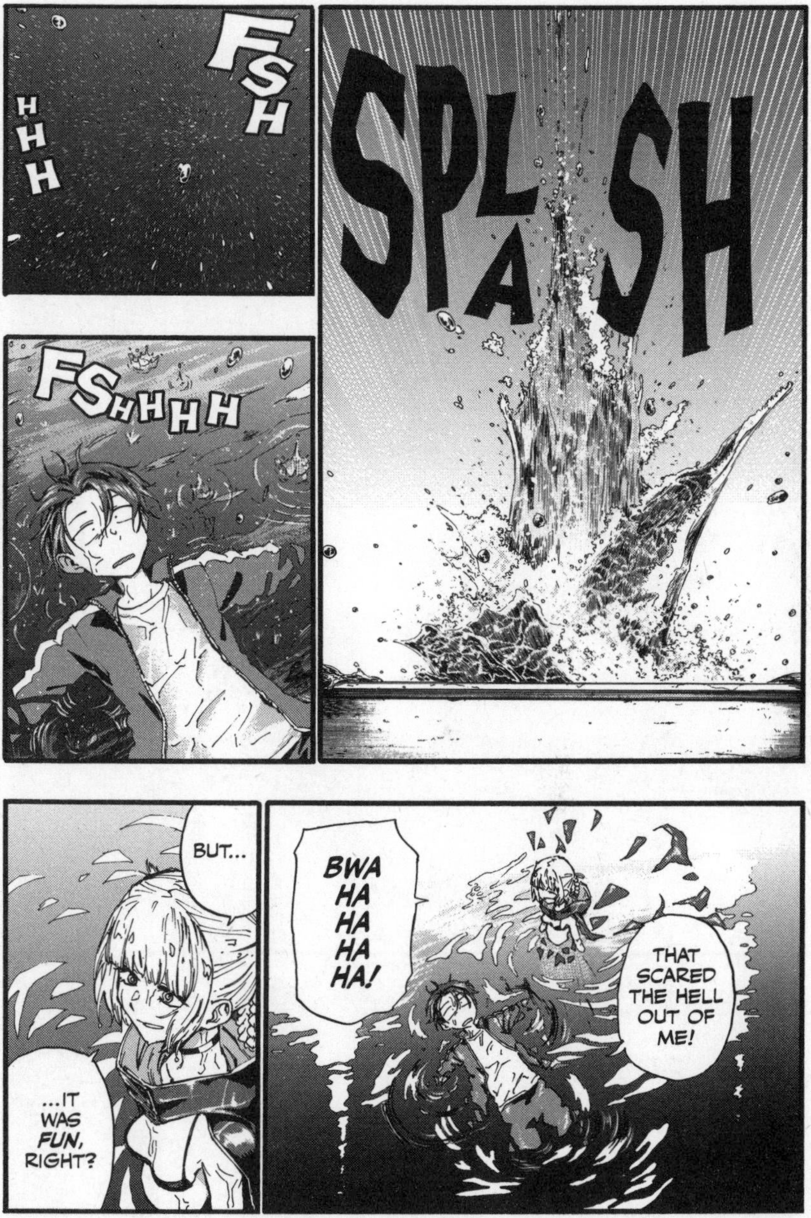
SPLASH
FSHHH
FSHHHHH
BWA HA HA HA HA!
THAT SCARED THE HELL OUT OF ME!
BUT...
...IT WAS FUN, RIGHT?

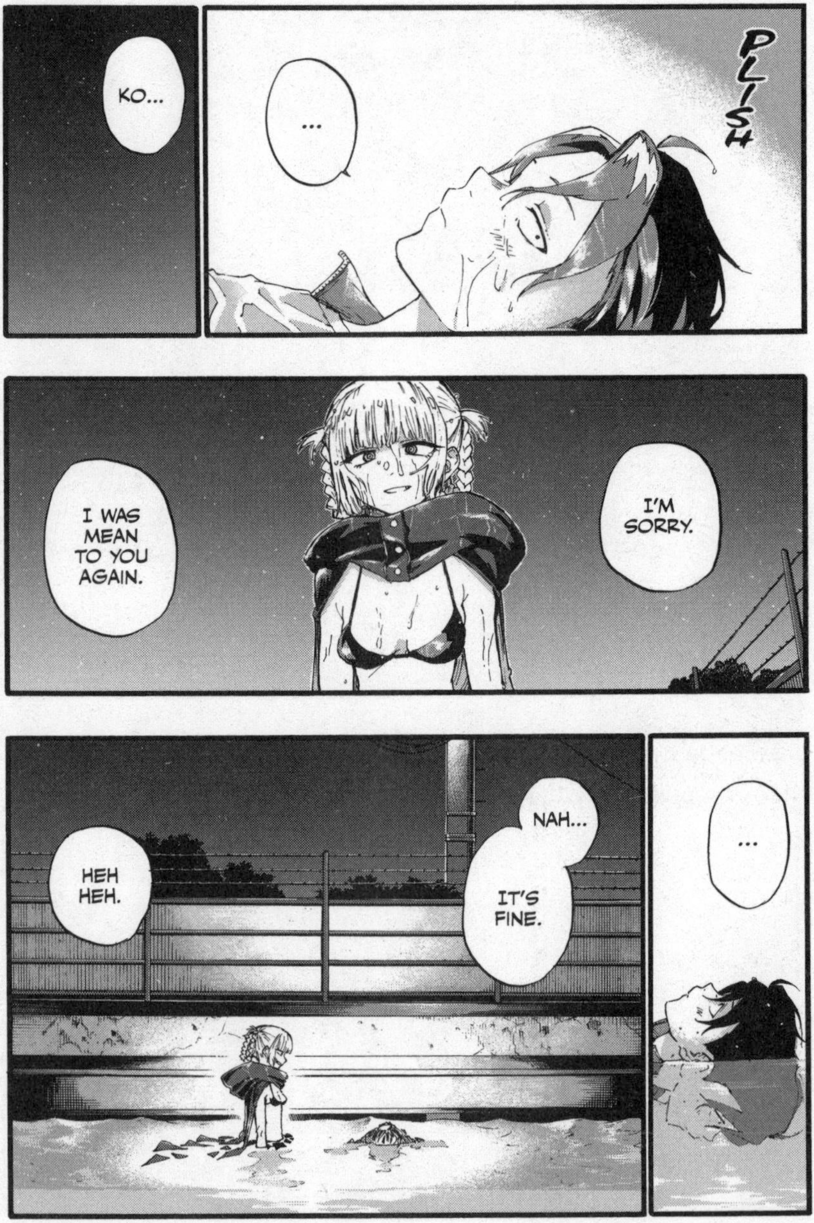
PLISH
...
KO...
I'M SORRY.
I WAS MEAN TO YOU AGAIN.
...
NAH...
IT'S FINE.
HEH HEH.

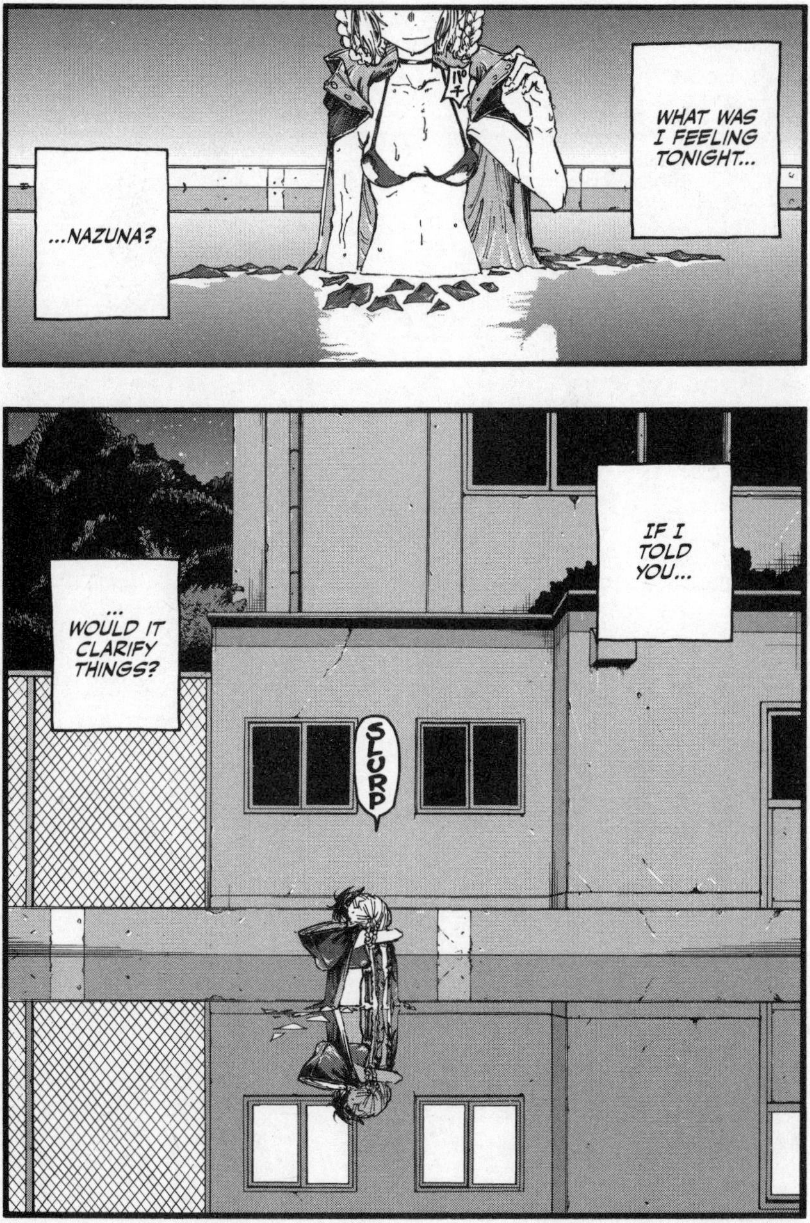
WHAT WAS I FEELING TONIGHT...
...NAZUNA?
IF I TOLD YOU...
...WOULD IT CLARIFY THINGS?
SLURP

Call of the Night

NIGHT 15: THE ROKYO PRESSURE POINT

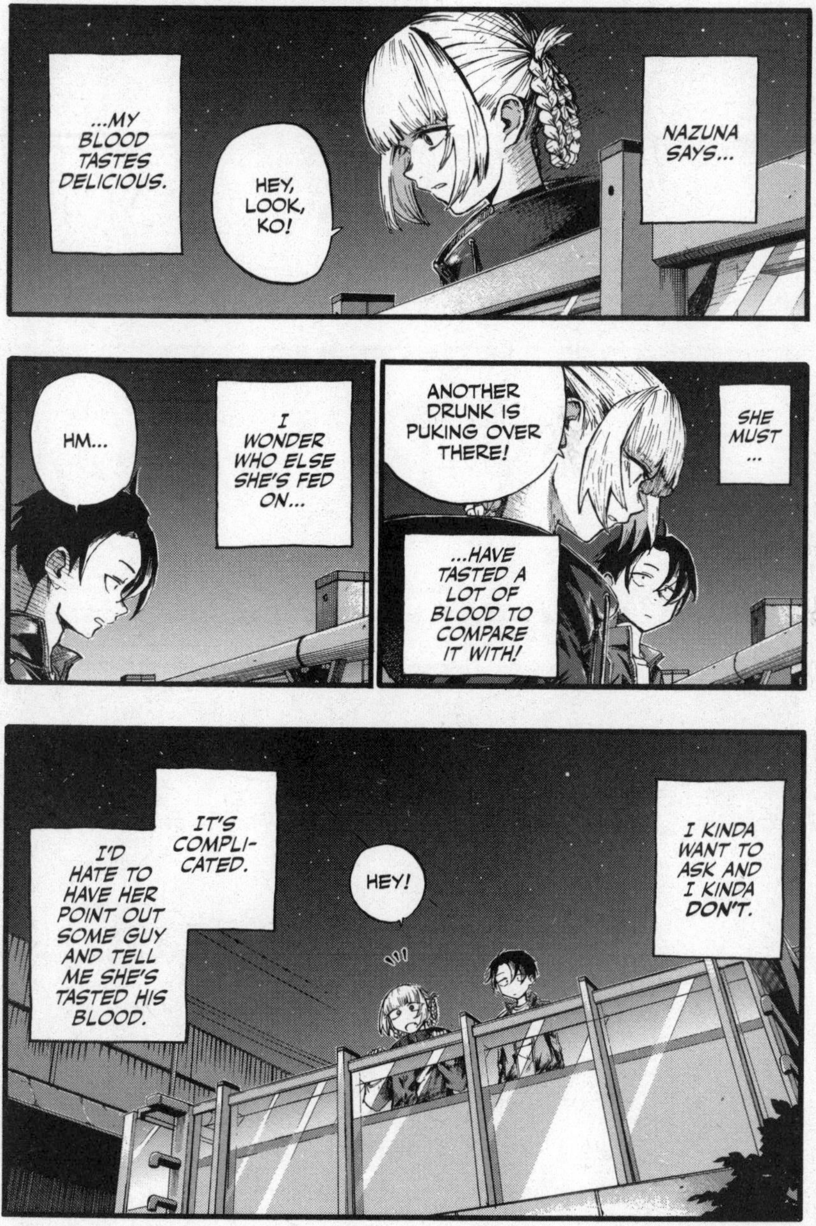
NAZUNA SAYS...
HEY, LOOK, KO!
...MY BLOOD TASTES DELICIOUS.
SHE MUST ...
ANOTHER DRUNK IS PUKING OVER THERE!
...HAVE TASTED A LOT OF BLOOD TO COMPARE IT WITH!
I WONDER WHO ELSE SHE'S FED ON...
HM...
I KINDA WANT TO ASK AND I KINDA DON'T.
HEY!
!!!
IT'S COMPLI-CATED.
I'D HATE TO HAVE HER POINT OUT SOME GUY AND TELL ME SHE'S TASTED HIS BLOOD.

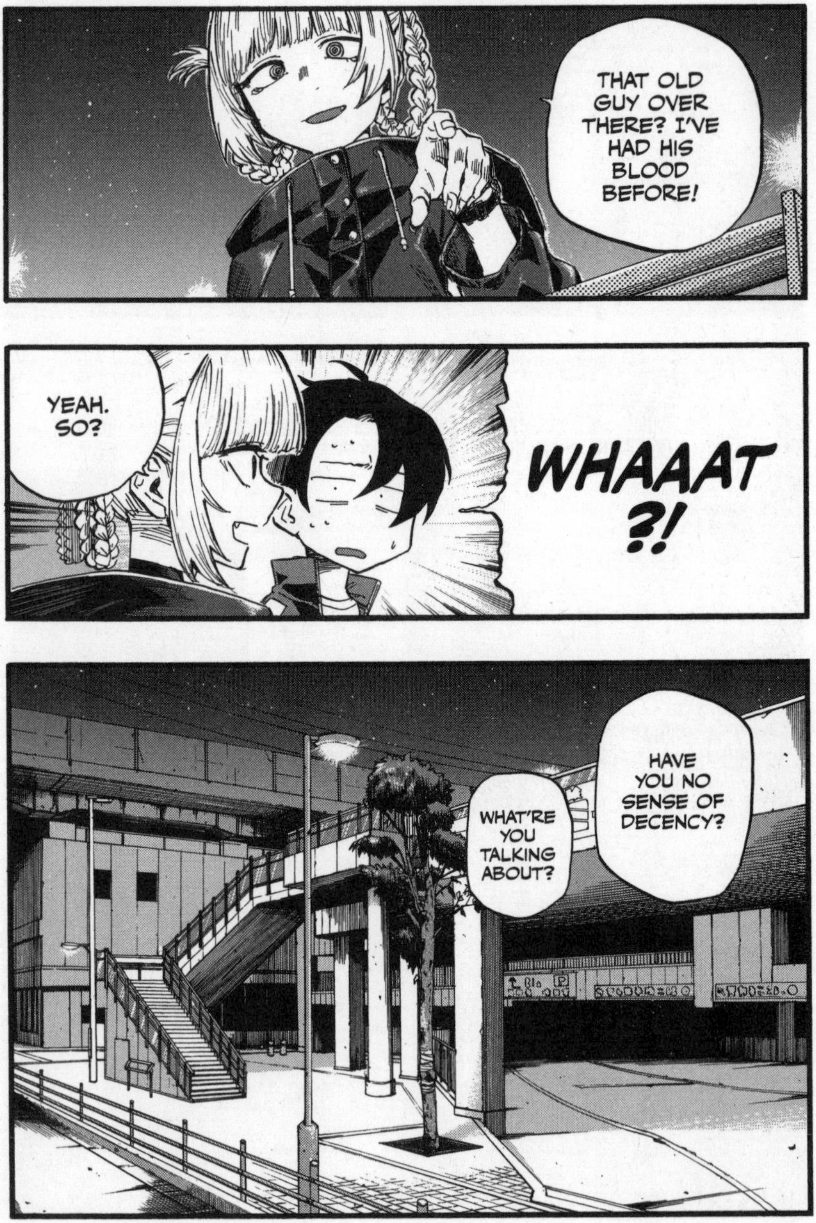
THAT OLD GUY OVER THERE? I'VE HAD HIS BLOOD BEFORE!
WHAAAT ?!
YEAH. SO?
HAVE YOU NO SENSE OF DECENCY?
WHAT'RE YOU TALKING ABOUT?

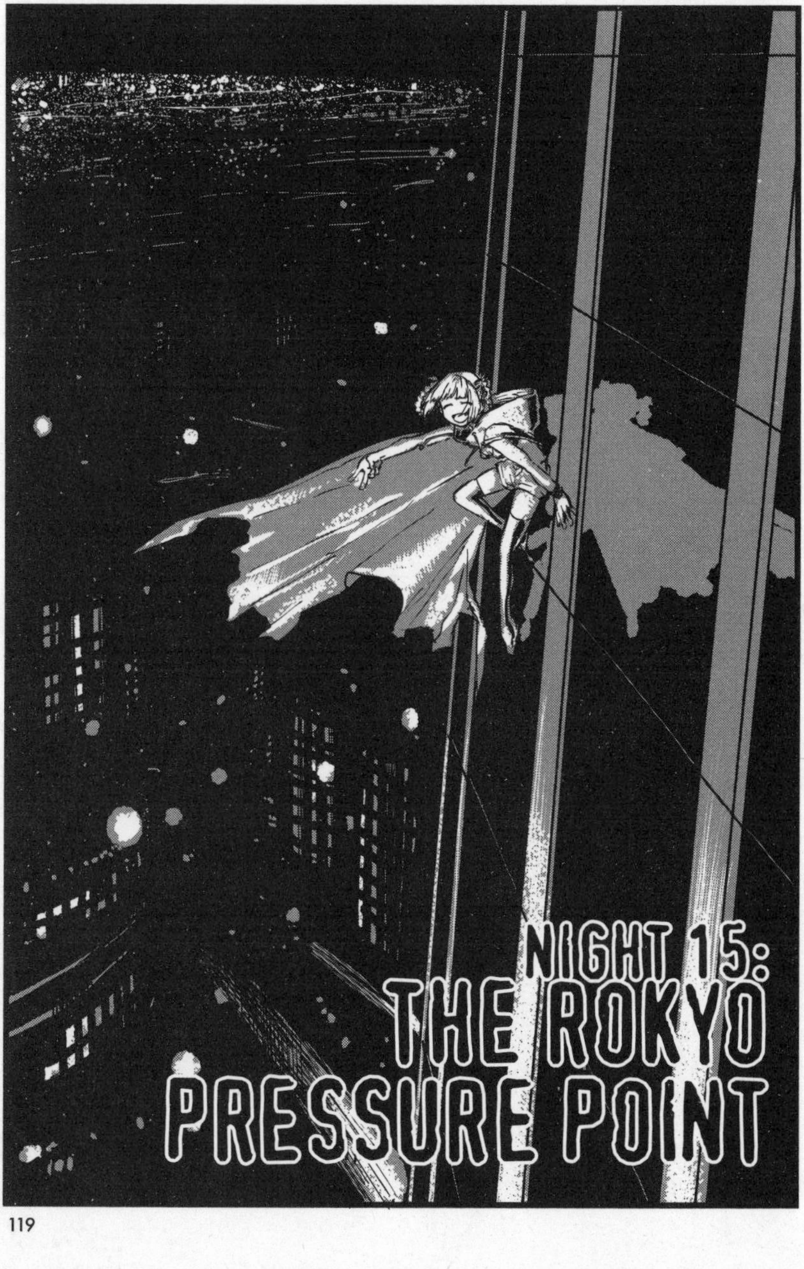
NIGHT 15:
THE ROKYO PRESSURE POINT

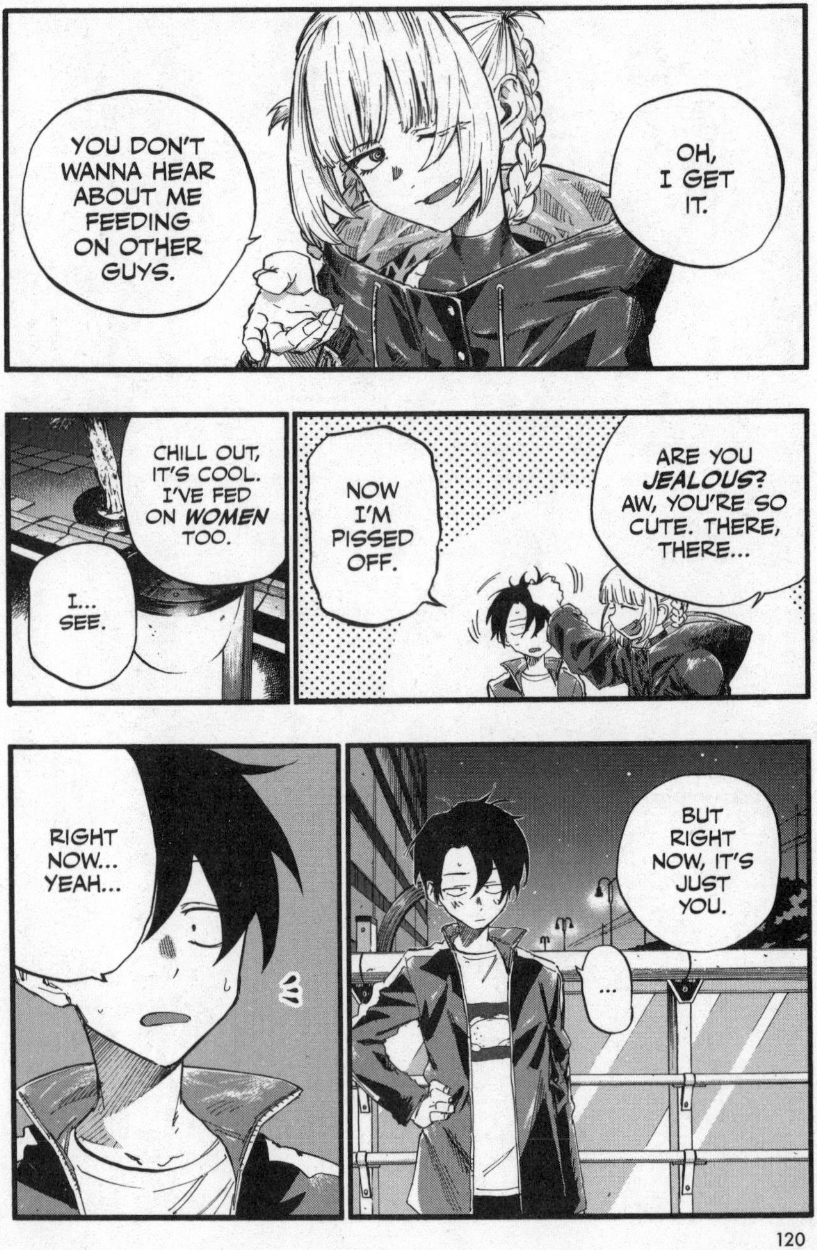
OH, I GET IT.
YOU DON'T WANNA HEAR ABOUT ME FEEDING ON OTHER GUYS.
ARE YOU *JEALOUS?* AW, YOU'RE SO CUTE. THERE, THERE...
NOW I'M PISSED OFF.
CHILL OUT, IT'S COOL. I'VE FED ON *WOMEN* TOO.
I... SEE.
BUT RIGHT NOW, IT'S JUST YOU.
...
RIGHT NOW... YEAH...

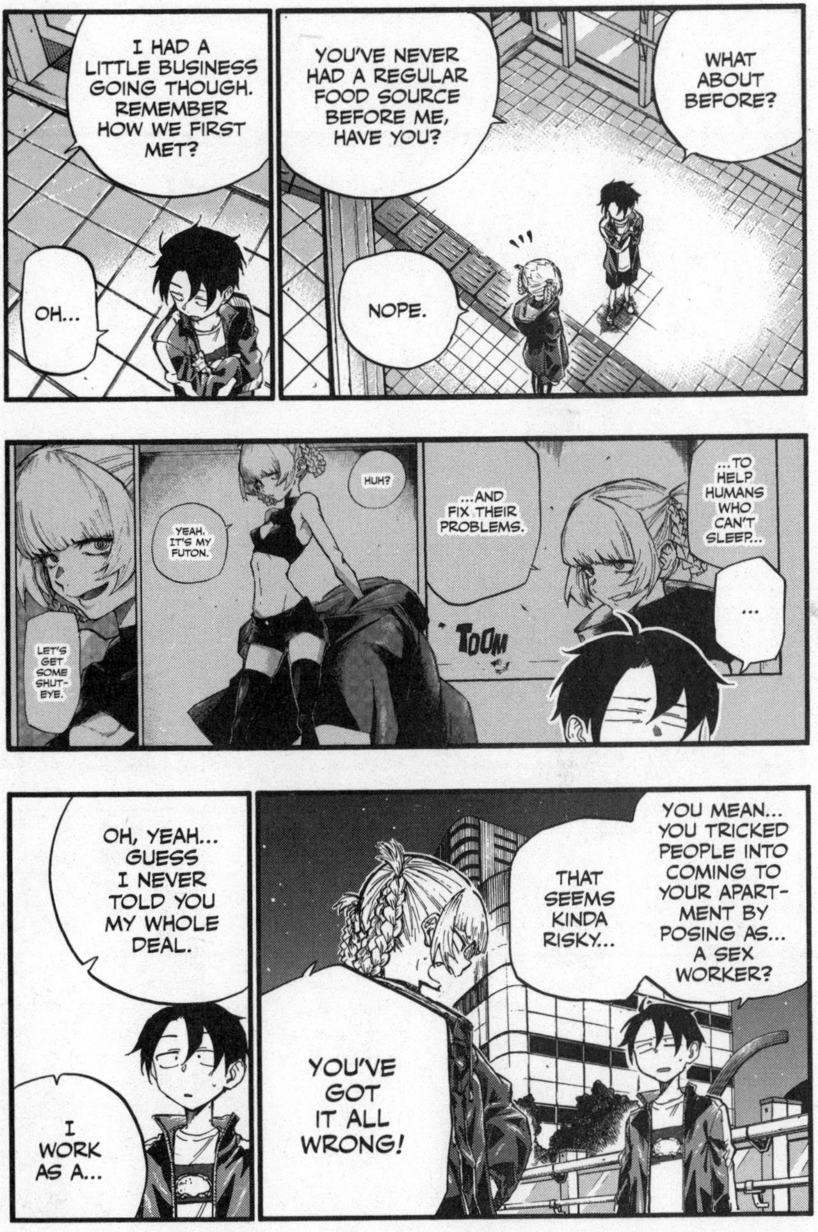

WHAT ABOUT BEFORE?
YOU'VE NEVER HAD A REGULAR FOOD SOURCE BEFORE ME, HAVE YOU?
NOPE.
I HAD A LITTLE BUSINESS GOING THOUGH. REMEMBER HOW WE FIRST MET?
OH...
...TO HELP HUMANS WHO CAN'T SLEEP...
...
...AND FIX THEIR PROBLEMS.
TOOM
HUH?
YEAH. IT'S MY FUTON.
LET'S GET SOME SHUT-EYE.
YOU MEAN... YOU TRICKED PEOPLE INTO COMING TO YOUR APARTMENT BY POSING AS... A SEX WORKER?
THAT SEEMS KINDA RISKY...
YOU'VE GOT IT ALL WRONG!
OH, YEAH... GUESS I NEVER TOLD YOU MY WHOLE DEAL.
I WORK AS A...

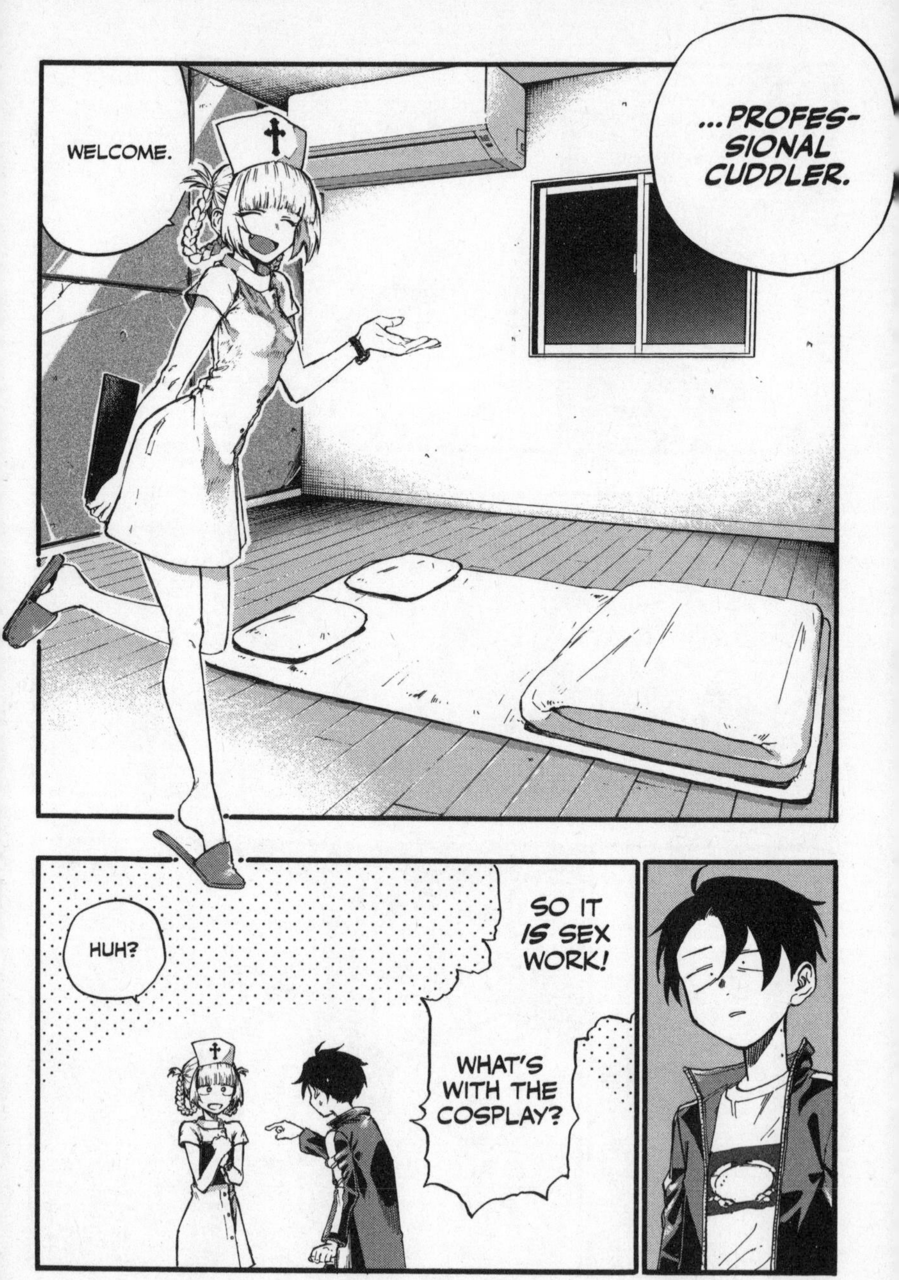
...PROFES-SIONAL CUDDLER.
WELCOME.
SO IT *IS* SEX WORK!
WHAT'S WITH THE COSPLAY?
HUH?

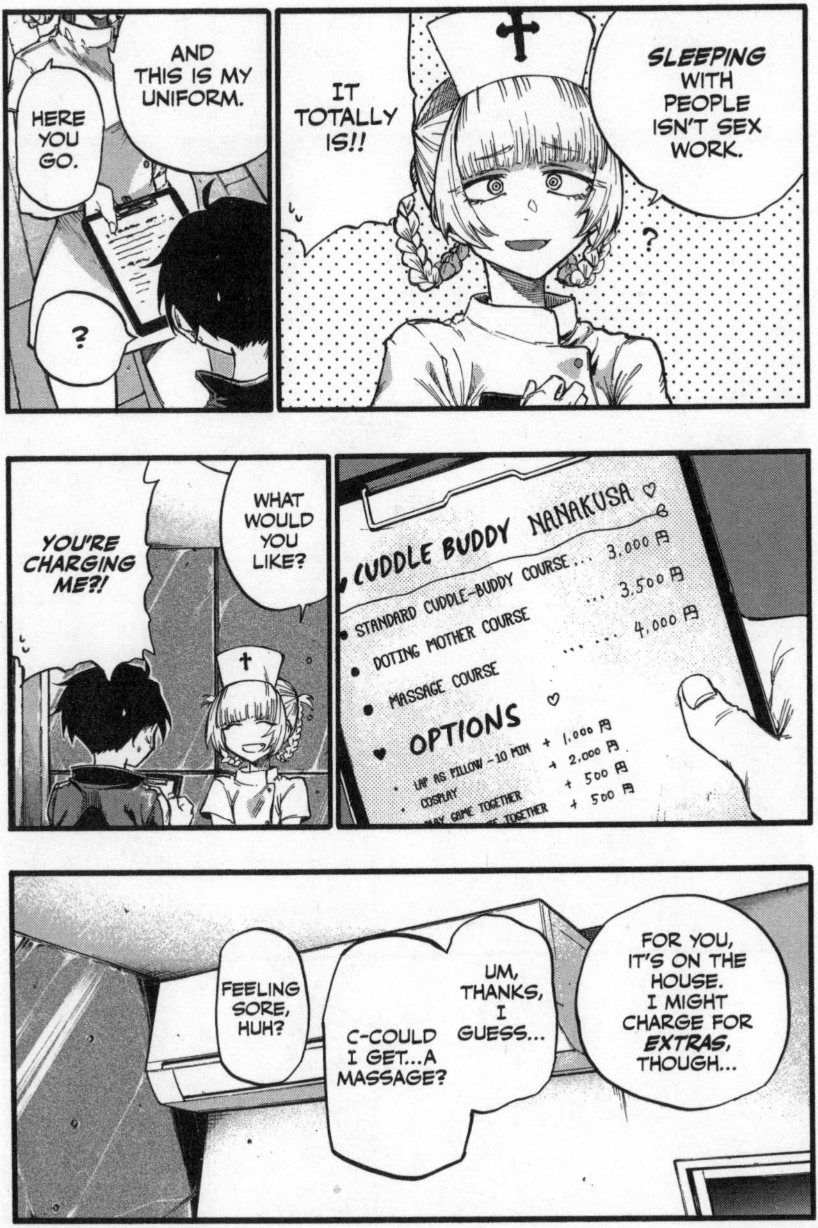
SLEEPING WITH PEOPLE ISN'T SEX WORK.
IT TOTALLY IS!!
?
AND THIS IS MY UNIFORM.
HERE YOU GO.
?
CUDDLE BUDDY NANAKUSA
STANDARD CUDDLE-BUDDY COURSE... 3,000 円
DOTING MOTHER COURSE ... 3,500 円
MASSAGE COURSE ...... 4,000 円
OPTIONS
LAP AS PILLOW - 10 MIN + 1,000 円
COSPLAY + 2,000 円
LAY GAME TOGETHER + 500 円
+ 500 円
WHAT WOULD YOU LIKE?
YOU'RE CHARGING ME?!
FOR YOU, IT'S ON THE HOUSE. I MIGHT CHARGE FOR EXTRAS, THOUGH...
UM, THANKS, I GUESS...
C-COULD I GET...A MASSAGE?
FEELING SORE, HUH?

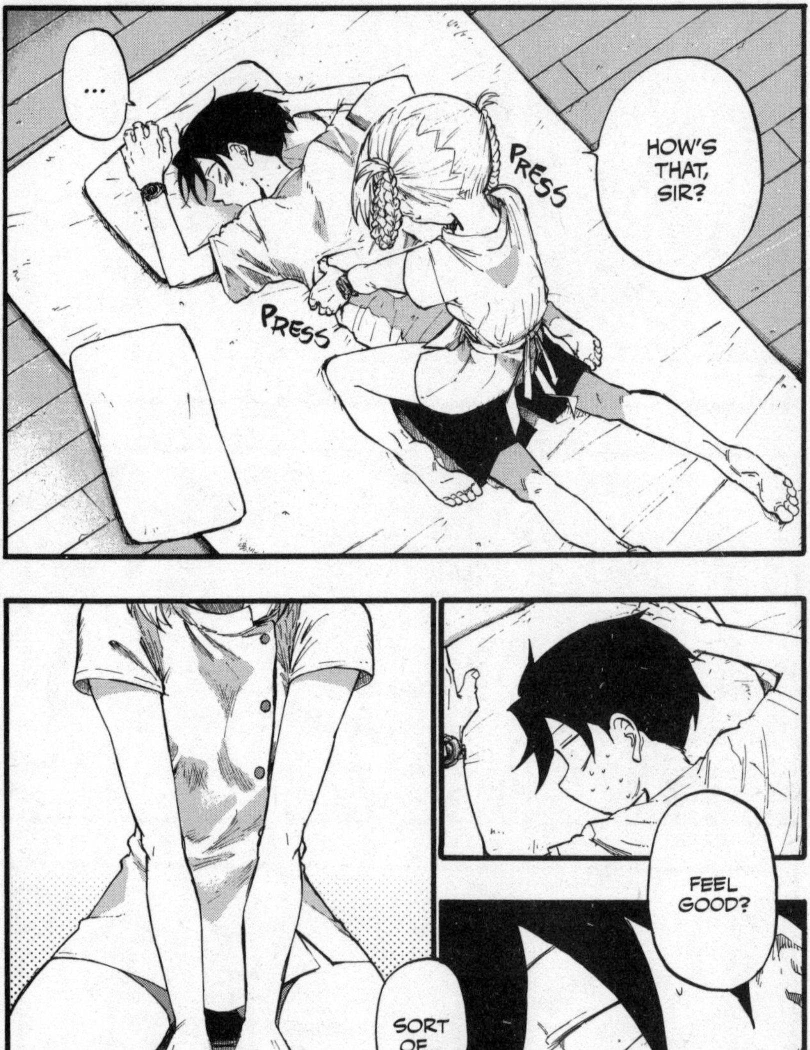
HOW'S THAT, SIR?
PRESS
PRESS
...
FEEL GOOD?
SORT OF...

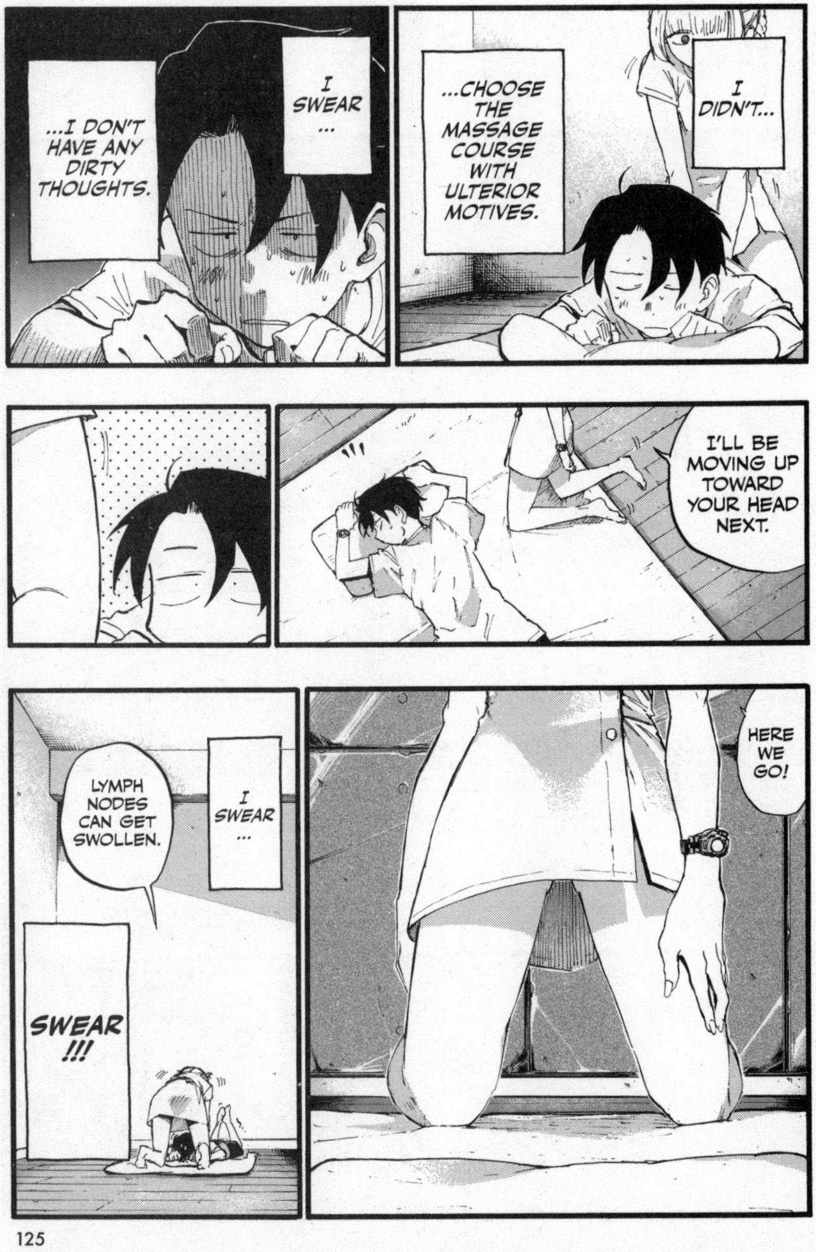
I DIDN'T...
...CHOOSE THE MASSAGE COURSE WITH ULTERIOR MOTIVES.
I SWEAR ...
...I DON'T HAVE ANY DIRTY THOUGHTS.
I'LL BE MOVING UP TOWARD YOUR HEAD NEXT.
HERE WE GO!
I SWEAR ...
LYMPH NODES CAN GET SWOLLEN.
SWEAR !!!

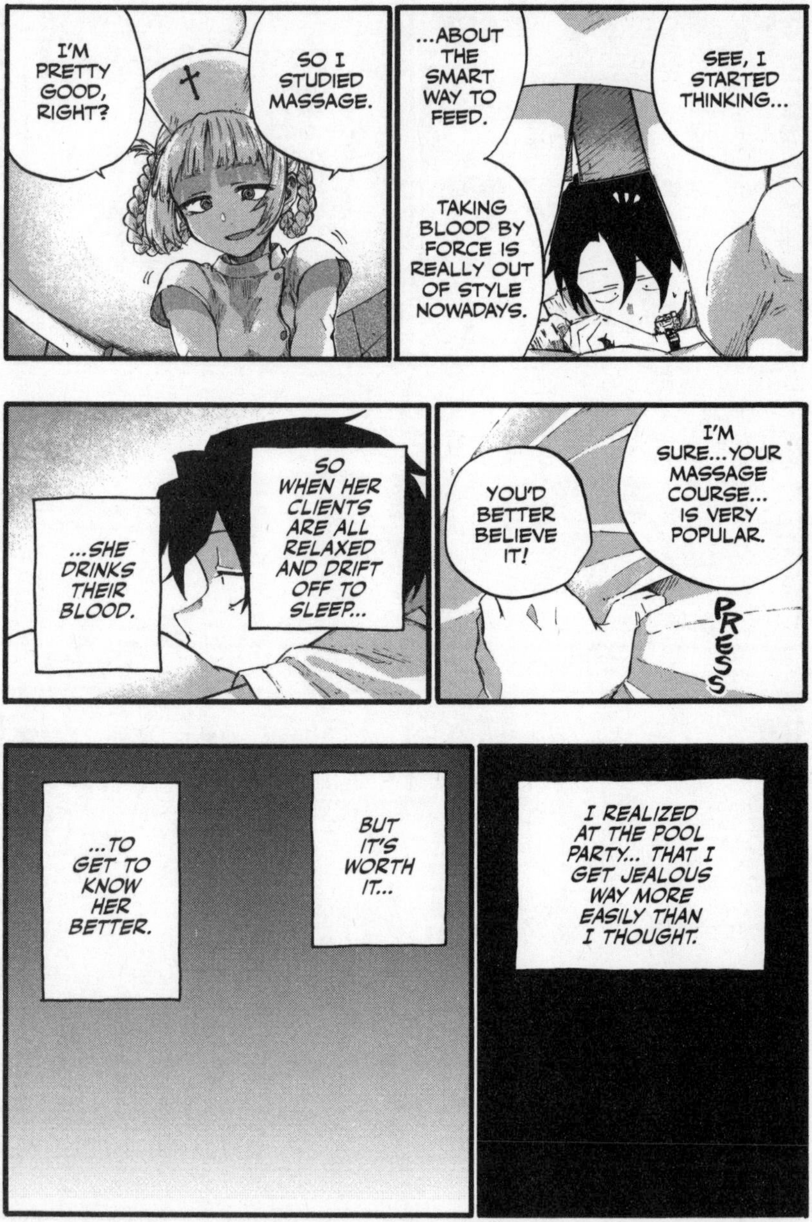
SEE, I STARTED THINKING...
...ABOUT THE SMART WAY TO FEED.
TAKING BLOOD BY FORCE IS REALLY OUT OF STYLE NOWADAYS.
SO I STUDIED MASSAGE.
I'M PRETTY GOOD, RIGHT?
I'M SURE...YOUR MASSAGE COURSE... IS VERY POPULAR.
YOU'D BETTER BELIEVE IT!
PRESS
SO WHEN HER CLIENTS ARE ALL RELAXED AND DRIFT OFF TO SLEEP...
...SHE DRINKS THEIR BLOOD.
I REALIZED AT THE POOL PARTY... THAT I GET JEALOUS WAY MORE EASILY THAN I THOUGHT.
BUT IT'S WORTH IT...
...TO GET TO KNOW HER BETTER.

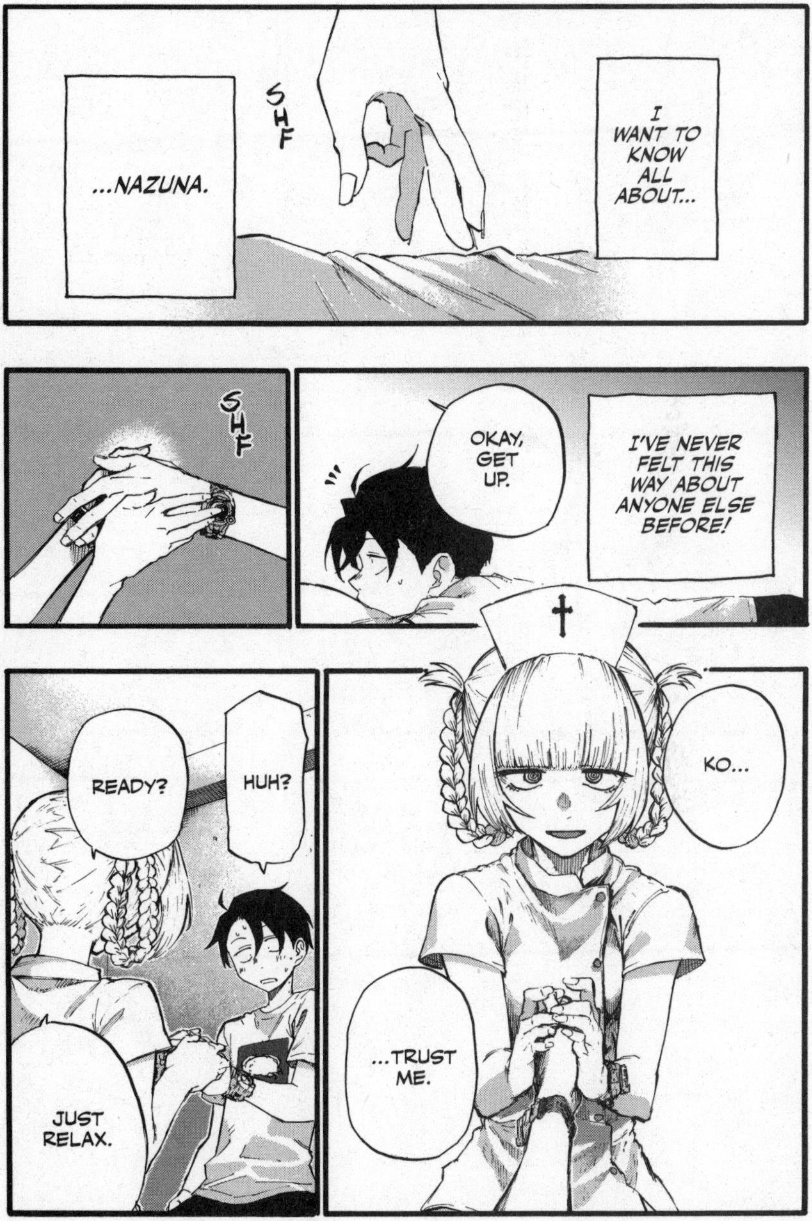
I WANT TO KNOW ALL ABOUT...
SHF
...NAZUNA.
I'VE NEVER FELT THIS WAY ABOUT ANYONE ELSE BEFORE!
OKAY, GET UP.
SHF
KO...
...TRUST ME.
HUH?
READY?
JUST RELAX.

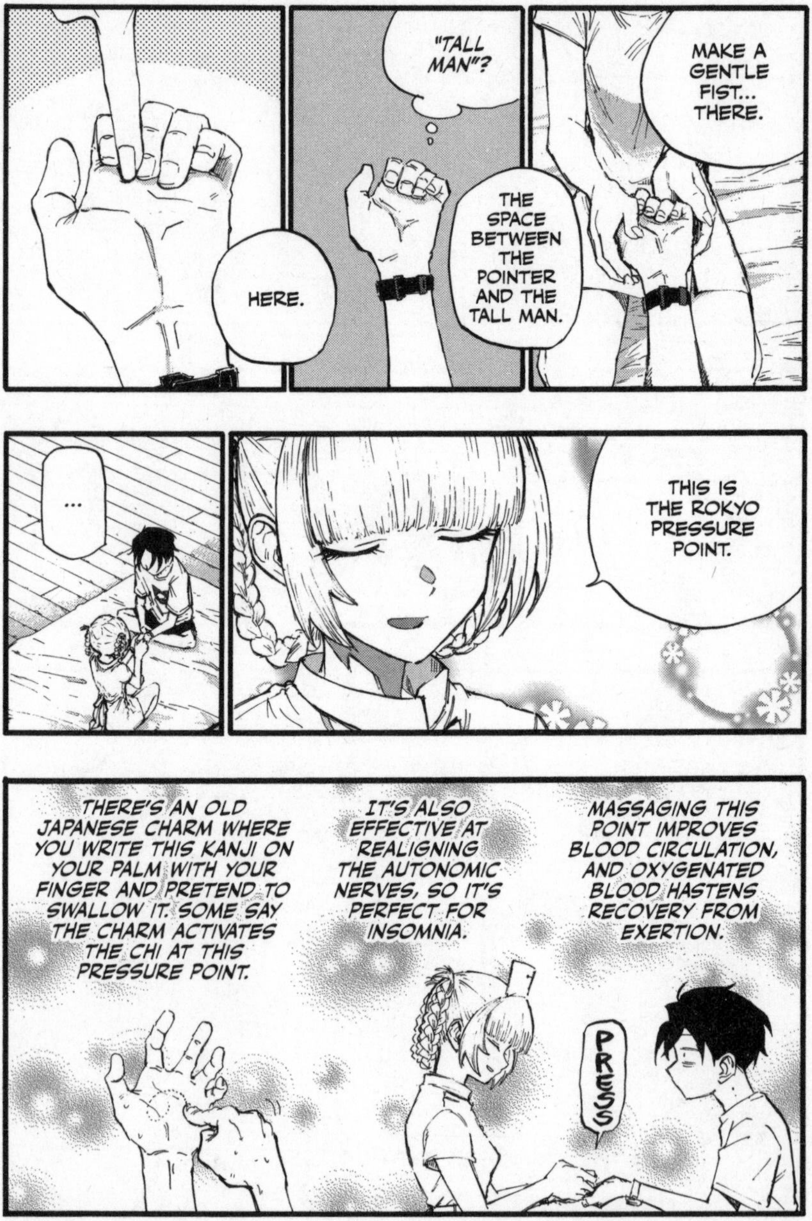
MAKE A GENTLE FIST... THERE.
"TALL MAN"?
THE SPACE BETWEEN THE POINTER AND THE TALL MAN.
HERE.
THIS IS THE ROKYO PRESSURE POINT.
...
MASSAGING THIS POINT IMPROVES BLOOD CIRCULATION, AND OXYGENATED BLOOD HASTENS RECOVERY FROM EXERTION.
IT'S ALSO EFFECTIVE AT REALIGNING THE AUTONOMIC NERVES, SO IT'S PERFECT FOR INSOMNIA.
THERE'S AN OLD JAPANESE CHARM WHERE YOU WRITE THIS KANJI ON YOUR PALM WITH YOUR FINGER AND PRETEND TO SWALLOW IT. SOME SAY THE CHARM ACTIVATES THE CHI AT THIS PRESSURE POINT.
PRESS

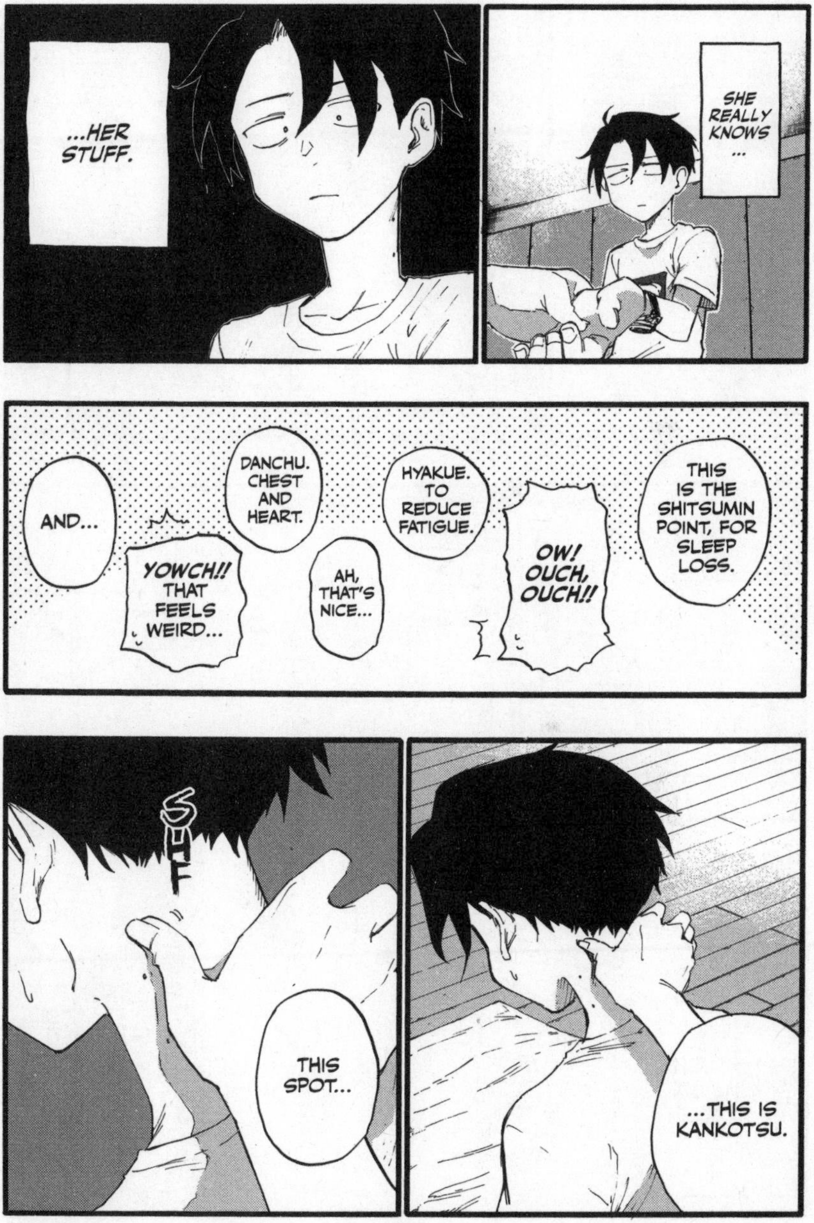
SHE REALLY KNOWS ...
...HER STUFF.
THIS IS THE SHITSUMIN POINT, FOR SLEEP LOSS.
OW! OUCH, OUCH!!
HYAKUE. TO REDUCE FATIGUE.
AH, THAT'S NICE...
DANCHU. CHEST AND HEART.
YOWCH!! THAT FEELS WEIRD...
AND...
...THIS IS KANKOTSU.
THIS SPOT...

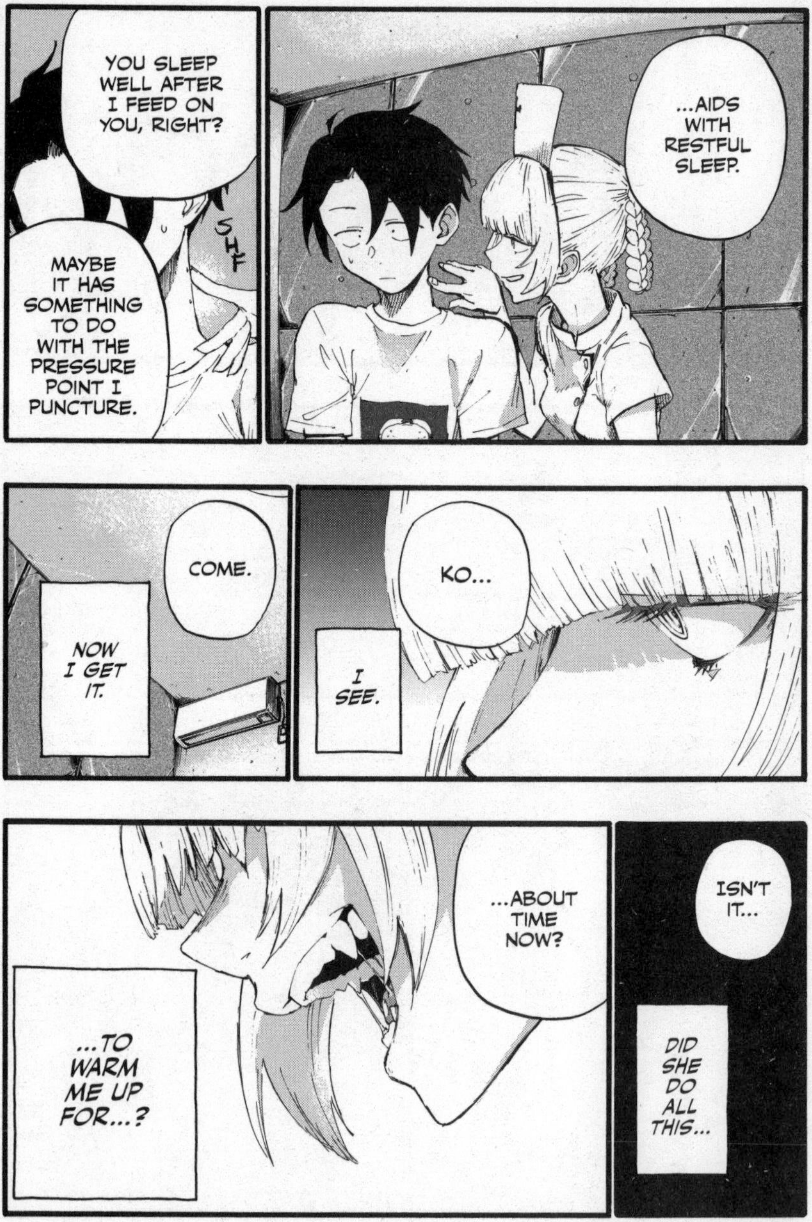
...AIDS WITH RESTFUL SLEEP.
YOU SLEEP WELL AFTER I FEED ON YOU, RIGHT?
SHF
MAYBE IT HAS SOMETHING TO DO WITH THE PRESSURE POINT I PUNCTURE.
KO...
I SEE.
COME.
NOW I GET IT.
ISN'T IT...
DID SHE DO ALL THIS...
...ABOUT TIME NOW?
...TO WARM ME UP FOR...?

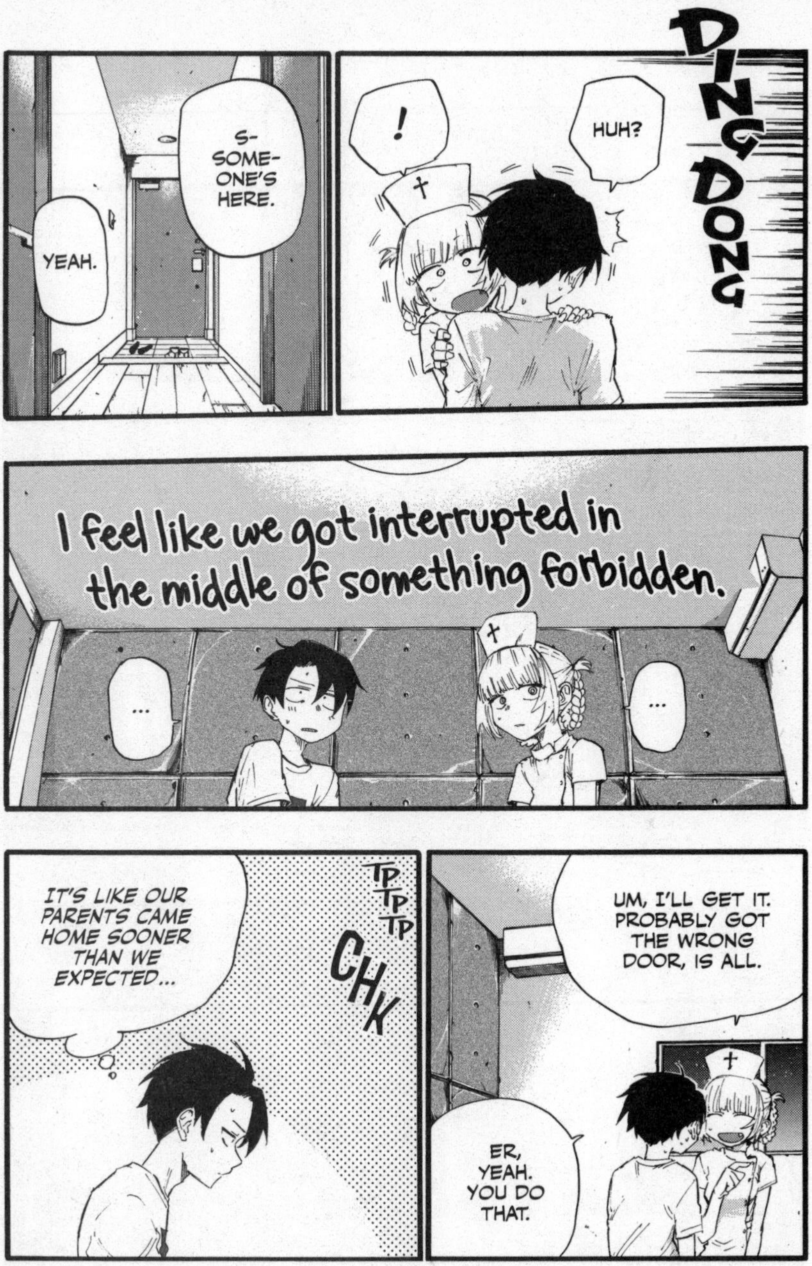
DING DONG
HUH?
!
S-SOME-ONE'S HERE.
YEAH.
I feel like we got interrupted in the middle of something forbidden.
...
...
UM, I'LL GET IT. PROBABLY GOT THE WRONG DOOR, IS ALL.
ER, YEAH. YOU DO THAT.
TP TP TP
CHK
IT'S LIKE OUR PARENTS CAME HOME SOONER THAN WE EXPECTED...

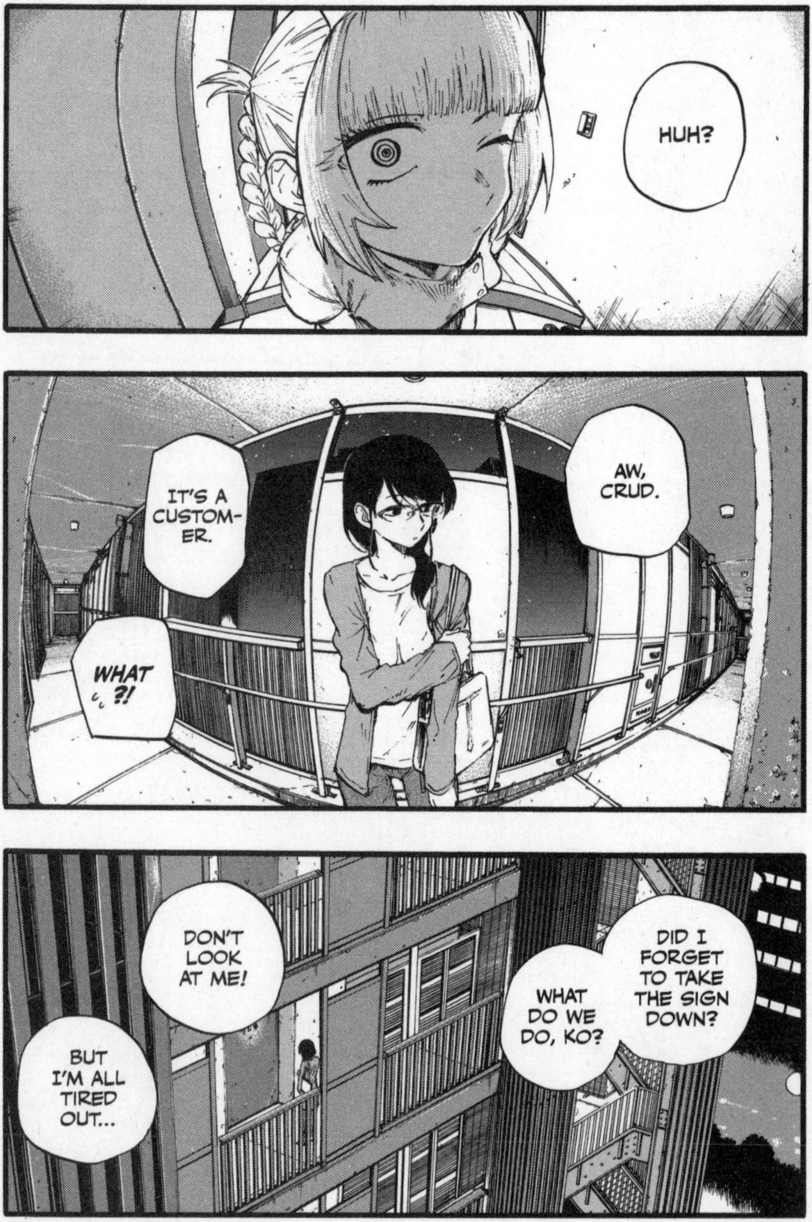
HUH?
AW, CRUD.
IT'S A CUSTOM-ER.
WHAT ?!
DID I FORGET TO TAKE THE SIGN DOWN?
WHAT DO WE DO, KO?
DON'T LOOK AT ME!
BUT I'M ALL TIRED OUT...

Call of the Night

Call of the Night

NIGHT 16: BOOZING WITH COWORKERS IS THE WORST

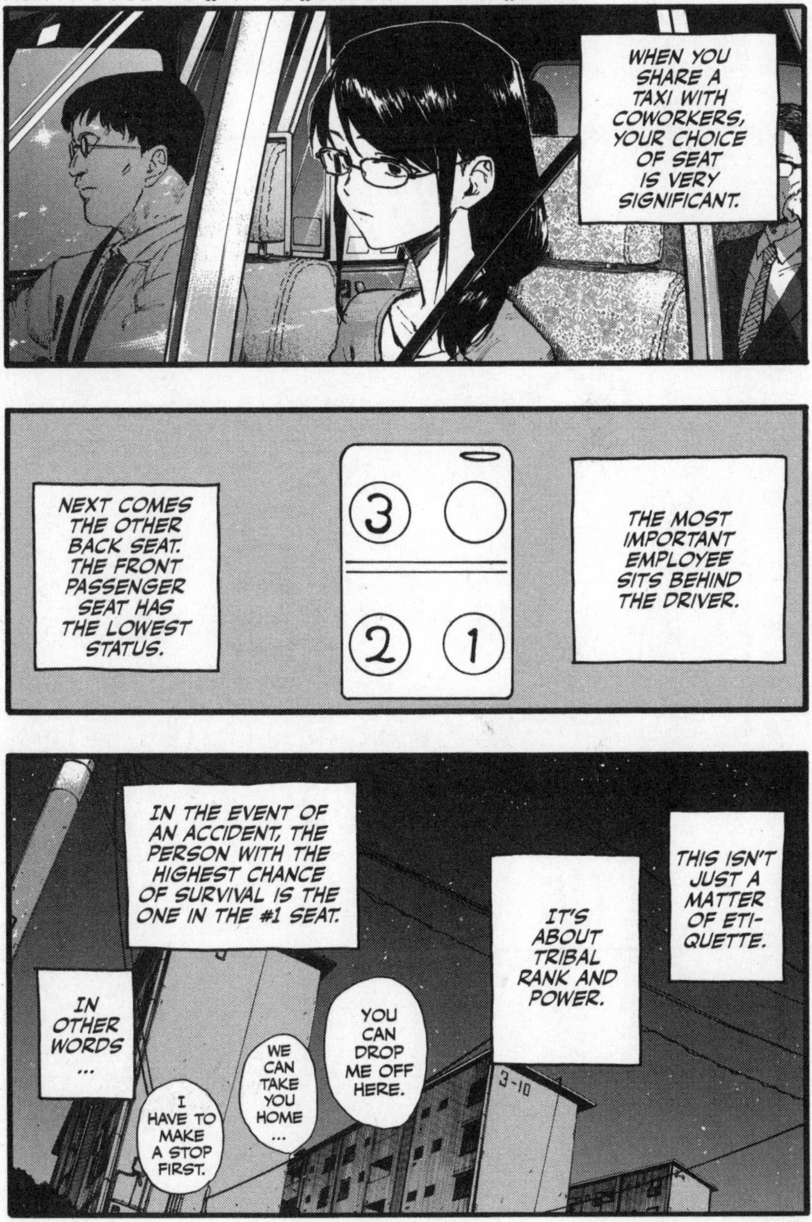
WHEN YOU SHARE A TAXI WITH COWORKERS, YOUR CHOICE OF SEAT IS VERY SIGNIFICANT.
THE MOST IMPORTANT EMPLOYEE SITS BEHIND THE DRIVER.
3
2
1
NEXT COMES THE OTHER BACK SEAT. THE FRONT PASSENGER SEAT HAS THE LOWEST STATUS.
THIS ISN'T JUST A MATTER OF ETI-QUETTE.
IT'S ABOUT TRIBAL RANK AND POWER.
IN THE EVENT OF AN ACCIDENT, THE PERSON WITH THE HIGHEST CHANCE OF SURVIVAL IS THE ONE IN THE #1 SEAT.
3-10
YOU CAN DROP ME OFF HERE.
WE CAN TAKE YOU HOME ...
IN OTHER WORDS ...
I HAVE TO MAKE A STOP FIRST.

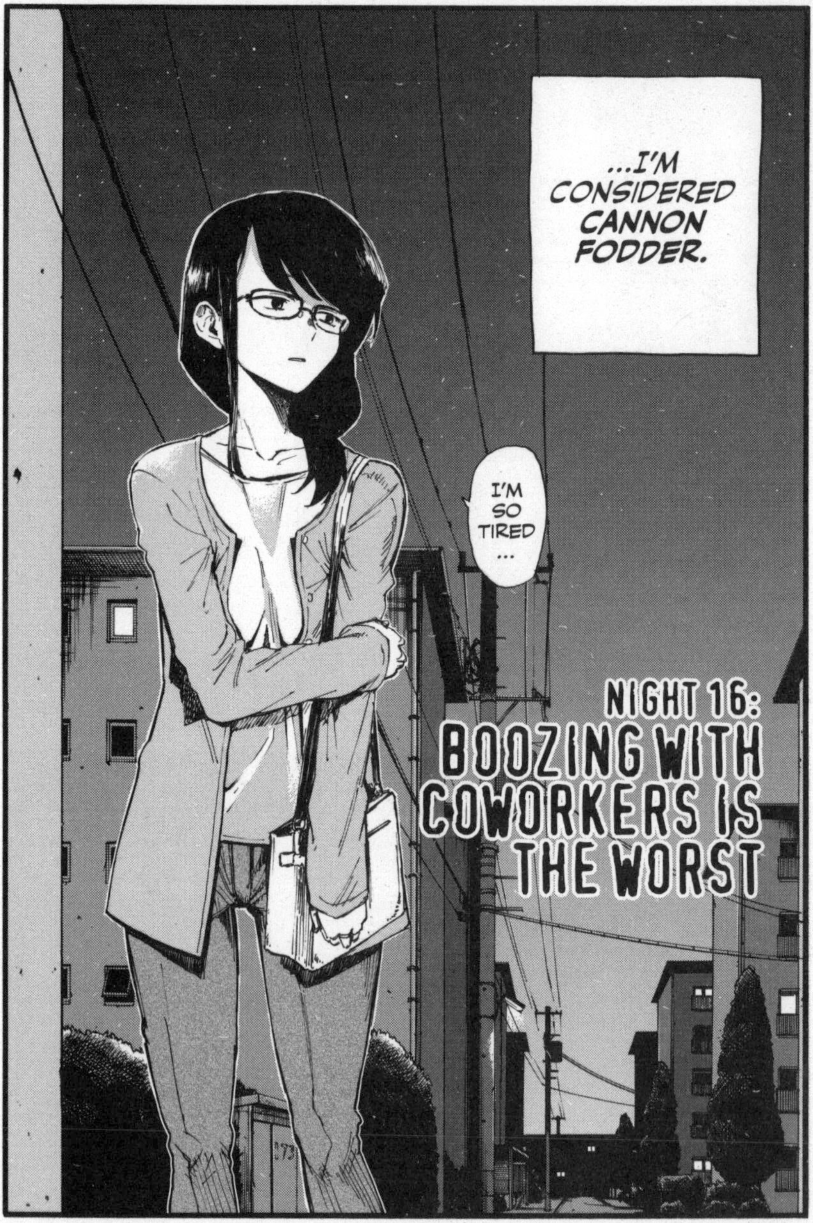
...I'M CONSIDERED CANNON FODDER.
I'M SO TIRED ...
NIGHT 16:
BOOZING WITH COWORKERS IS THE WORST

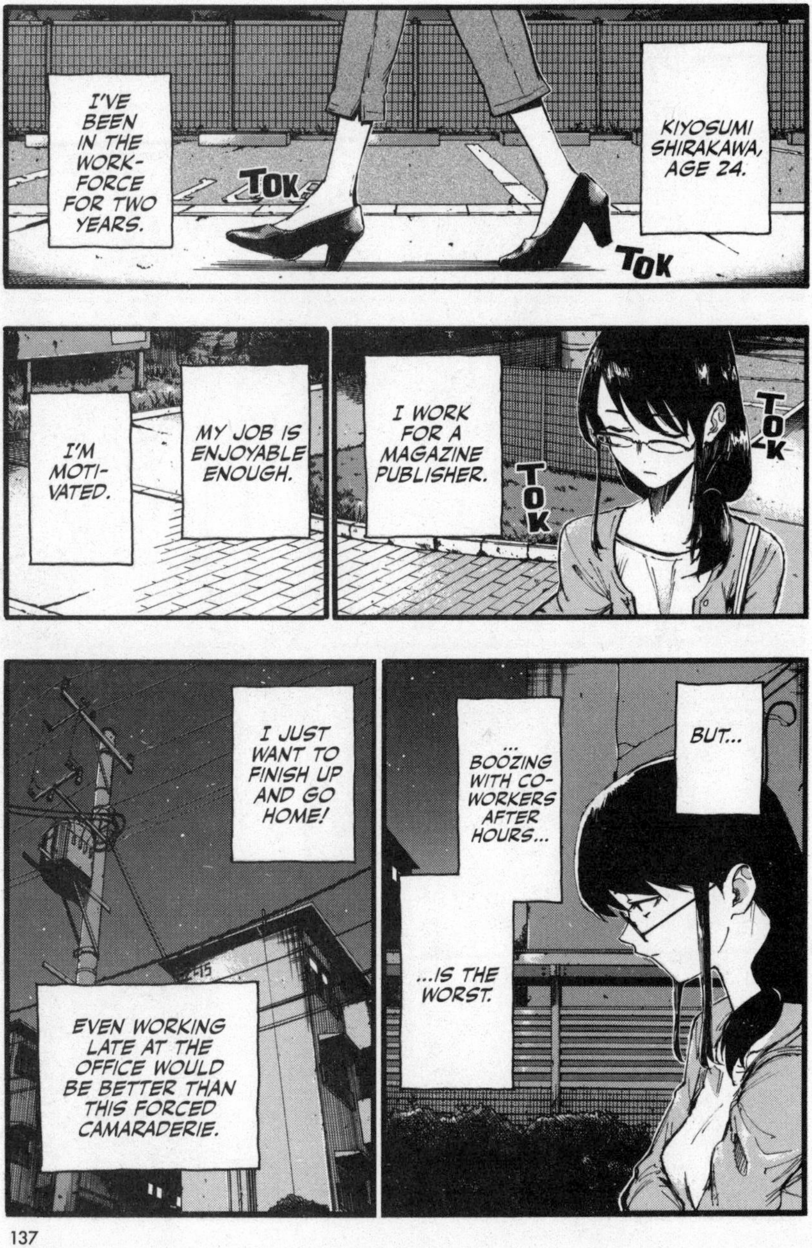
KIYOSUMI SHIRAKAWA, AGE 24.
I'VE BEEN IN THE WORK-FORCE FOR TWO YEARS.
TOK
TOK
TOK
TOK
I WORK FOR A MAGAZINE PUBLISHER.
MY JOB IS ENJOYABLE ENOUGH.
I'M MOTI-VATED.
BUT...
...BOOZING WITH CO-WORKERS AFTER HOURS...
...IS THE WORST.
I JUST WANT TO FINISH UP AND GO HOME!
EVEN WORKING LATE AT THE OFFICE WOULD BE BETTER THAN THIS FORCED CAMARADERIE.

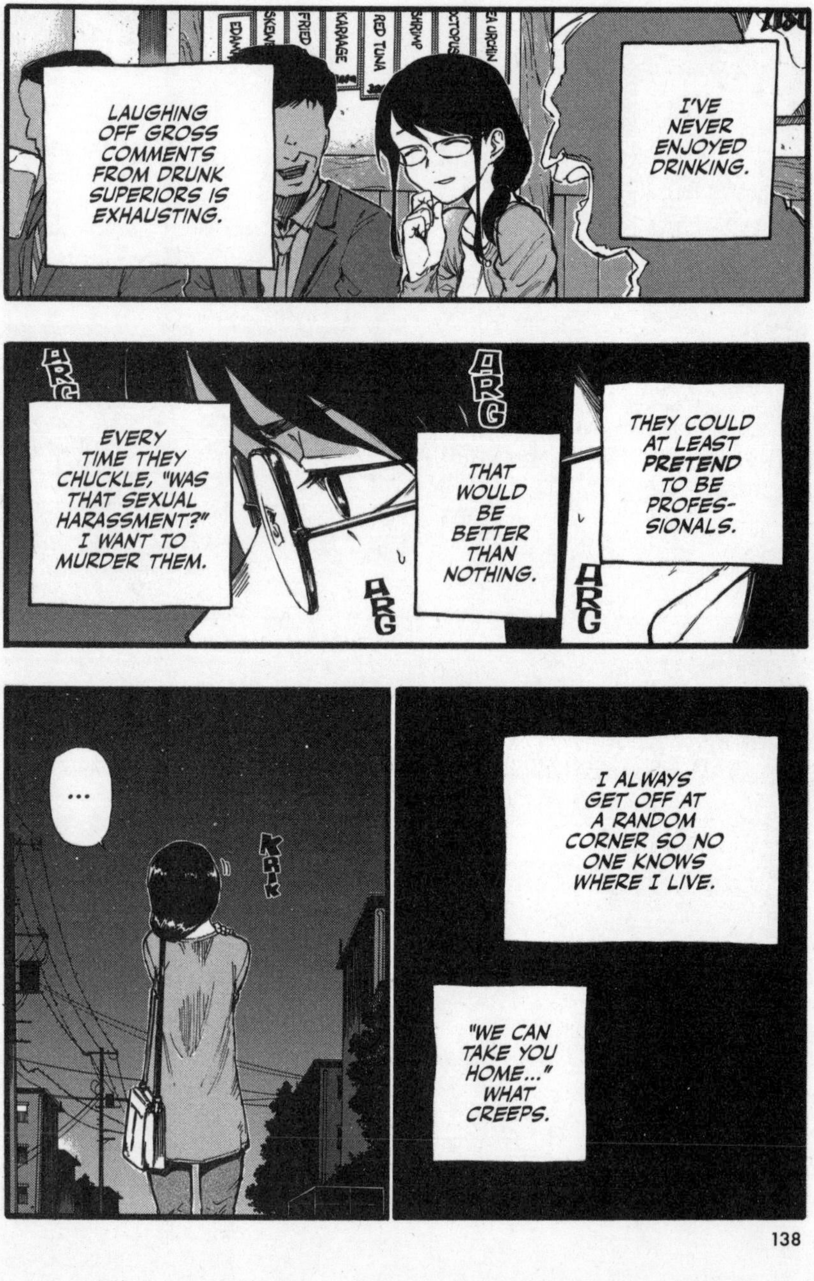
I'VE NEVER ENJOYED DRINKING.
SHRIMP
RED TUNA
KARAAGE
FRIED
LAUGHING OFF GROSS COMMENTS FROM DRUNK SUPERIORS IS EXHAUSTING.
ARG
THEY COULD AT LEAST PRETEND TO BE PROFES-SIONALS.
ARG
ARG
THAT WOULD BE BETTER THAN NOTHING.
ARG
EVERY TIME THEY CHUCKLE, "WAS THAT SEXUAL HARASSMENT?" I WANT TO MURDER THEM.
I ALWAYS GET OFF AT A RANDOM CORNER SO NO ONE KNOWS WHERE I LIVE.
"WE CAN TAKE YOU HOME..." WHAT CREEPS.
...
KRIK

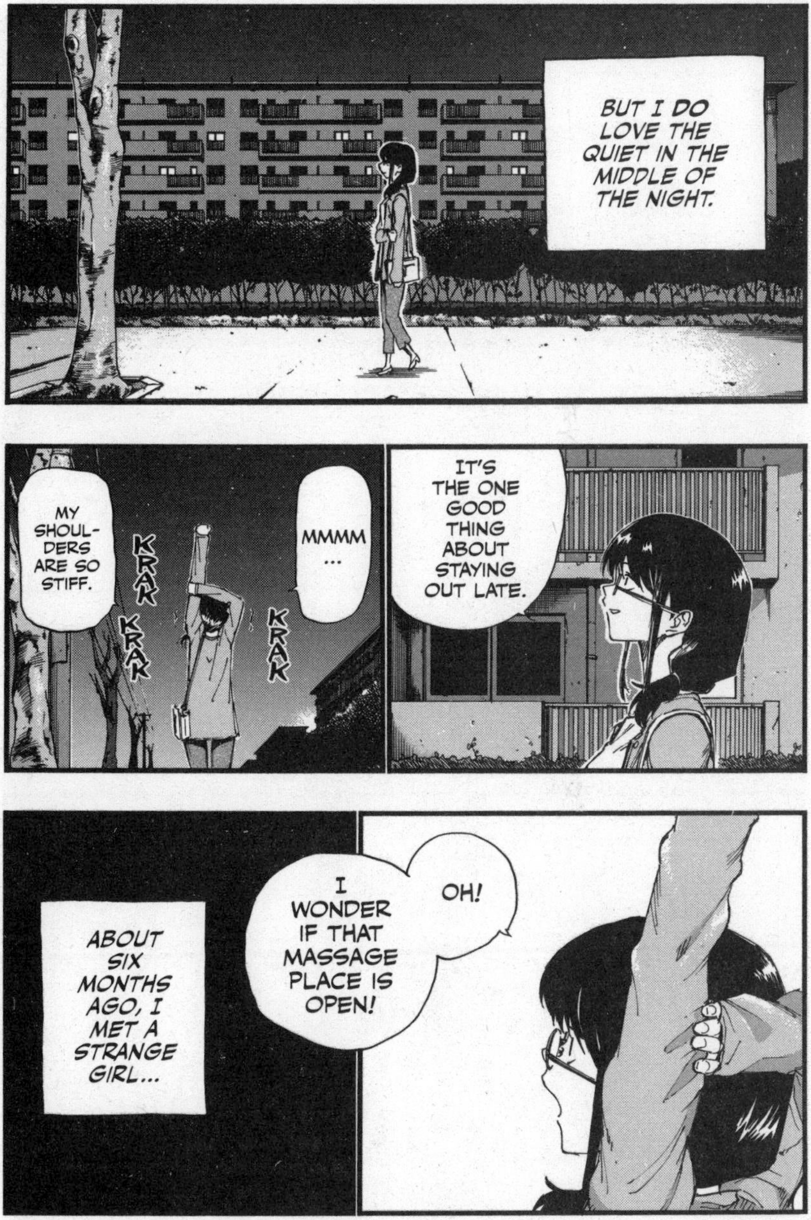
BUT I DO LOVE THE QUIET IN THE MIDDLE OF THE NIGHT.
IT'S THE ONE GOOD THING ABOUT STAYING OUT LATE.
MMMM ...
KRAK
MY SHOULDERS ARE SO STIFF.
KRAK KRAK
OH!
I WONDER IF THAT MASSAGE PLACE IS OPEN!
ABOUT SIX MONTHS AGO, I MET A STRANGE GIRL...

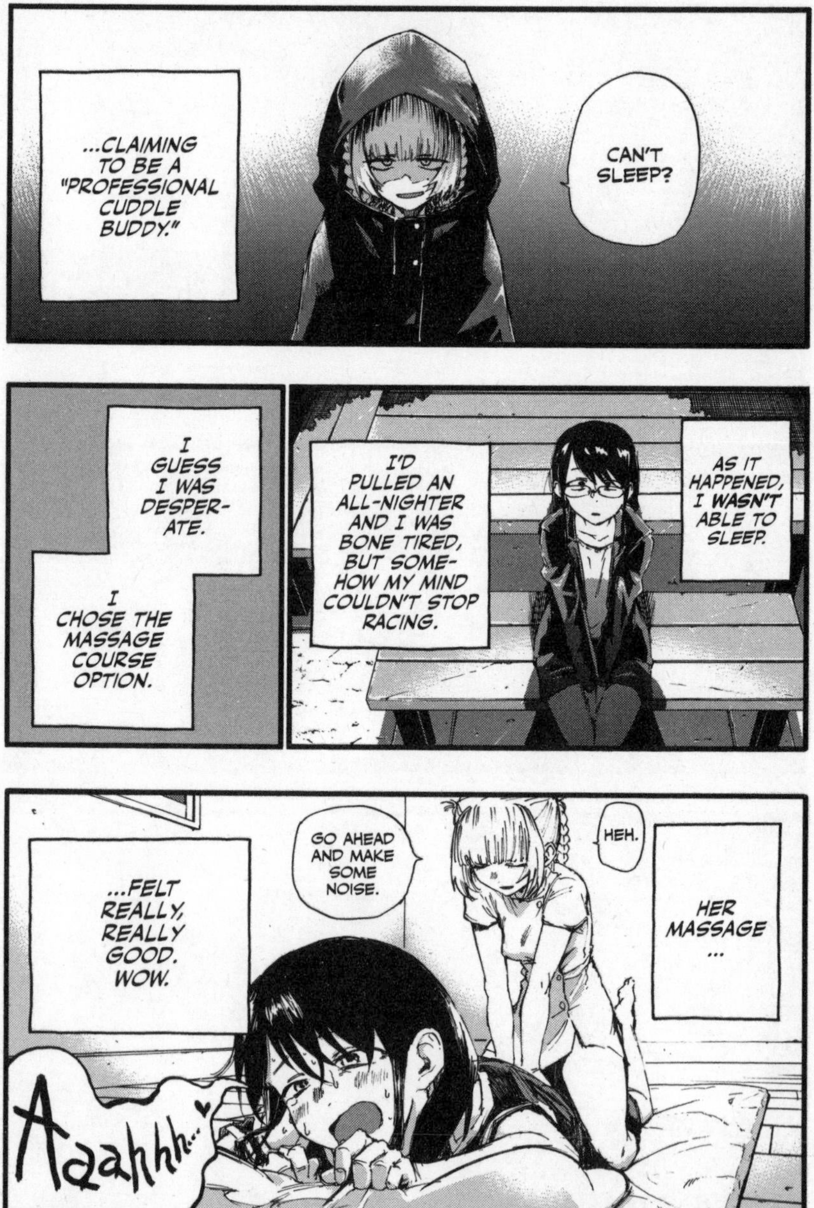
CAN'T SLEEP?
...CLAIMING TO BE A "PROFESSIONAL CUDDLE BUDDY."
AS IT HAPPENED, I WASN'T ABLE TO SLEEP.
I'D PULLED AN ALL-NIGHTER AND I WAS BONE TIRED, BUT SOME-HOW MY MIND COULDN'T STOP RACING.
I GUESS I WAS DESPER-ATE.
I CHOSE THE MASSAGE COURSE OPTION.
HER MASSAGE ...
HEH.
GO AHEAD AND MAKE SOME NOISE.
...FELT REALLY, REALLY GOOD. WOW.
Aaahhh...♥

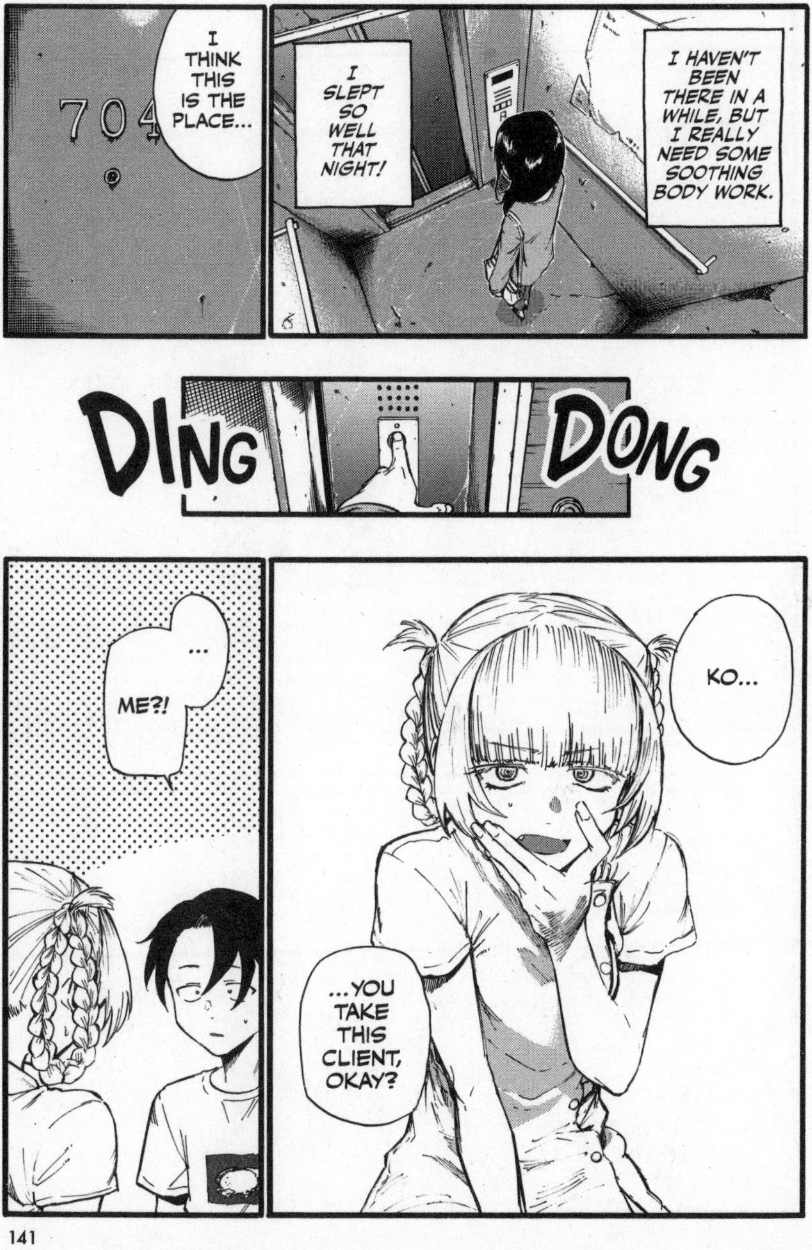
I HAVEN'T BEEN THERE IN A WHILE, BUT I REALLY NEED SOME SOOTHING BODY WORK.
I SLEPT SO WELL THAT NIGHT!
704
I THINK THIS IS THE PLACE...
DING
DONG
KO...
...YOU TAKE THIS CLIENT, OKAY?
... ME?!

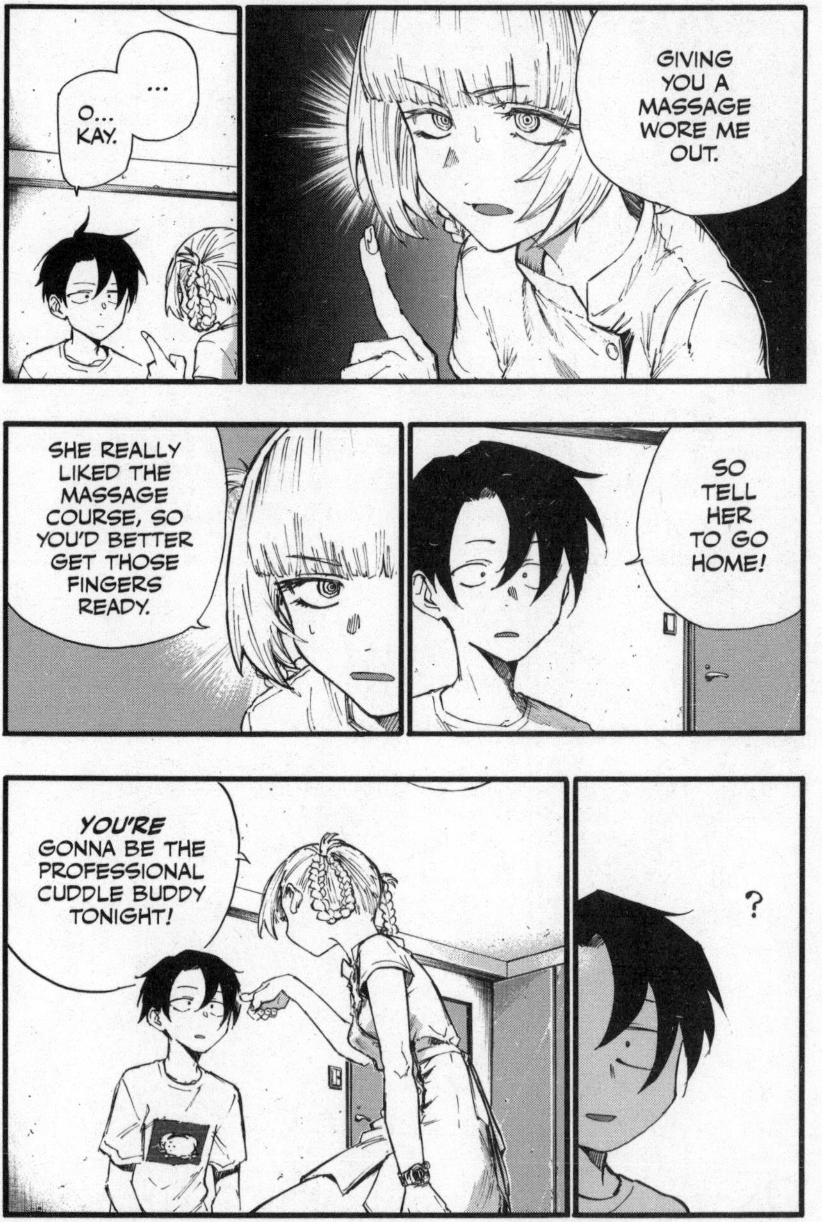
...
O... KAY.
GIVING YOU A MASSAGE WORE ME OUT.
SHE REALLY LIKED THE MASSAGE COURSE, SO YOU'D BETTER GET THOSE FINGERS READY.
SO TELL HER TO GO HOME!
YOU'RE GONNA BE THE PROFESSIONAL CUDDLE BUDDY TONIGHT!
?

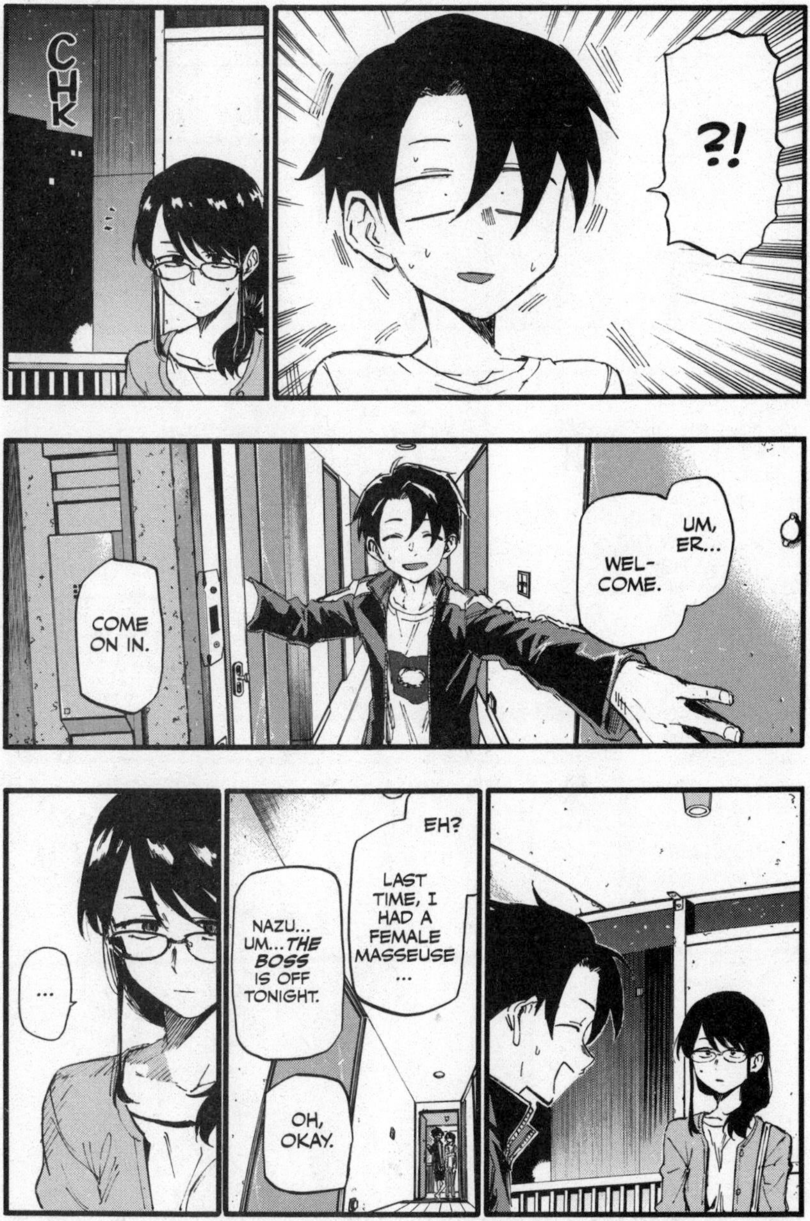
?!
CHK
UM, ER...
WEL-COME.
COME ON IN.
EH?
LAST TIME, I HAD A FEMALE MASSEUSE ...
NAZU... UM... *THE BOSS* IS OFF TONIGHT.
OH, OKAY.
...

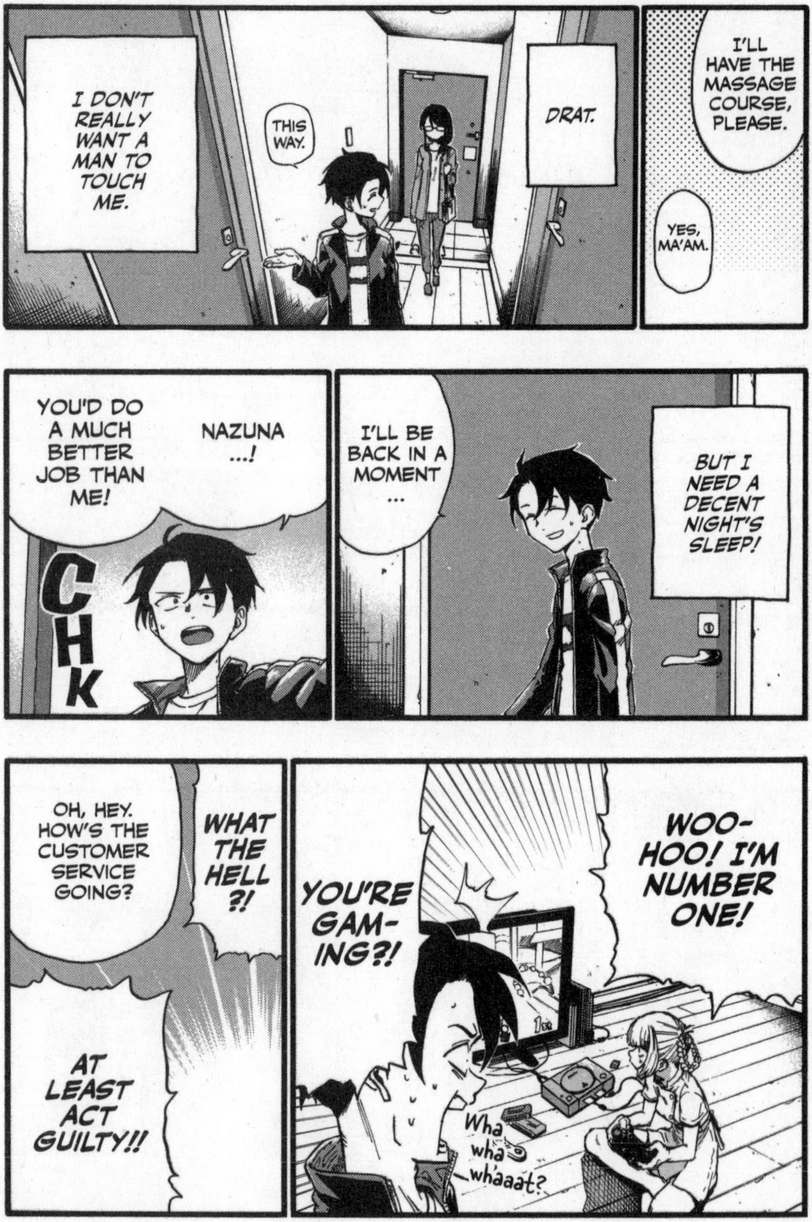
I'LL HAVE THE MASSAGE COURSE, PLEASE.
YES, MA'AM.
DRAT.
THIS WAY.
I DON'T REALLY WANT A MAN TO TOUCH ME.
BUT I NEED A DECENT NIGHT'S SLEEP!
I'LL BE BACK IN A MOMENT ...
NAZUNA ...!
YOU'D DO A MUCH BETTER JOB THAN ME!
CHK
WOO-HOO! I'M NUMBER ONE!
YOU'RE GAM-ING?!
Wha wha wha'aaat?
OH, HEY. HOW'S THE CUSTOMER SERVICE GOING?
WHAT THE HELL ?!
AT LEAST ACT GUILTY!!

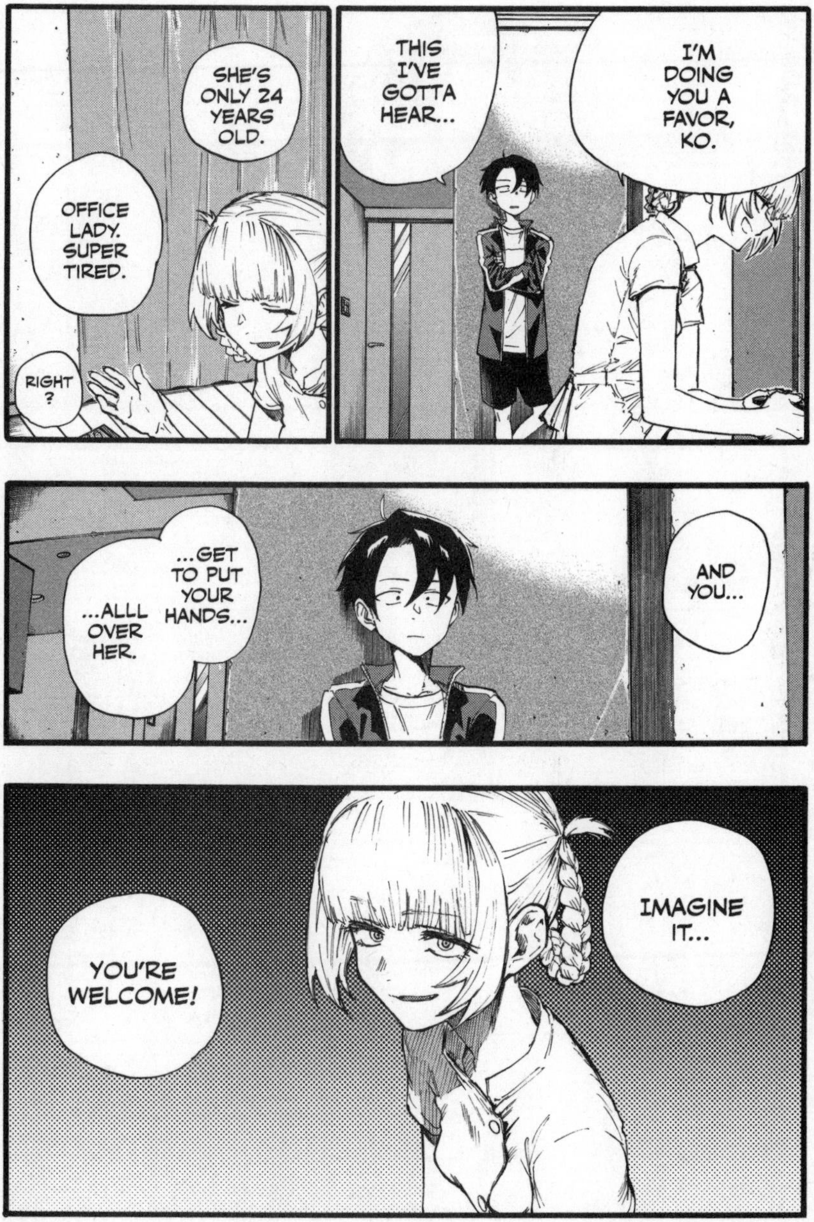
I'M DOING YOU A FAVOR, KO.
THIS I'VE GOTTA HEAR...
SHE'S ONLY 24 YEARS OLD.
OFFICE LADY. SUPER TIRED.
RIGHT?
AND YOU...
...GET TO PUT YOUR HANDS...
...ALLL OVER HER.
IMAGINE IT...
YOU'RE WELCOME!

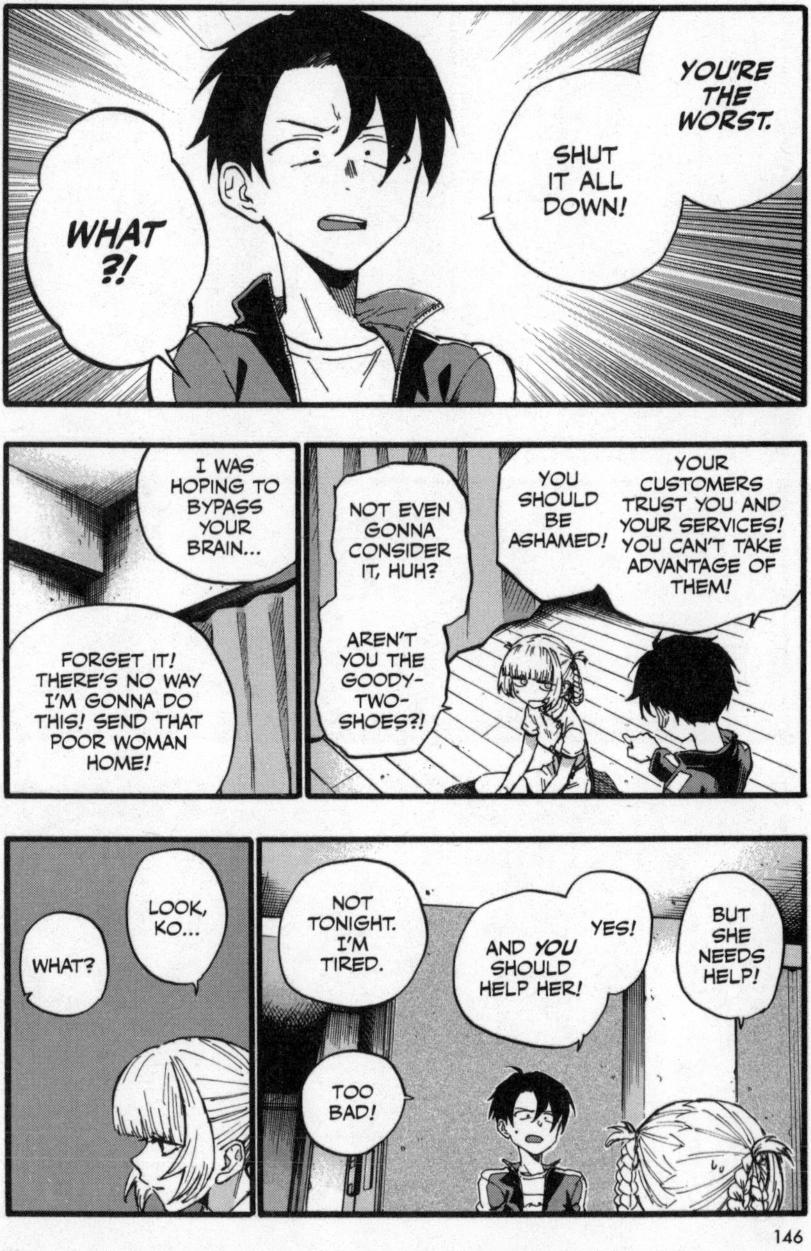
YOU'RE THE WORST.
SHUT IT ALL DOWN!
WHAT?!
YOUR CUSTOMERS TRUST YOU AND YOUR SERVICES! YOU CAN'T TAKE ADVANTAGE OF THEM!
YOU SHOULD BE ASHAMED!
NOT EVEN GONNA CONSIDER IT, HUH?
AREN'T YOU THE GOODY-TWO-SHOES?!
I WAS HOPING TO BYPASS YOUR BRAIN...
FORGET IT! THERE'S NO WAY I'M GONNA DO THIS! SEND THAT POOR WOMAN HOME!
BUT SHE NEEDS HELP!
YES!
AND *YOU* SHOULD HELP HER!
NOT TONIGHT. I'M TIRED.
TOO BAD!
LOOK, KO...
WHAT?

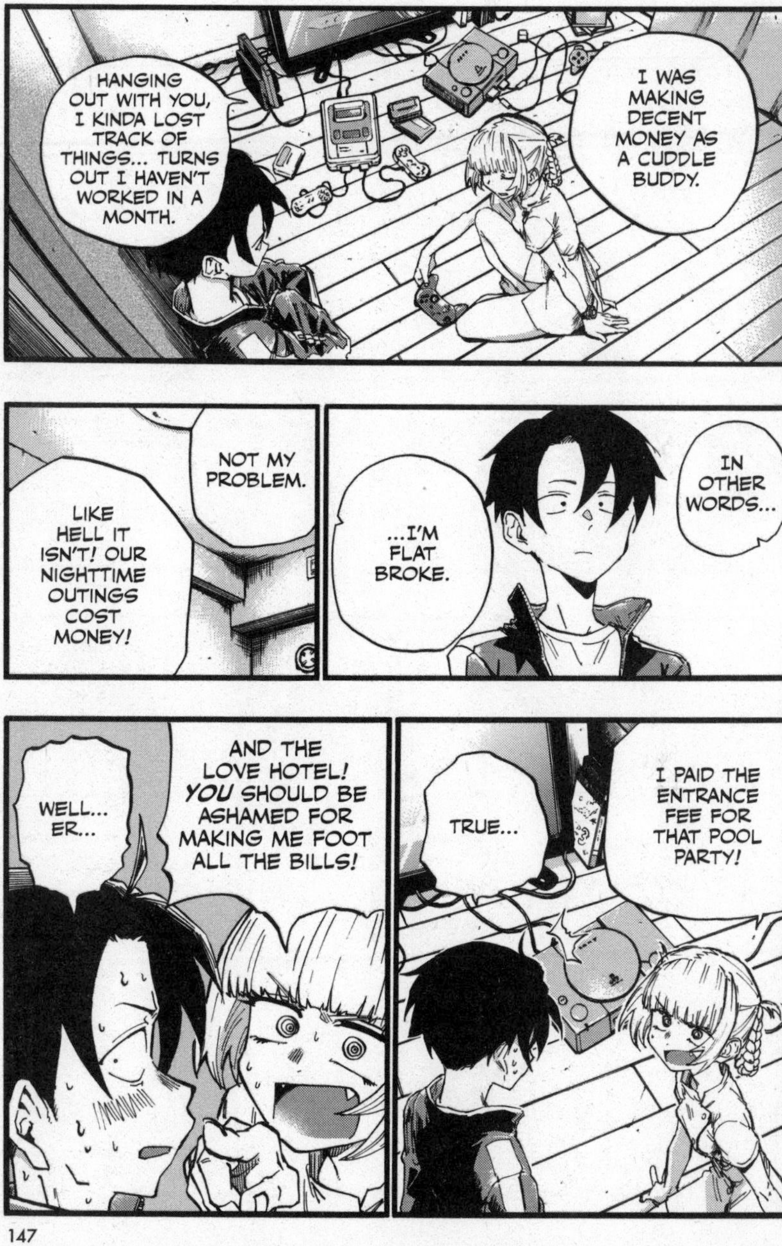
I WAS MAKING DECENT MONEY AS A CUDDLE BUDDY.
HANGING OUT WITH YOU, I KINDA LOST TRACK OF THINGS... TURNS OUT I HAVEN'T WORKED IN A MONTH.
IN OTHER WORDS...
...I'M FLAT BROKE.
NOT MY PROBLEM.
LIKE HELL IT ISN'T! OUR NIGHTTIME OUTINGS COST MONEY!
I PAID THE ENTRANCE FEE FOR THAT POOL PARTY!
TRUE...
AND THE LOVE HOTEL! *YOU* SHOULD BE ASHAMED FOR MAKING ME FOOT ALL THE BILLS!
WELL... ER...

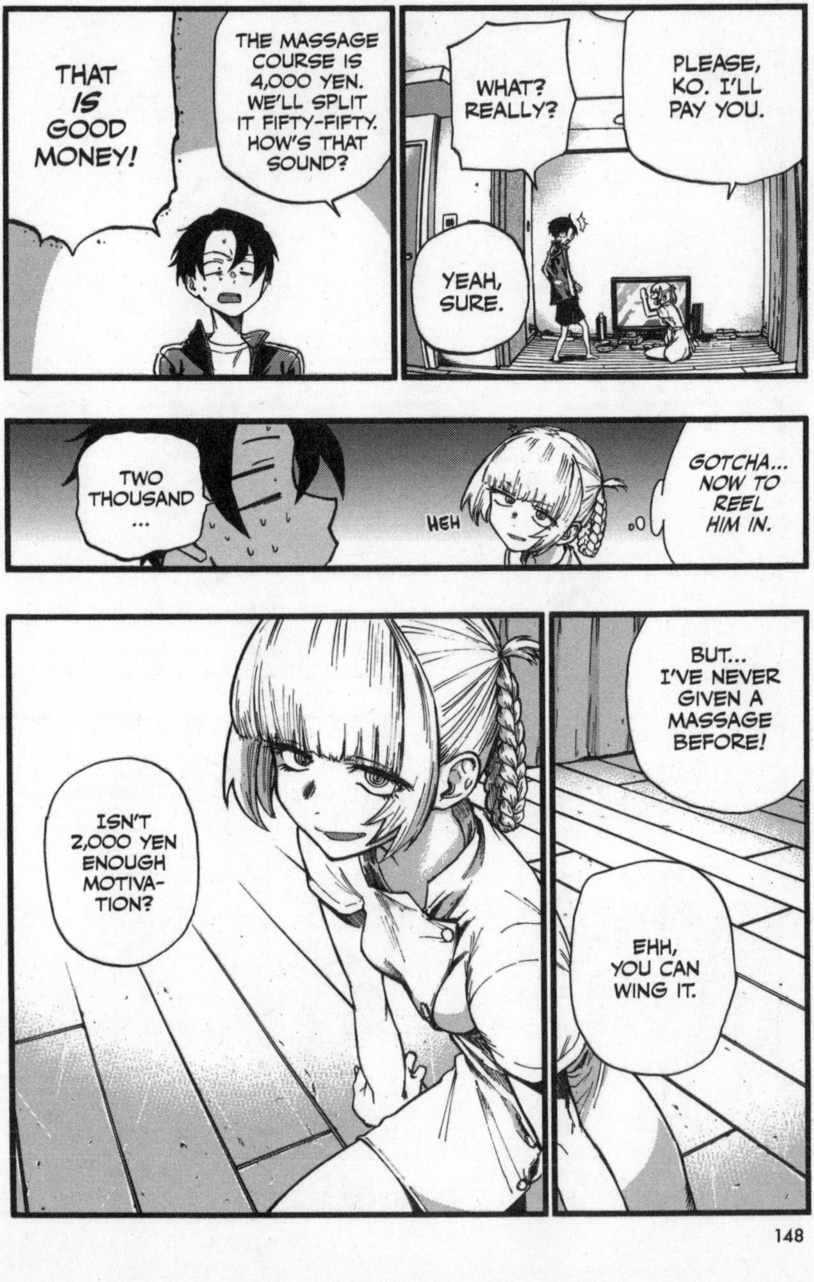
PLEASE, KO. I'LL PAY YOU.
WHAT? REALLY?
YEAH, SURE.
THE MASSAGE COURSE IS 4,000 YEN. WE'LL SPLIT IT FIFTY-FIFTY. HOW'S THAT SOUND?
THAT *IS* GOOD MONEY!
GOTCHA... NOW TO REEL HIM IN.
HEH
TWO THOUSAND ...
BUT... I'VE NEVER GIVEN A MASSAGE BEFORE!
EHH, YOU CAN WING IT.
ISN'T 2,000 YEN ENOUGH MOTIVA-TION?

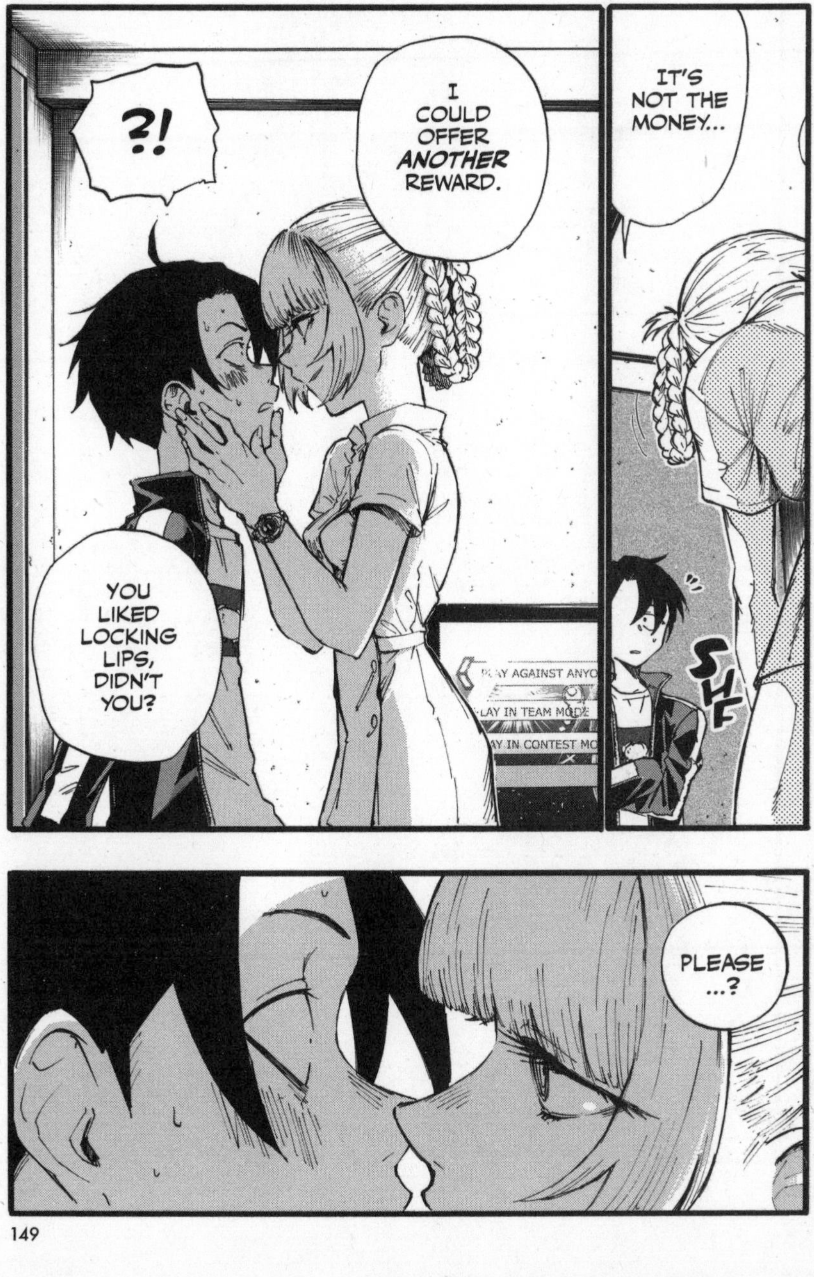
IT'S NOT THE MONEY...
SHF
I COULD OFFER ANOTHER REWARD.
?!
YOU LIKED LOCKING LIPS, DIDN'T YOU?
PLEASE ...?

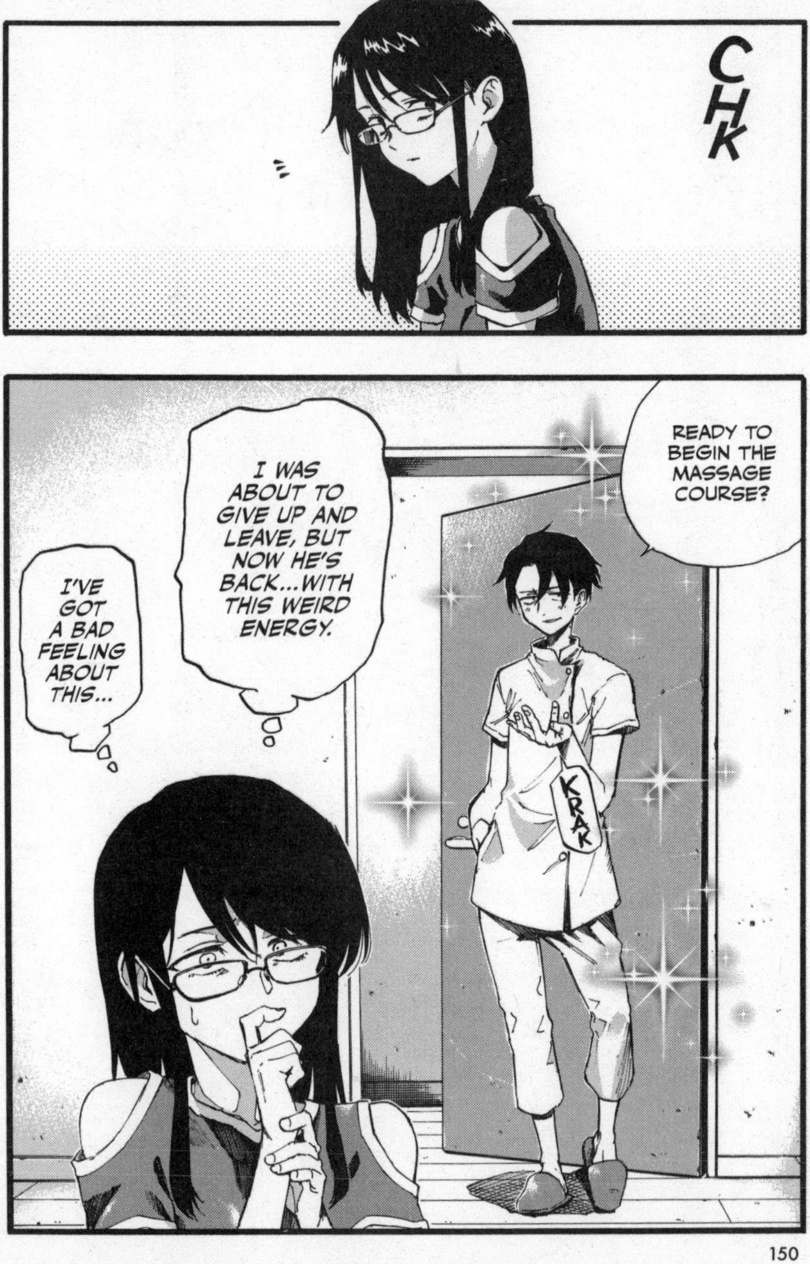
CHK
READY TO BEGIN THE MASSAGE COURSE?
I WAS ABOUT TO GIVE UP AND LEAVE, BUT NOW HE'S BACK...WITH THIS WEIRD ENERGY.
I'VE GOT A BAD FEELING ABOUT THIS...
KRAK

NIGHT 17: I'LL KEEP YOU ALL NIGHT

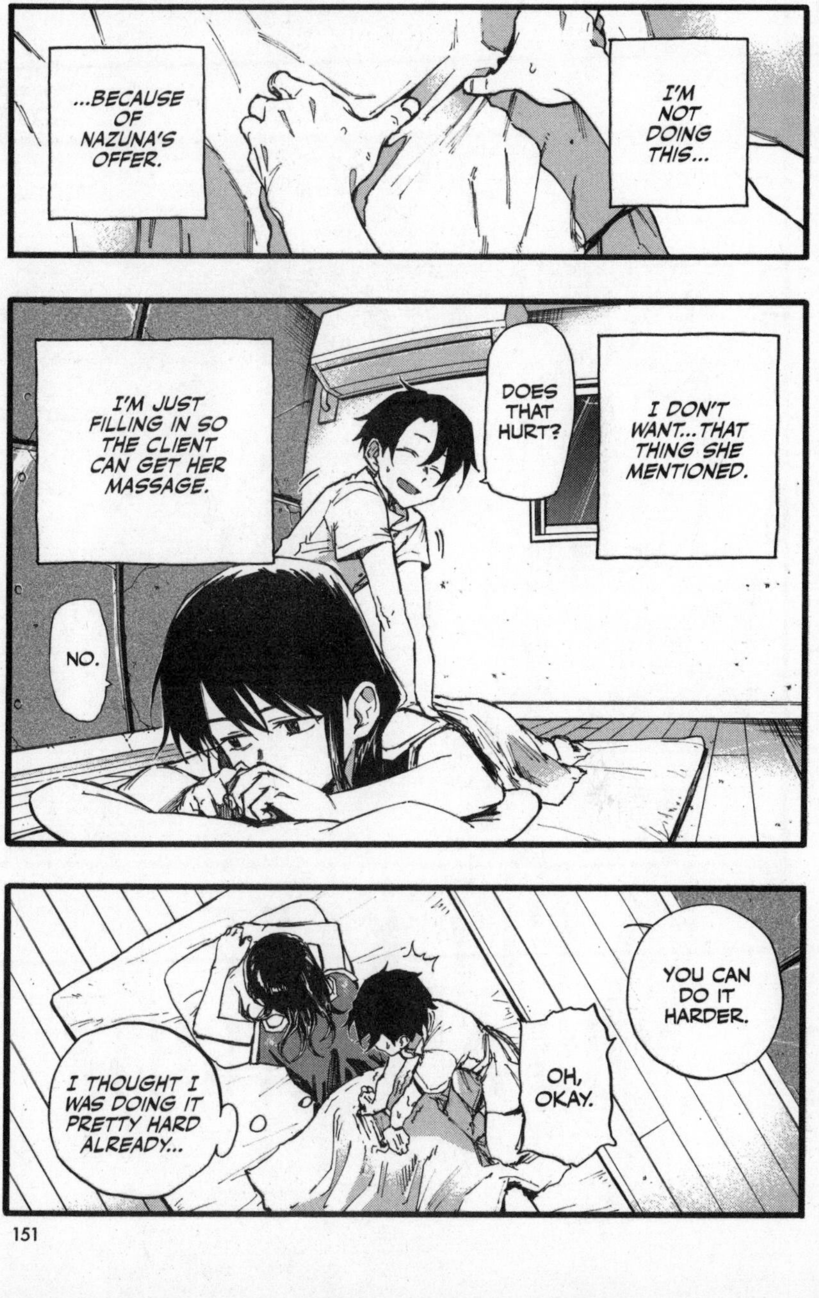
I'M NOT DOING THIS...
...BECAUSE OF NAZUNA'S OFFER.
I DON'T WANT...THAT THING SHE MENTIONED.
DOES THAT HURT?
I'M JUST FILLING IN SO THE CLIENT CAN GET HER MASSAGE.
NO.
YOU CAN DO IT HARDER.
OH, OKAY.
I THOUGHT I WAS DOING IT PRETTY HARD ALREADY...

NIGHT 17:

I'LL KEEP
YOU ALL NIGHT

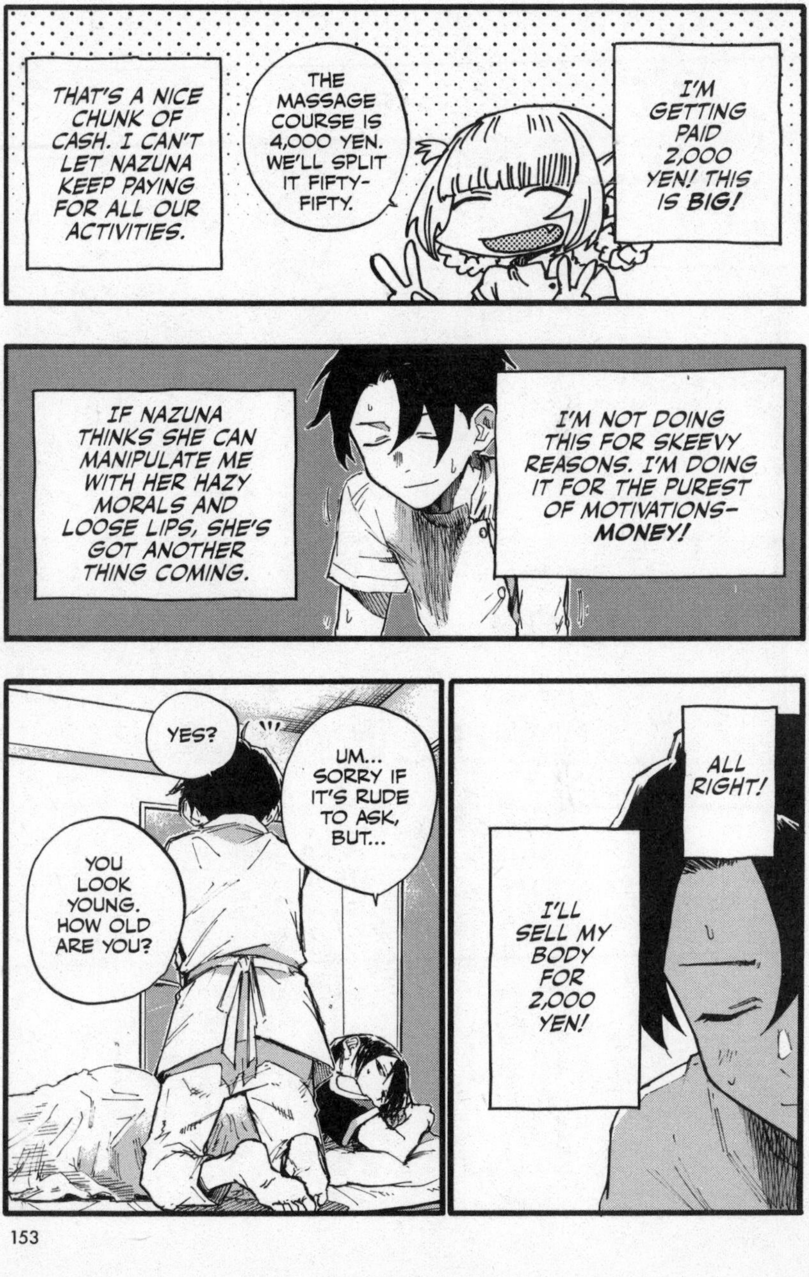
I'M GETTING PAID 2,000 YEN! THIS IS BIG!
THE MASSAGE COURSE IS 4,000 YEN. WE'LL SPLIT IT FIFTY-FIFTY.
THAT'S A NICE CHUNK OF CASH. I CAN'T LET NAZUNA KEEP PAYING FOR ALL OUR ACTIVITIES.
I'M NOT DOING THIS FOR SKEEVY REASONS. I'M DOING IT FOR THE PUREST OF MOTIVATIONS-MONEY!
IF NAZUNA THINKS SHE CAN MANIPULATE ME WITH HER HAZY MORALS AND LOOSE LIPS, SHE'S GOT ANOTHER THING COMING.
ALL RIGHT!
I'LL SELL MY BODY FOR 2,000 YEN!
UM... SORRY IF IT'S RUDE TO ASK, BUT...
YES?
YOU LOOK YOUNG. HOW OLD ARE YOU?

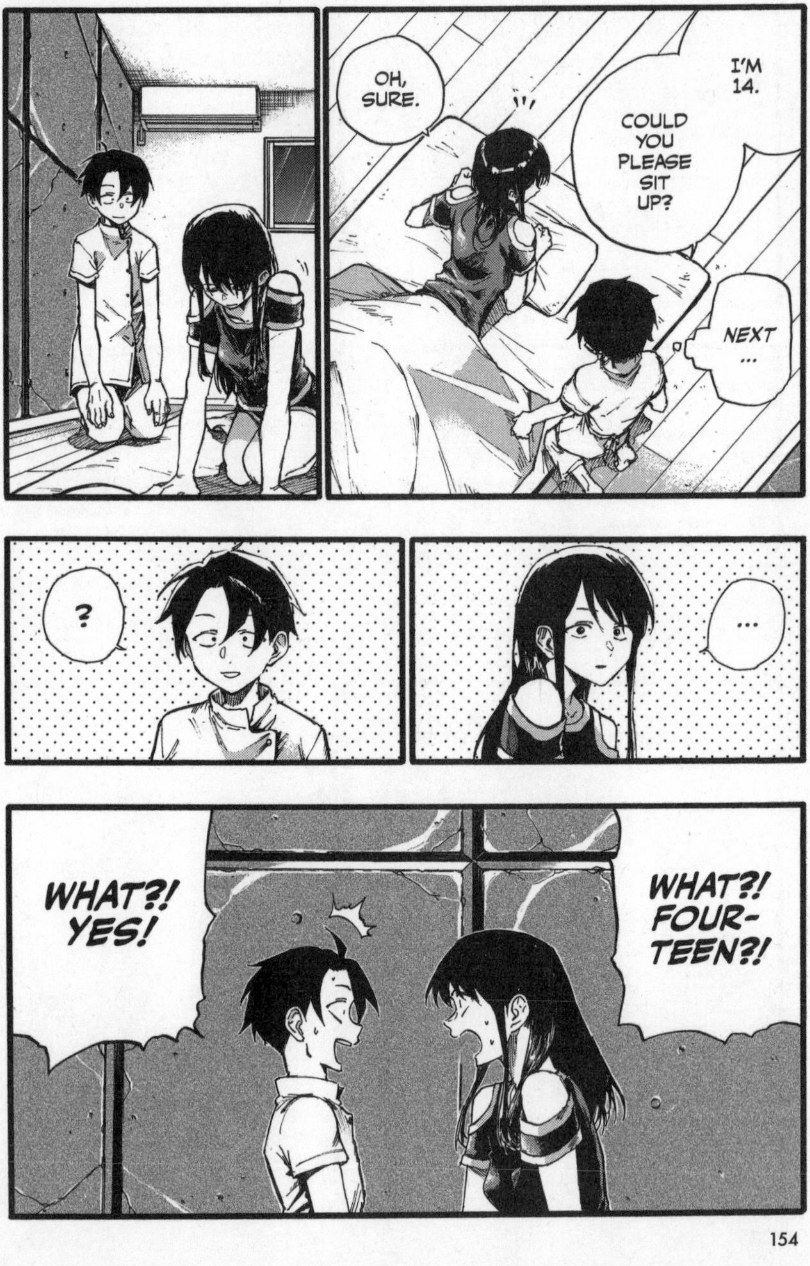

I'M 14.
COULD YOU PLEASE SIT UP?
OH, SURE.
NEXT ...
...
?
WHAT?! FOUR-TEEN?!
WHAT?! YES!

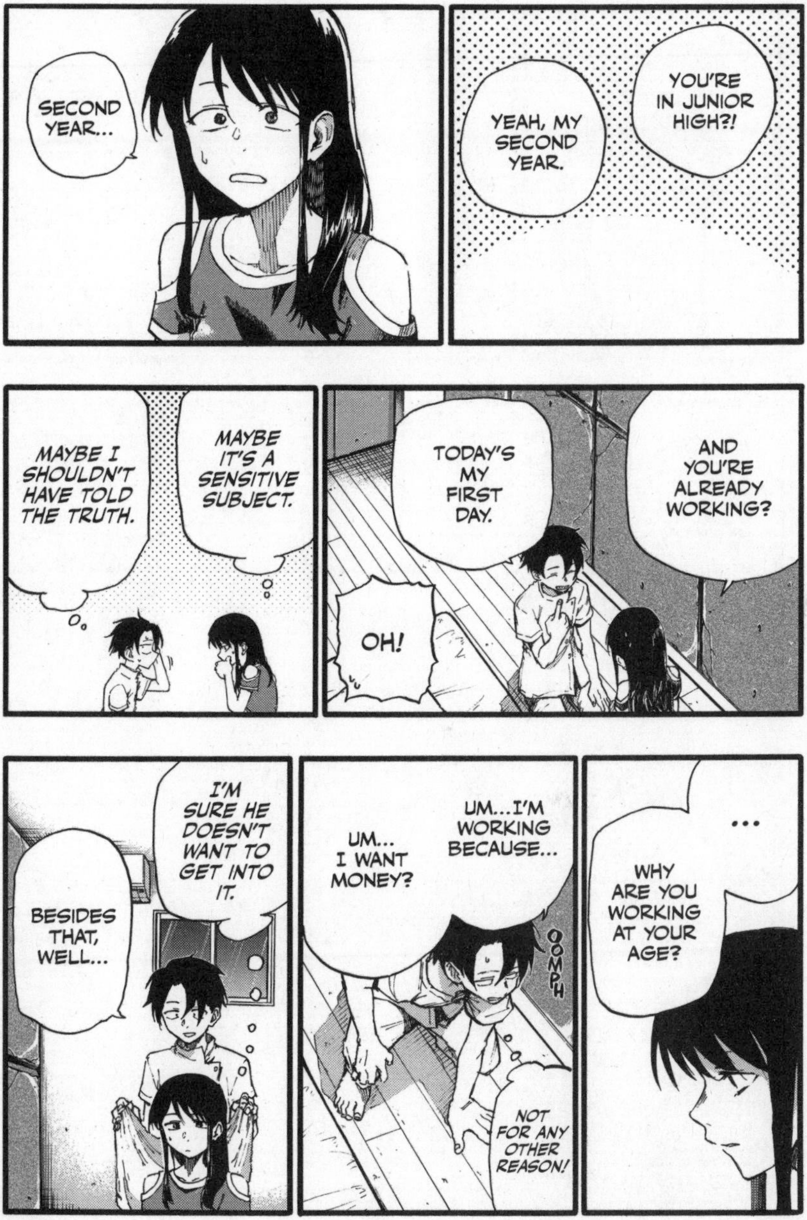
YOU'RE IN JUNIOR HIGH?!
YEAH, MY SECOND YEAR.
SECOND YEAR...
AND YOU'RE ALREADY WORKING?
TODAY'S MY FIRST DAY.
OH!
MAYBE IT'S A SENSITIVE SUBJECT.
MAYBE I SHOULDN'T HAVE TOLD THE TRUTH.
...
WHY ARE YOU WORKING AT YOUR AGE?
UM...I'M WORKING BECAUSE...
UM... I WANT MONEY?
OOMPH
NOT FOR ANY OTHER REASON!
I'M SURE HE DOESN'T WANT TO GET INTO IT.
BESIDES THAT, WELL...

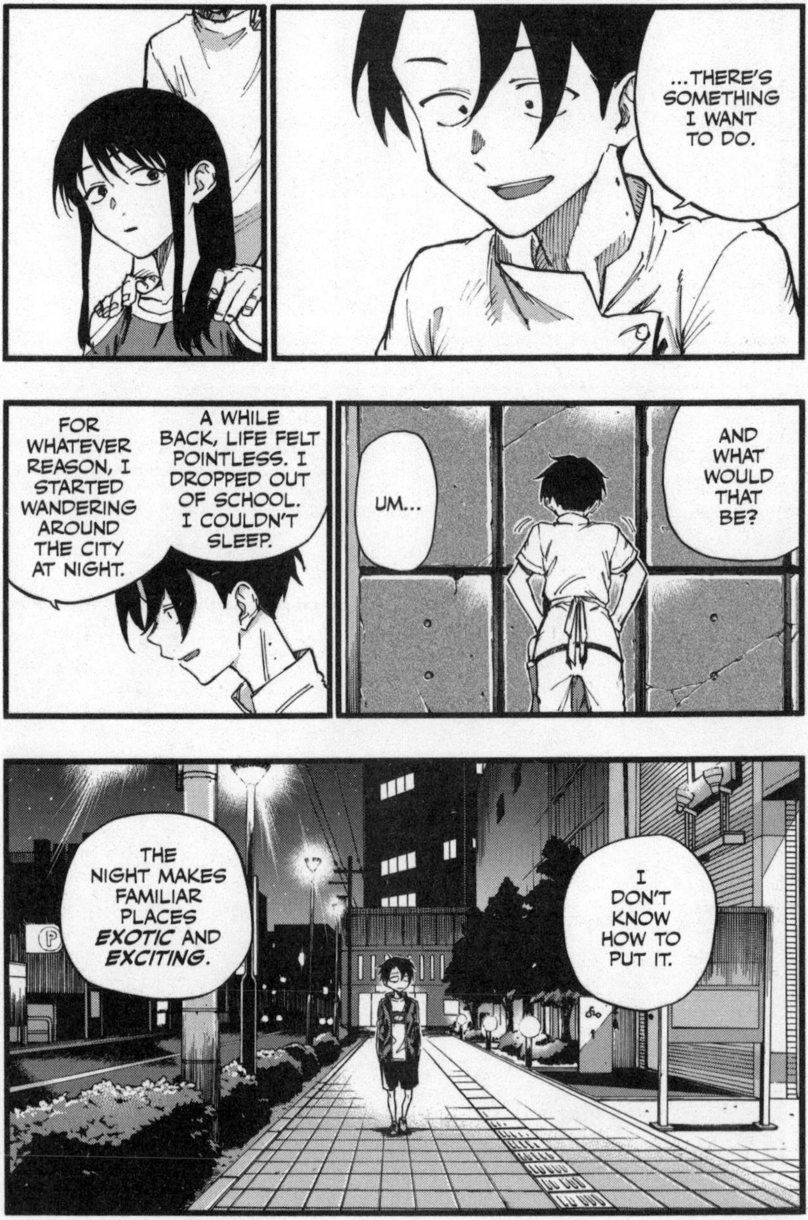
...THERE'S SOMETHING I WANT TO DO.
AND WHAT WOULD THAT BE?
UM...
A WHILE BACK, LIFE FELT POINTLESS. I DROPPED OUT OF SCHOOL. I COULDN'T SLEEP.
FOR WHATEVER REASON, I STARTED WANDERING AROUND THE CITY AT NIGHT.
I DON'T KNOW HOW TO PUT IT.
THE NIGHT MAKES FAMILIAR PLACES *EXOTIC* AND *EXCITING*.

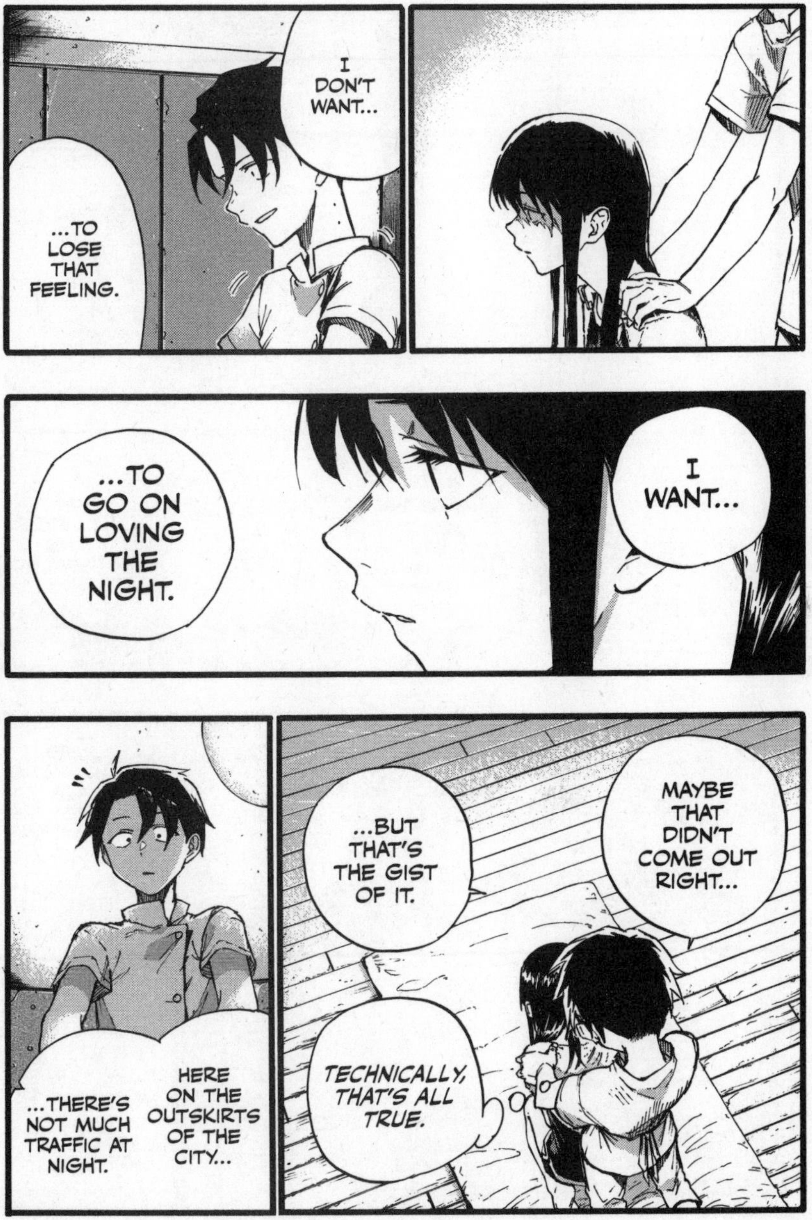
I DON'T WANT...
...TO LOSE THAT FEELING.
I WANT...
...TO GO ON LOVING THE NIGHT.
MAYBE THAT DIDN'T COME OUT RIGHT...
...BUT THAT'S THE GIST OF IT.
TECHNICALLY, THAT'S ALL TRUE.
HERE ON THE OUTSKIRTS OF THE CITY...
...THERE'S NOT MUCH TRAFFIC AT NIGHT.

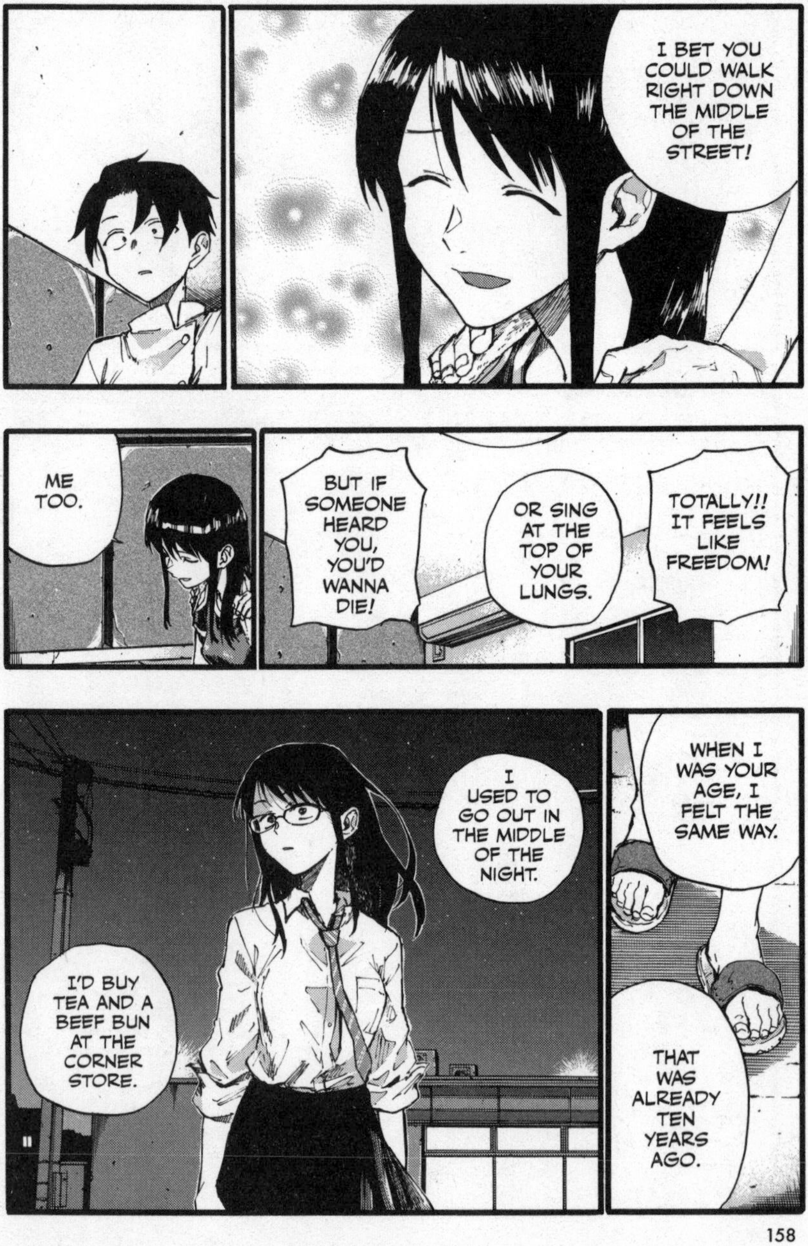
I BET YOU COULD WALK RIGHT DOWN THE MIDDLE OF THE STREET!
TOTALLY!! IT FEELS LIKE FREEDOM!
OR SING AT THE TOP OF YOUR LUNGS.
BUT IF SOMEONE HEARD YOU, YOU'D WANNA DIE!
ME TOO.
WHEN I WAS YOUR AGE, I FELT THE SAME WAY.
THAT WAS ALREADY TEN YEARS AGO.
I USED TO GO OUT IN THE MIDDLE OF THE NIGHT.
I'D BUY TEA AND A BEEF BUN AT THE CORNER STORE.

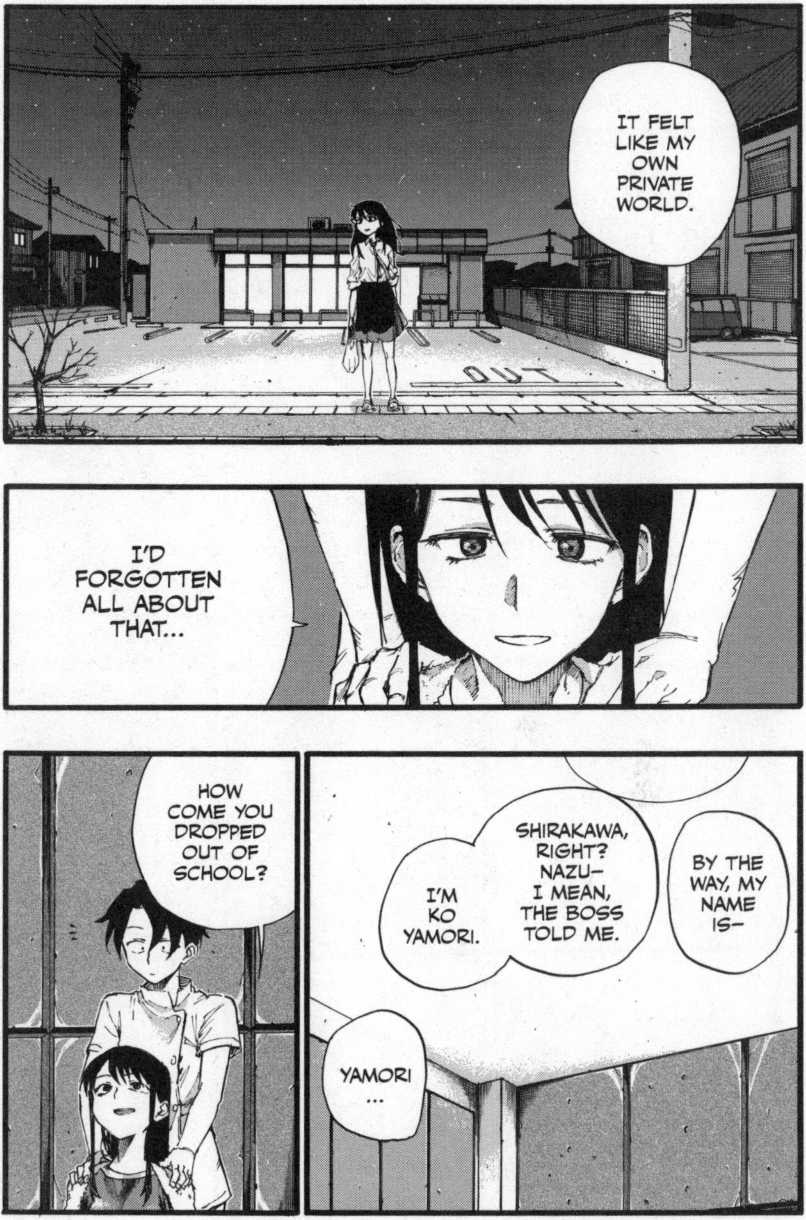
IT FELT LIKE MY OWN PRIVATE WORLD.
I'D FORGOTTEN ALL ABOUT THAT...
BY THE WAY, MY NAME IS–
SHIRAKAWA, RIGHT? NAZU– I MEAN, THE BOSS TOLD ME.
I'M KO YAMORI.
YAMORI ...
HOW COME YOU DROPPED OUT OF SCHOOL?

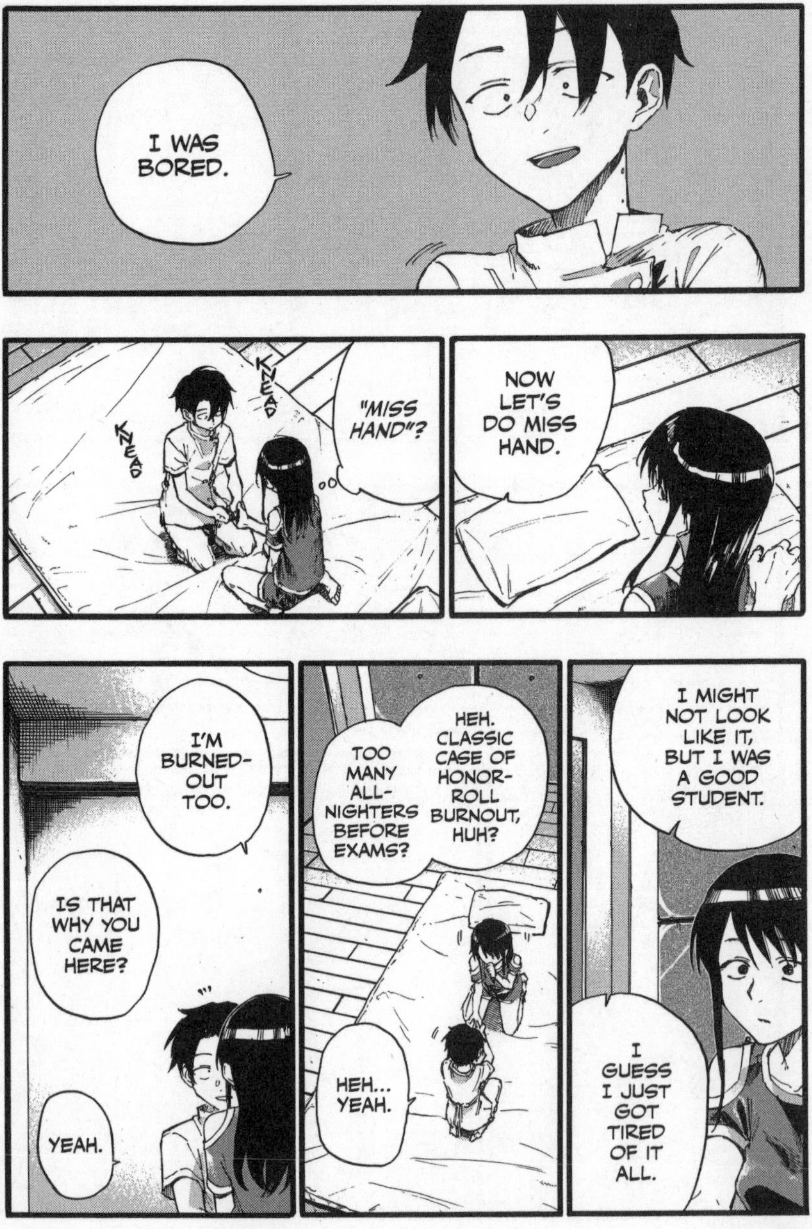
I WAS BORED.
NOW LET'S DO MISS HAND.
"MISS HAND"?
KNEAD
KNEAD
I MIGHT NOT LOOK LIKE IT, BUT I WAS A GOOD STUDENT.
I GUESS I JUST GOT TIRED OF IT ALL.
HEH. CLASSIC CASE OF HONOR-ROLL BURNOUT, HUH?
TOO MANY ALL-NIGHTERS BEFORE EXAMS?
HEH... YEAH.
I'M BURNED-OUT TOO.
IS THAT WHY YOU CAME HERE?
YEAH.

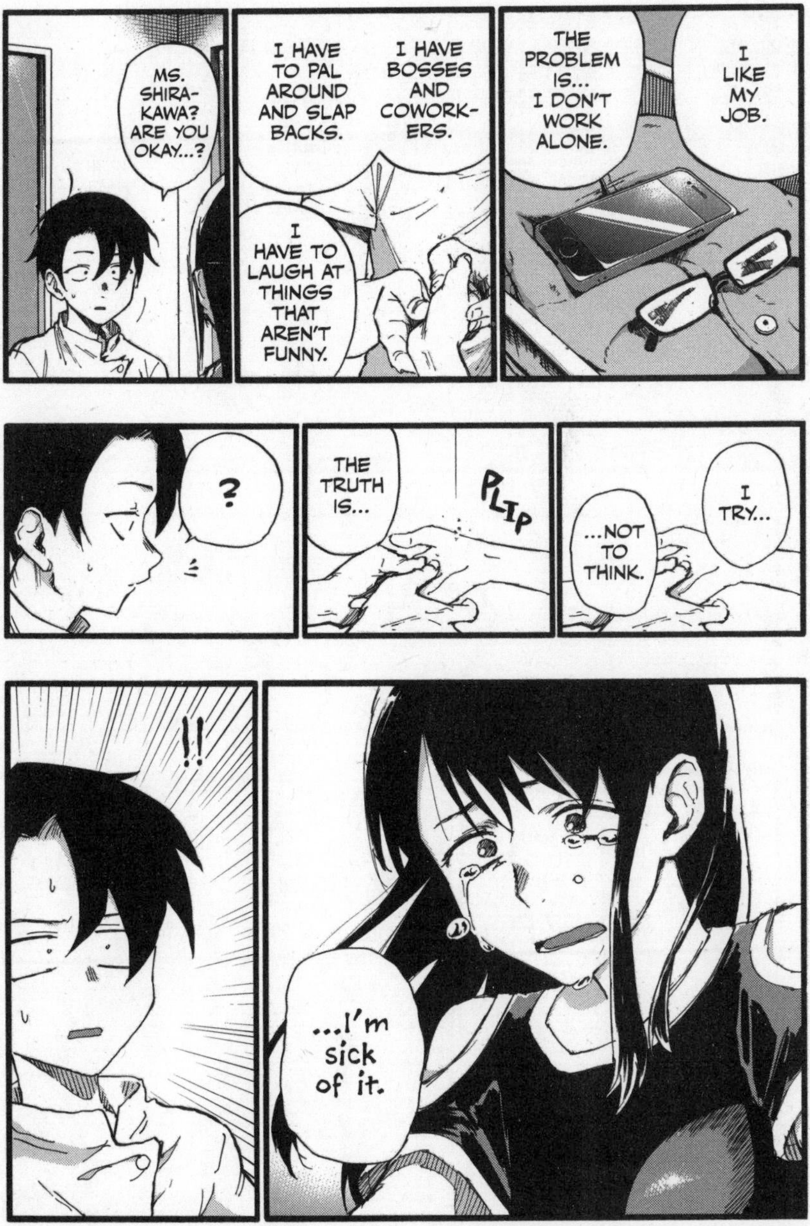
I LIKE MY JOB.
THE PROBLEM IS... I DON'T WORK ALONE.
I HAVE BOSSES AND COWORK-ERS.
I HAVE TO PAL AROUND AND SLAP BACKS.
I HAVE TO LAUGH AT THINGS THAT AREN'T FUNNY.
MS. SHIRA-KAWA? ARE YOU OKAY...?
I TRY...
...NOT TO THINK.
THE TRUTH IS...
PLIP
?
...I'm sick of it.
!!

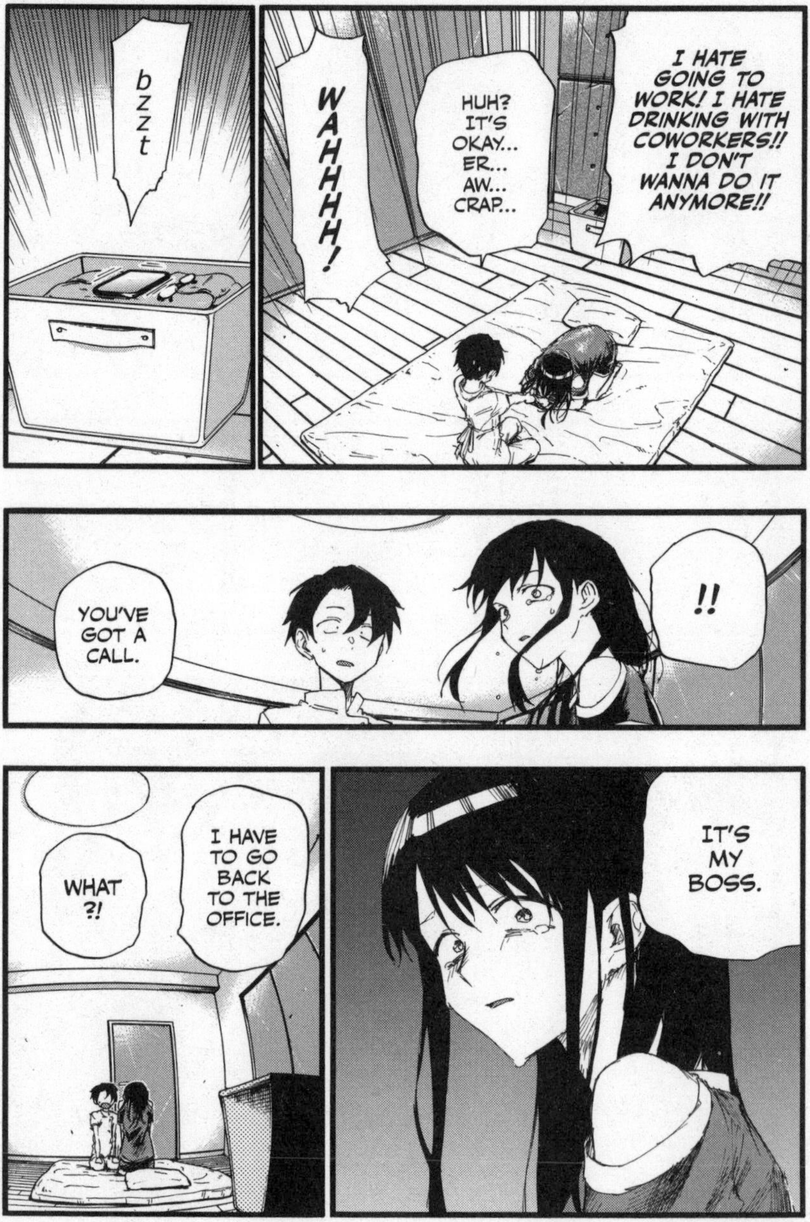
I HATE GOING TO WORK! I HATE DRINKING WITH COWORKERS!! I DON'T WANNA DO IT ANYMORE!!
HUH? IT'S OKAY... ER... AW... CRAP...
WAHHHHH!
bzzt
!!
YOU'VE GOT A CALL.
IT'S MY BOSS.
I HAVE TO GO BACK TO THE OFFICE.
WHAT ?!

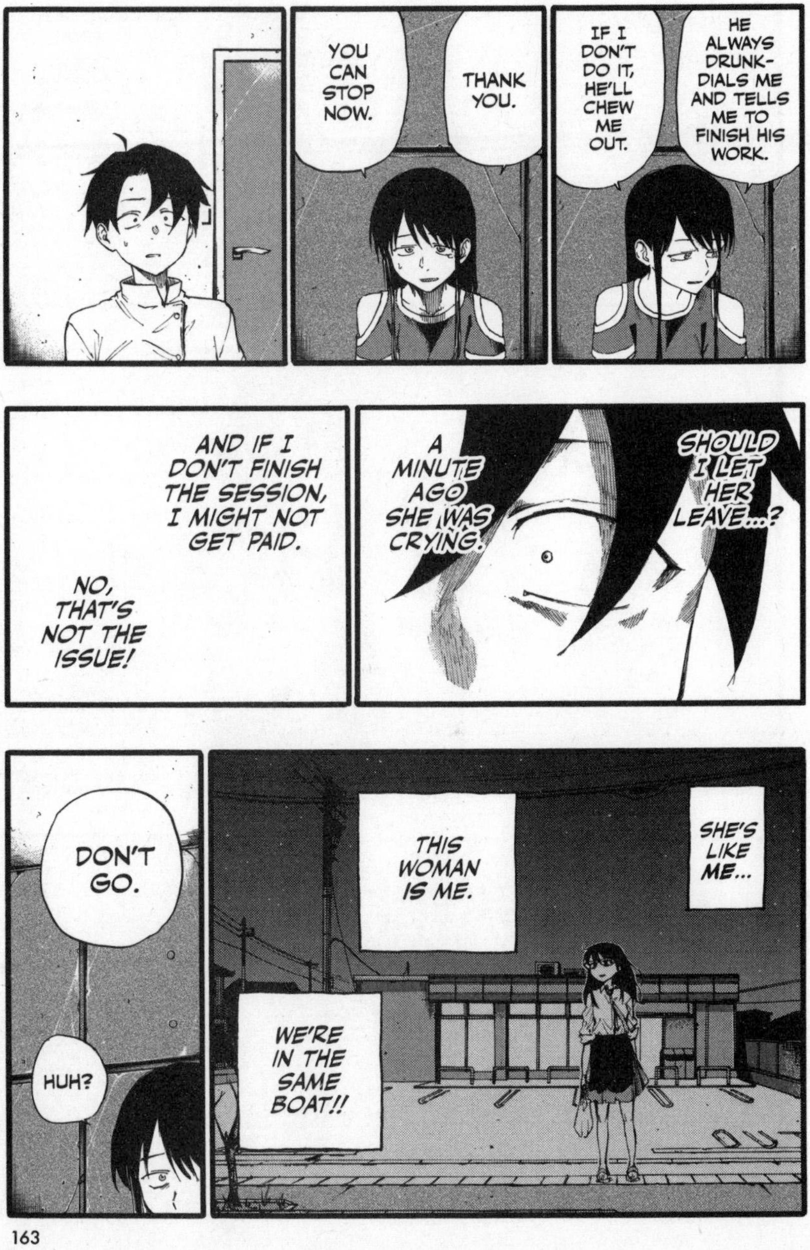
HE ALWAYS DRUNK-DIALS ME AND TELLS ME TO FINISH HIS WORK.
IF I DON'T DO IT, HE'LL CHEW ME OUT.
THANK YOU.
YOU CAN STOP NOW.
SHOULD I LET HER LEAVE...?
A MINUTE AGO SHE WAS CRYING.
AND IF I DON'T FINISH THE SESSION, I MIGHT NOT GET PAID.
NO, THAT'S NOT THE ISSUE!
SHE'S LIKE ME...
THIS WOMAN IS ME.
WE'RE IN THE SAME BOAT!!
DON'T GO.
HUH?

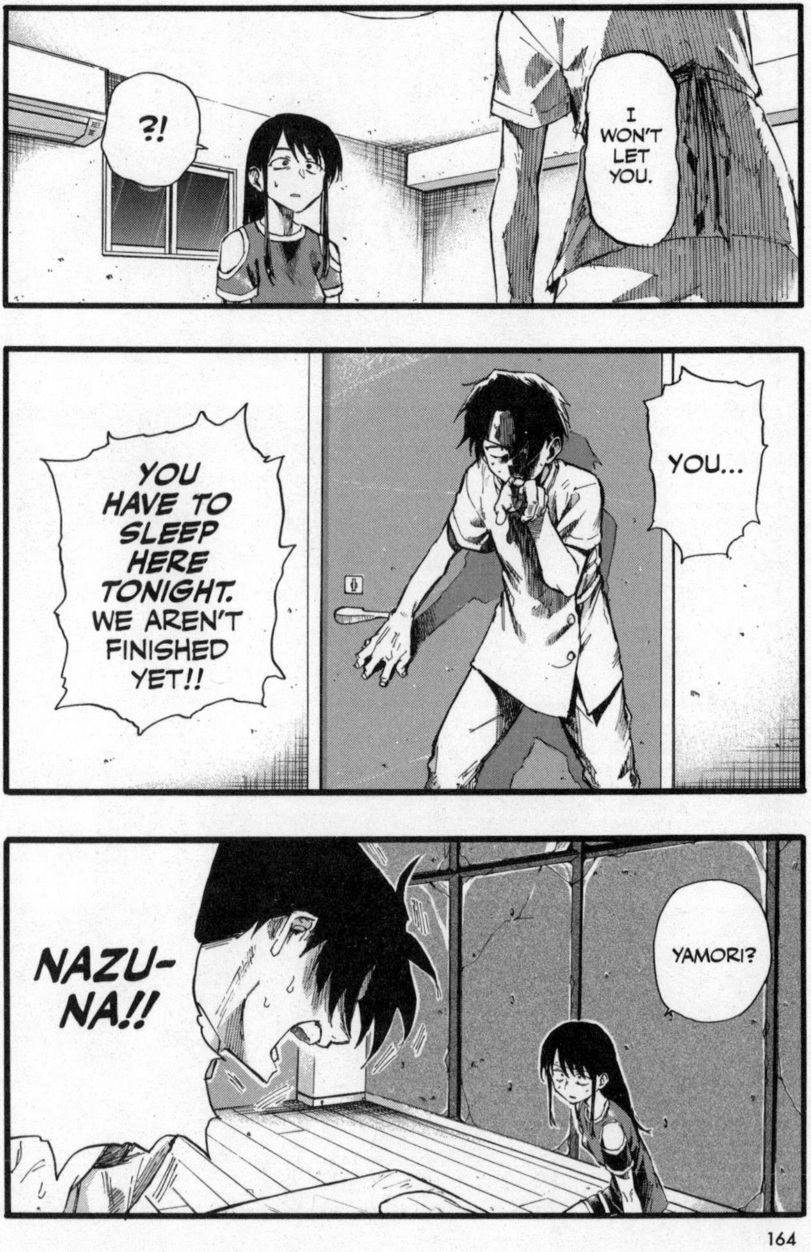
I WON'T LET YOU.
?!
YOU...
YOU HAVE TO SLEEP HERE TONIGHT. WE AREN'T FINISHED YET!!
YAMORI?
NAZU-NA!!

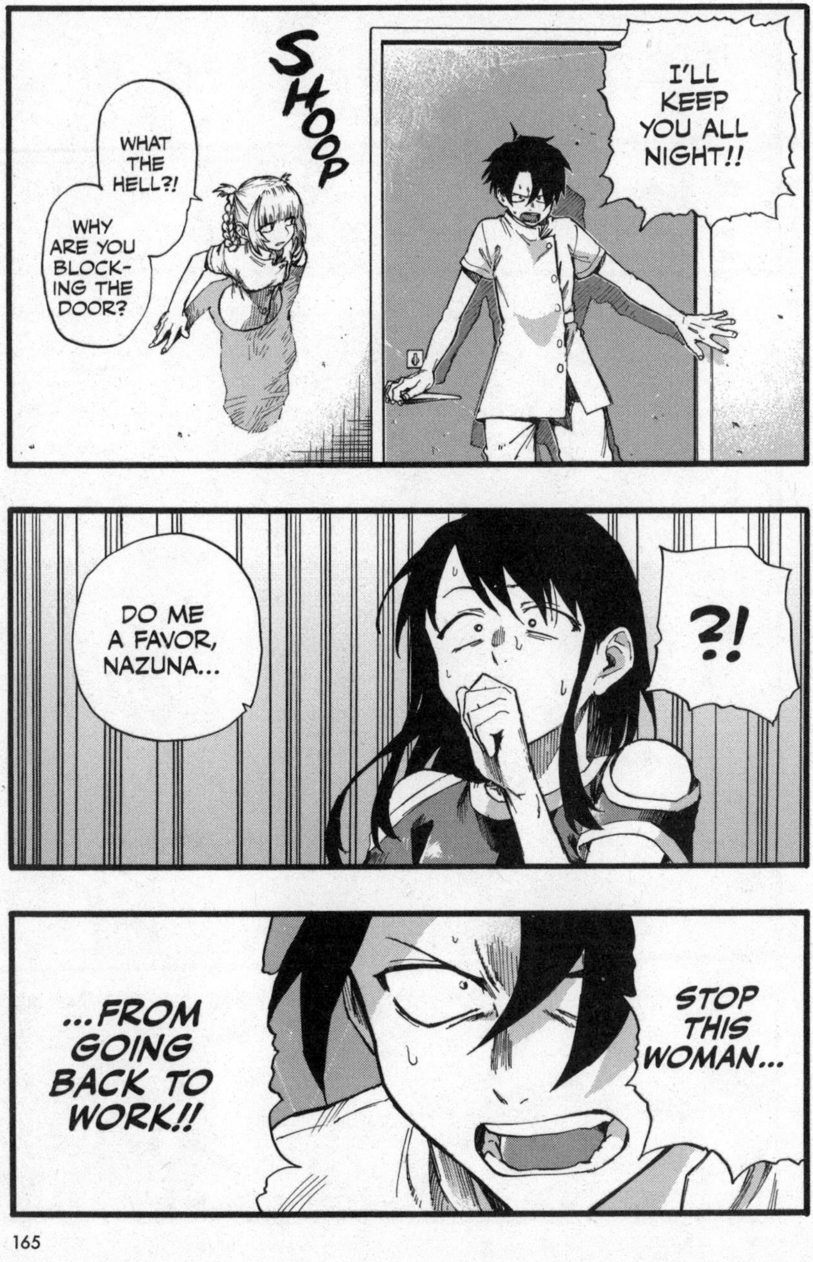
I'LL KEEP YOU ALL NIGHT!!
SHOOP
WHAT THE HELL?!
WHY ARE YOU BLOCKING THE DOOR?
?!
DO ME A FAVOR, NAZUNA...
STOP THIS WOMAN...
...FROM GOING BACK TO WORK!!

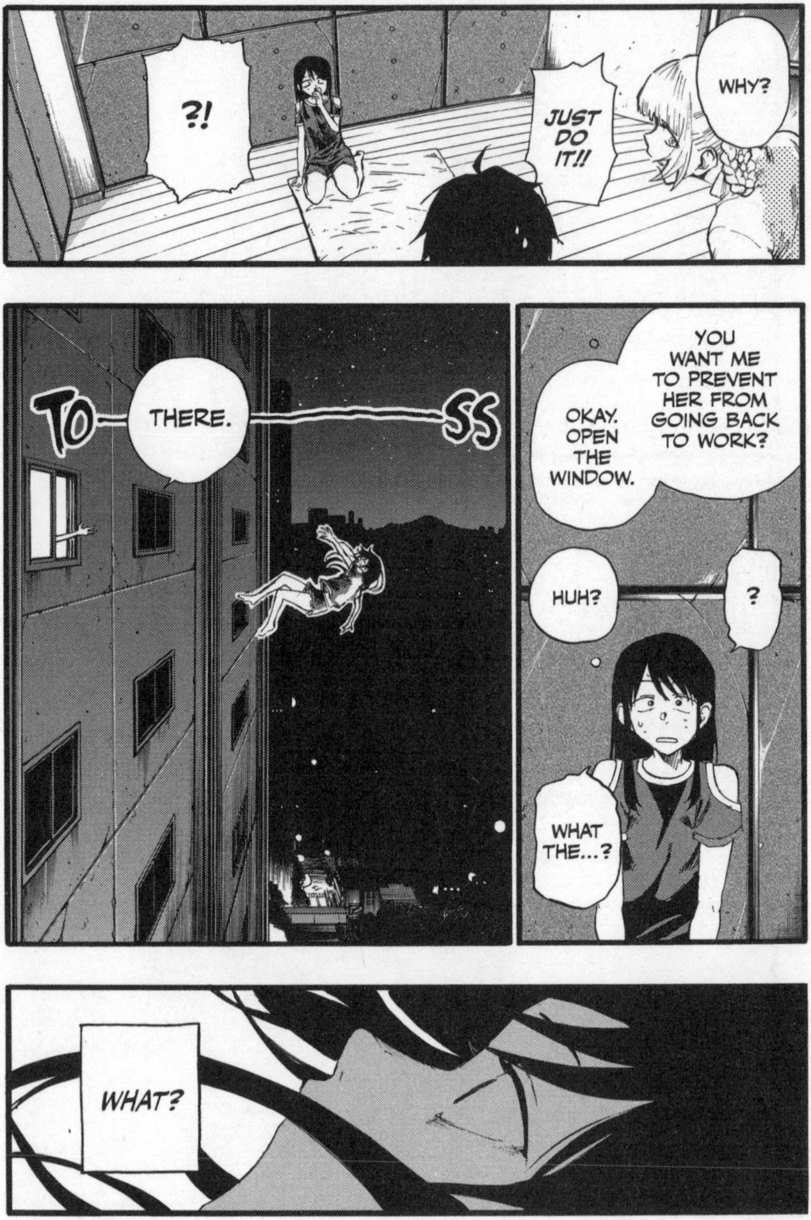
WHY?
JUST DO IT!!
?!
YOU WANT ME TO PREVENT HER FROM GOING BACK TO WORK?
OKAY. OPEN THE WINDOW.
?
HUH?
WHAT THE...?
THERE.
TO—SS
WHAT?

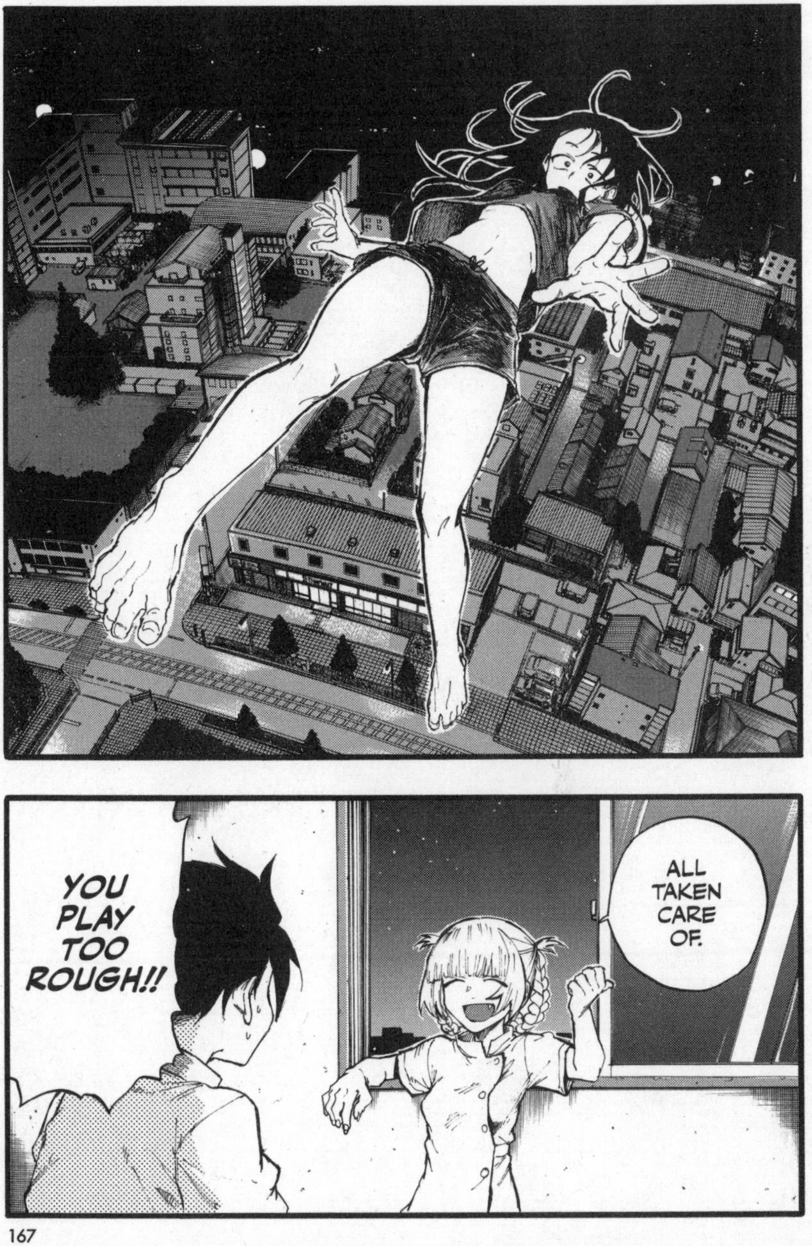
ALL TAKEN CARE OF.
YOU PLAY TOO ROUGH!!

Call of the Night

NIGHT 18: MIGHT AS WELL HAVE FUN

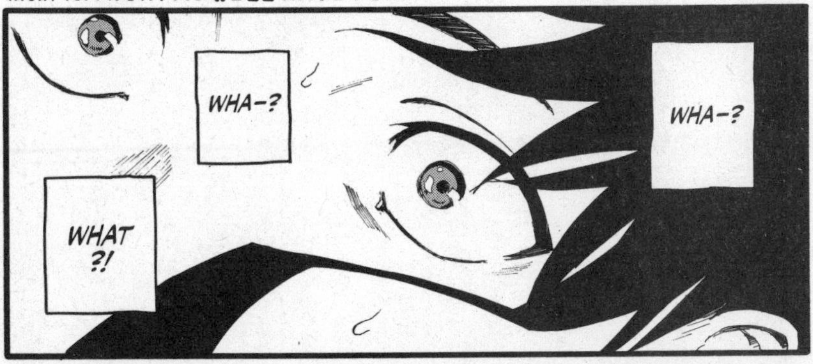
WHA-?
WHA-?
WHAT ?!

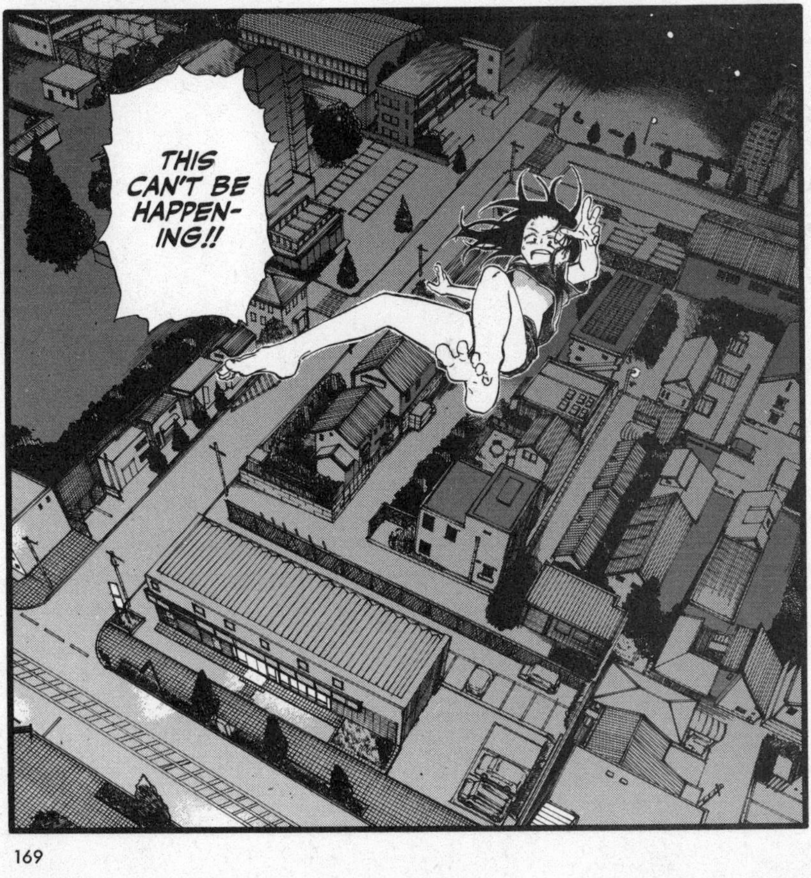
THIS CAN'T BE HAPPEN-ING!!

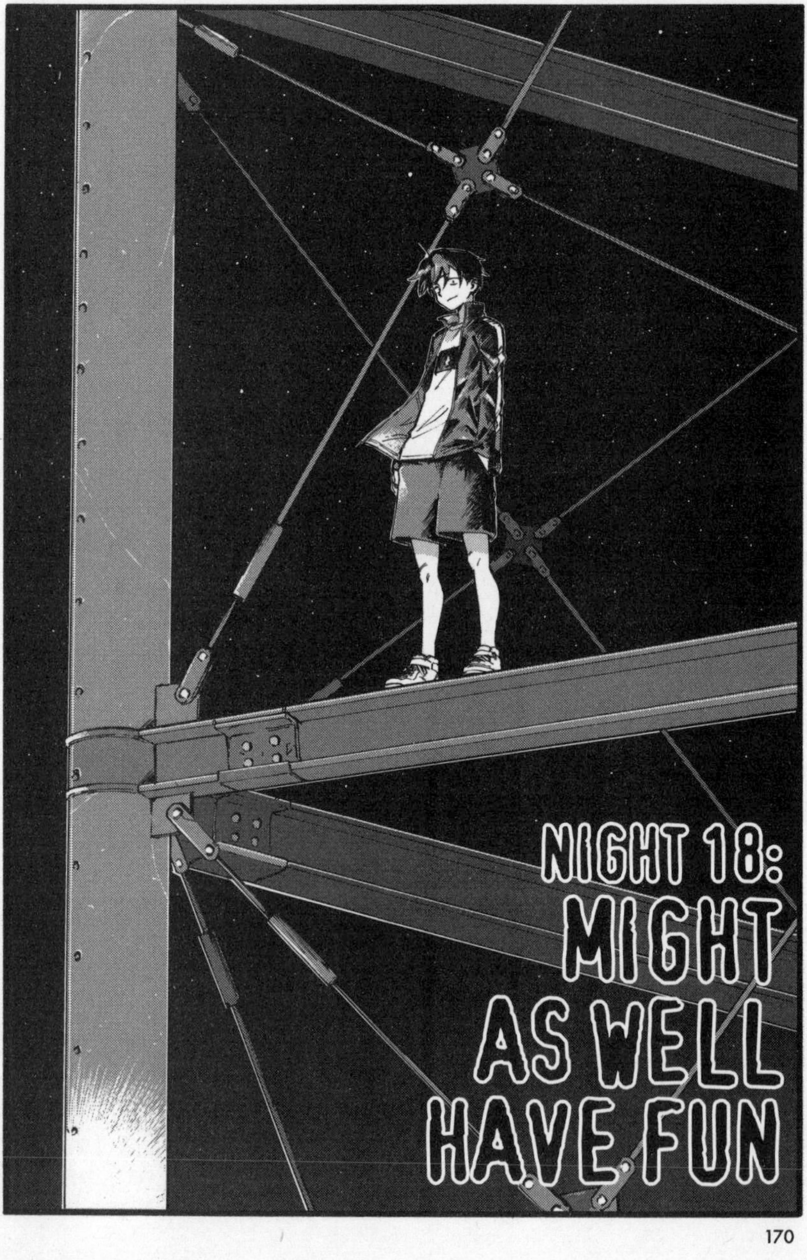
NIGHT 18:
MIGHT AS WELL HAVE FUN

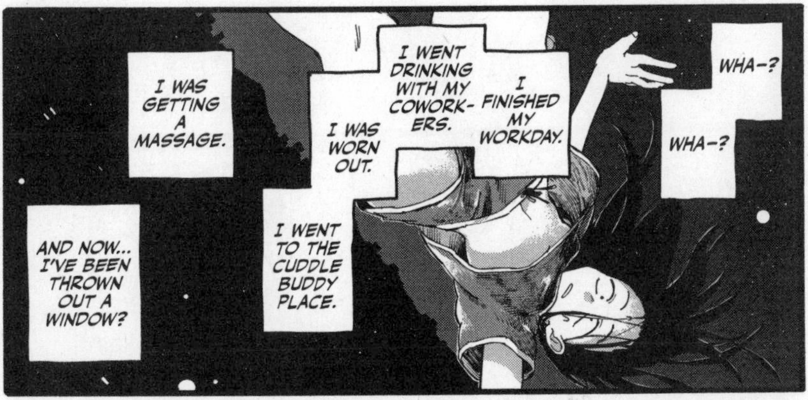
WHA-?
WHA-?
I FINISHED MY WORKDAY.
I WENT DRINKING WITH MY COWORK-ERS.
I WAS WORN OUT.
I WAS GETTING A MASSAGE.
I WENT TO THE CUDDLE BUDDY PLACE.
AND NOW... I'VE BEEN THROWN OUT A WINDOW?

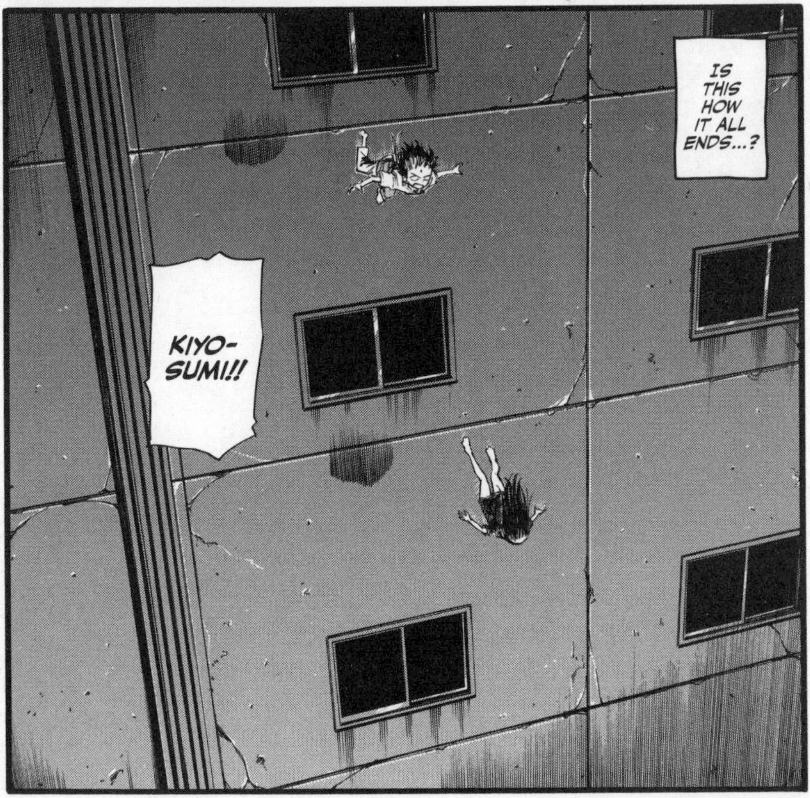
IS THIS HOW IT ALL ENDS...?
KIYO-SUMI!!

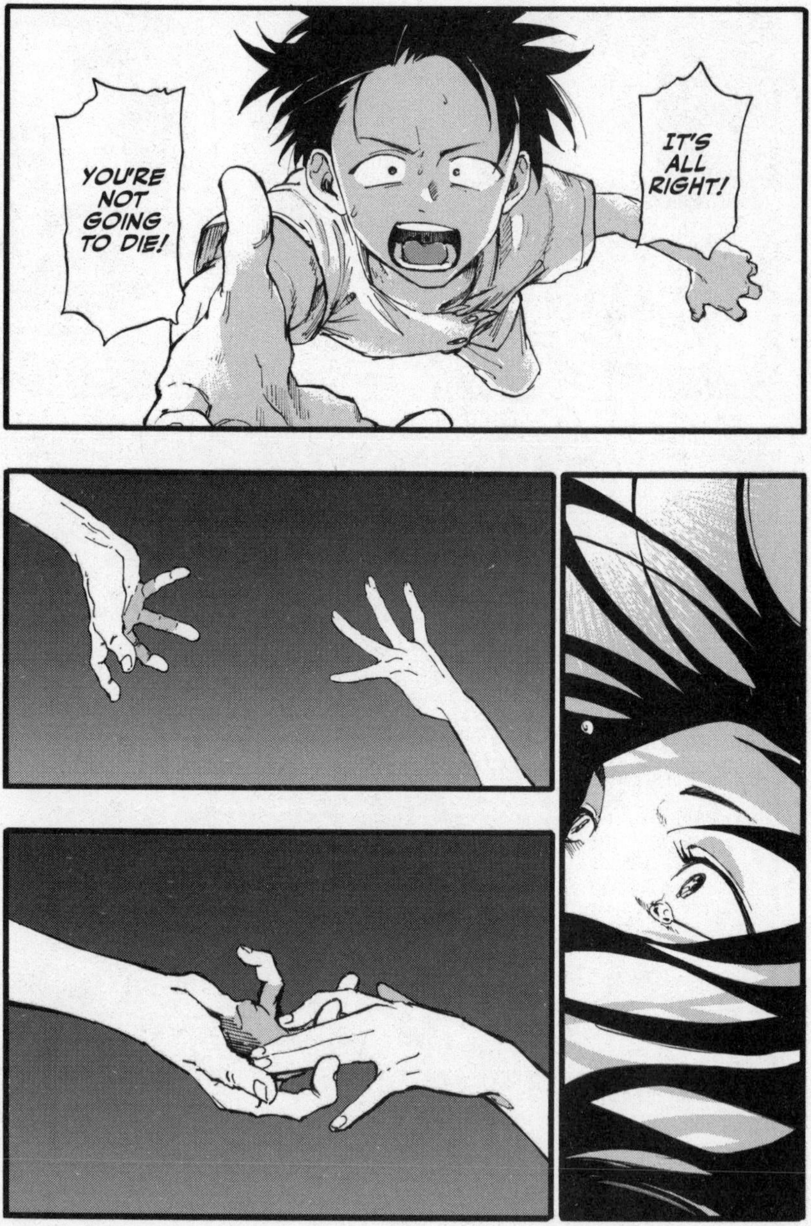
IT'S ALL RIGHT!
YOU'RE NOT GOING TO DIE!

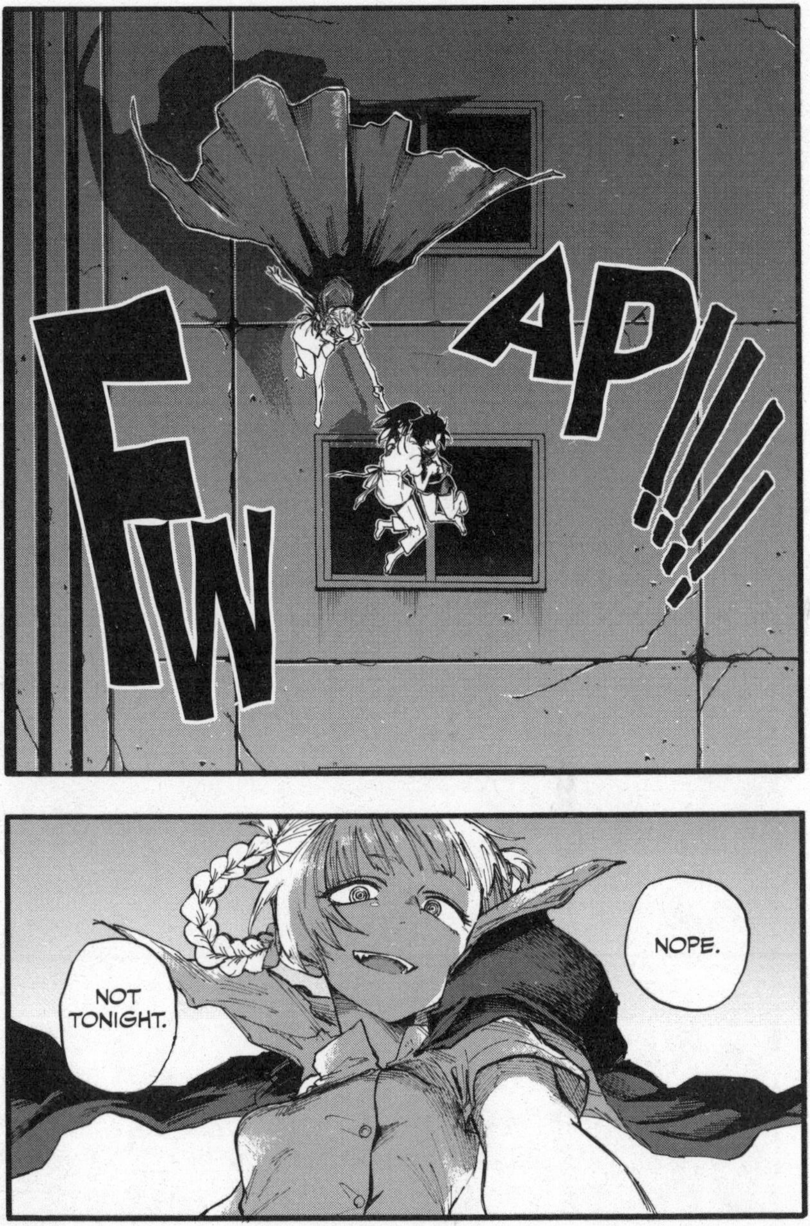
FWAP!!!!
NOPE.
NOT TONIGHT.

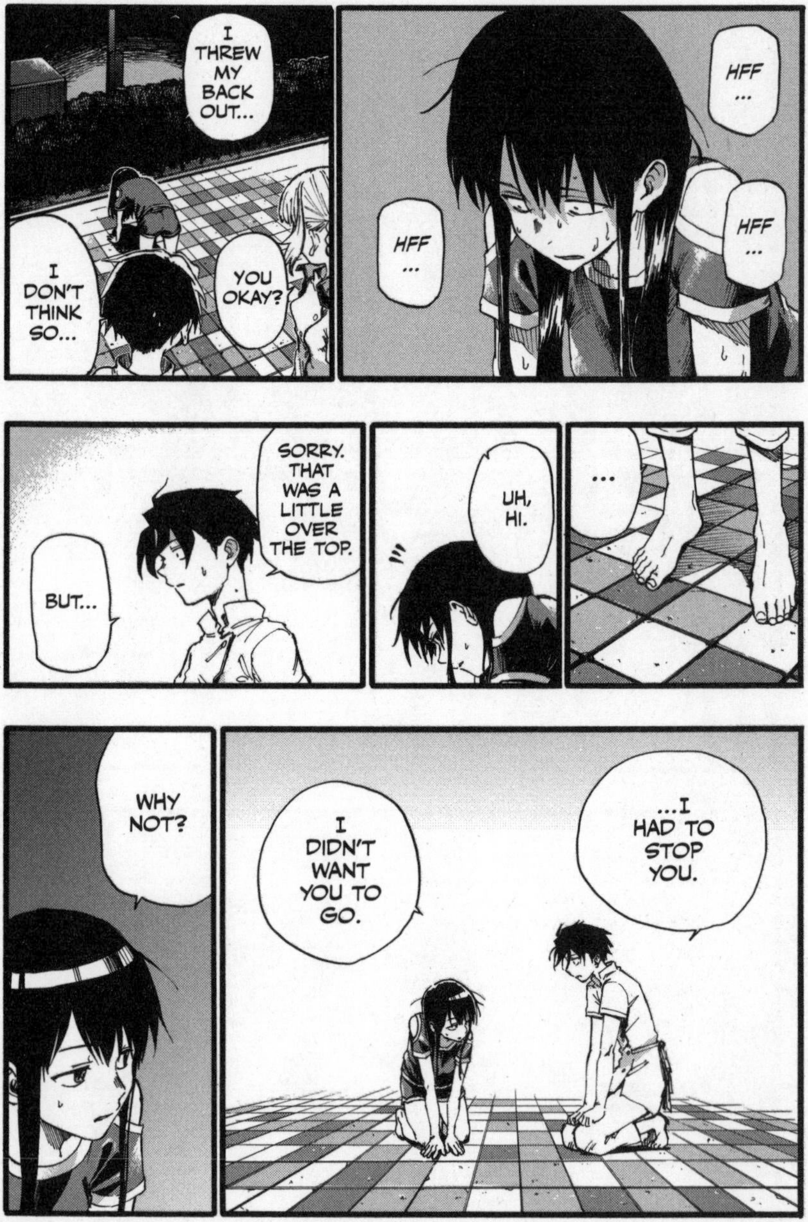

HFF ...
HFF ...
HFF ...
YOU OKAY?
I DON'T THINK SO...
I THREW MY BACK OUT...
...
UH, HI.
SORRY. THAT WAS A LITTLE OVER THE TOP.
BUT...
...I HAD TO STOP YOU.
I DIDN'T WANT YOU TO GO.
WHY NOT?

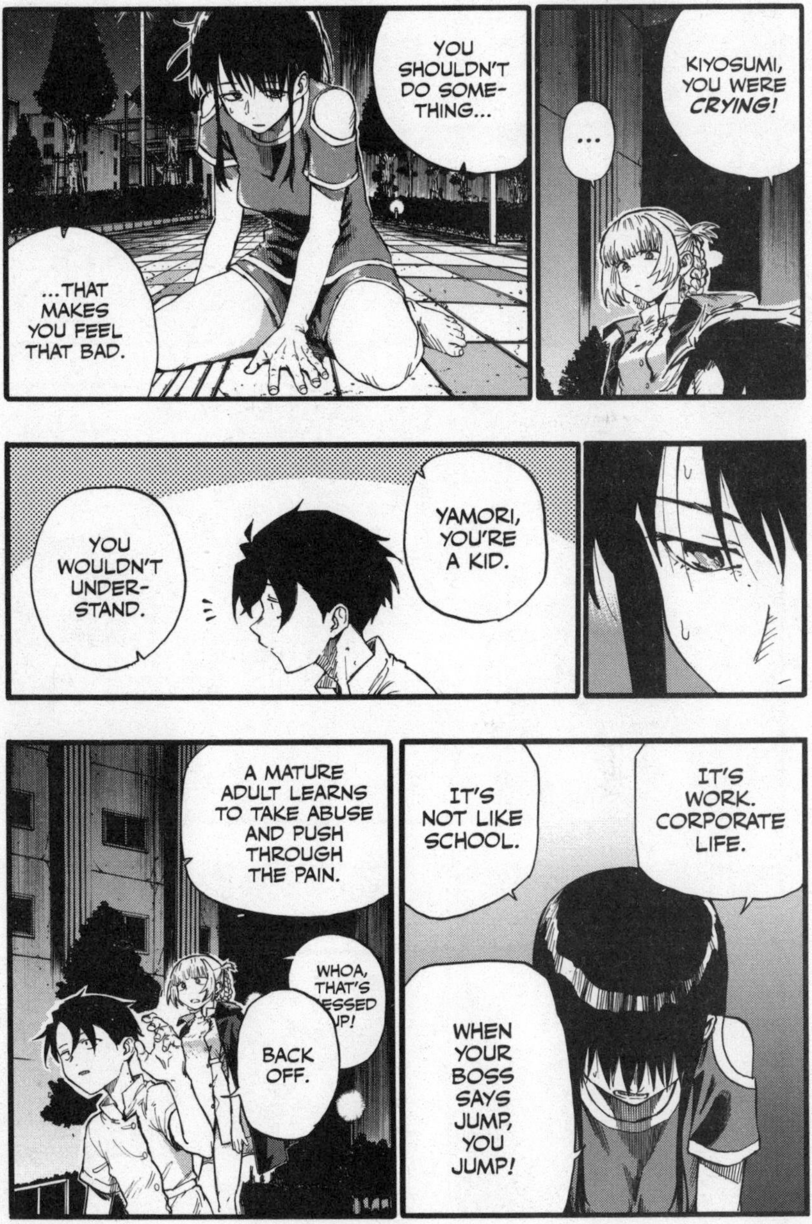
KIYOSUMI, YOU WERE *CRYING!*
...
YOU SHOULDN'T DO SOME-THING...
...THAT MAKES YOU FEEL THAT BAD.
YAMORI, YOU'RE A KID.
YOU WOULDN'T UNDER-STAND.
IT'S WORK. CORPORATE LIFE.
IT'S NOT LIKE SCHOOL.
WHEN YOUR BOSS SAYS JUMP, YOU JUMP!
A MATURE ADULT LEARNS TO TAKE ABUSE AND PUSH THROUGH THE PAIN.
WHOA, THAT'S
BACK OFF.

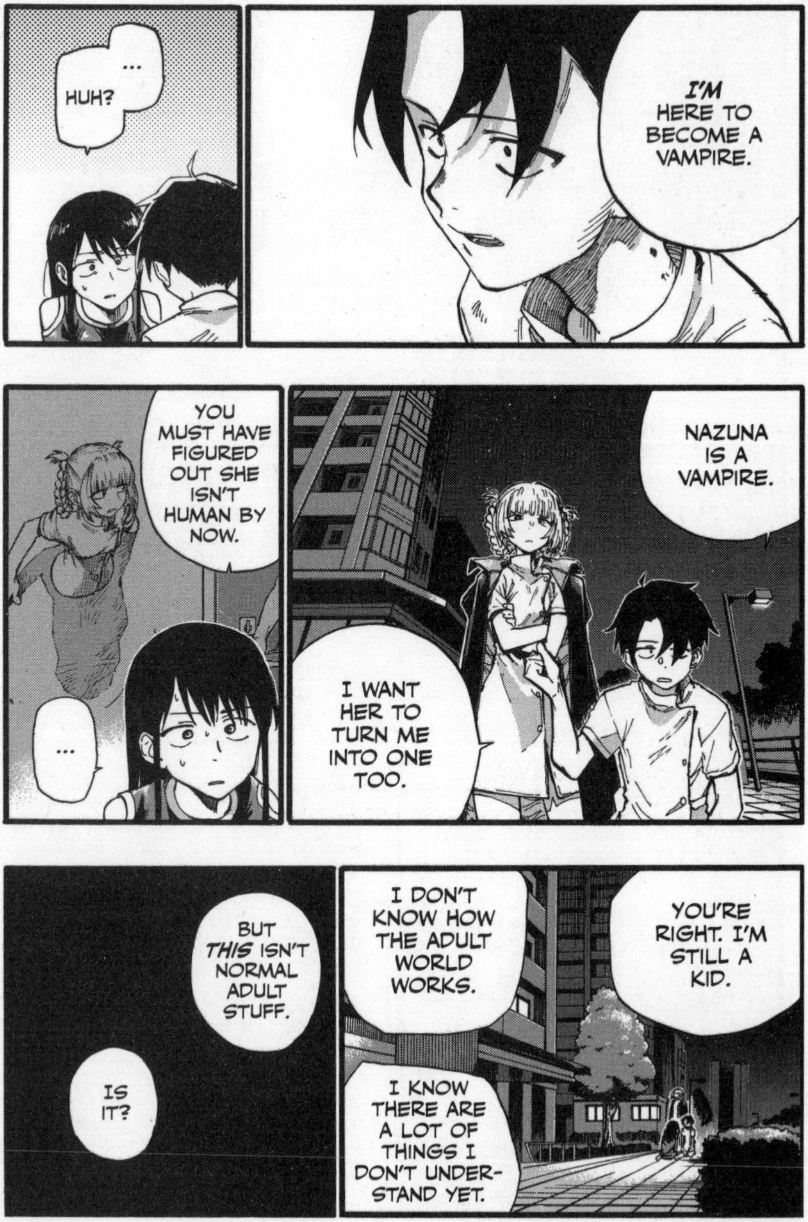
I'M HERE TO BECOME A VAMPIRE.
... HUH?
NAZUNA IS A VAMPIRE.
I WANT HER TO TURN ME INTO ONE TOO.
YOU MUST HAVE FIGURED OUT SHE ISN'T HUMAN BY NOW.
...
YOU'RE RIGHT. I'M STILL A KID.
I DON'T KNOW HOW THE ADULT WORLD WORKS.
I KNOW THERE ARE A LOT OF THINGS I DON'T UNDER-STAND YET.
BUT *THIS* ISN'T NORMAL ADULT STUFF.
IS IT?

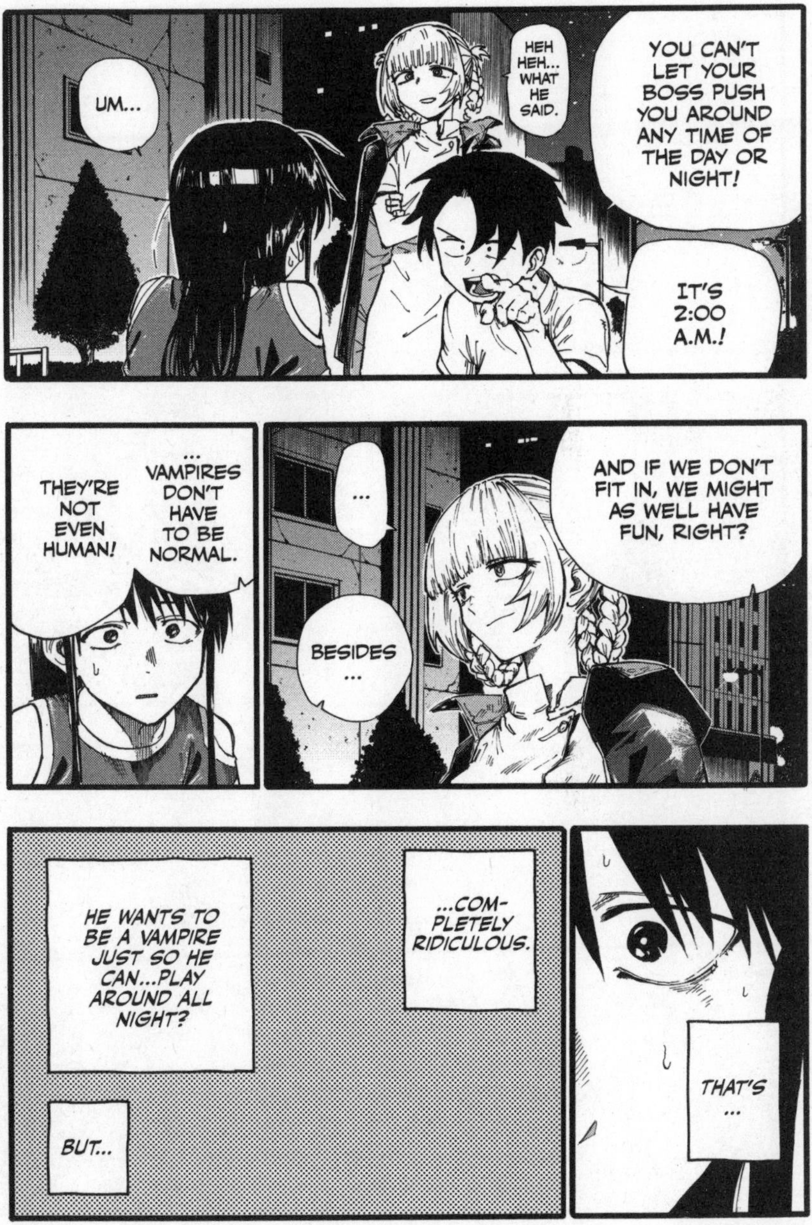
YOU CAN'T LET YOUR BOSS PUSH YOU AROUND ANY TIME OF THE DAY OR NIGHT!
IT'S 2:00 A.M.!
HEH HEH... WHAT HE SAID.
UM...
AND IF WE DON'T FIT IN, WE MIGHT AS WELL HAVE FUN, RIGHT?
...
BESIDES ...
... VAMPIRES DON'T HAVE TO BE NORMAL.
THEY'RE NOT EVEN HUMAN!
THAT'S ...
...COM-PLETELY RIDICULOUS.
HE WANTS TO BE A VAMPIRE JUST SO HE CAN...PLAY AROUND ALL NIGHT?
BUT...

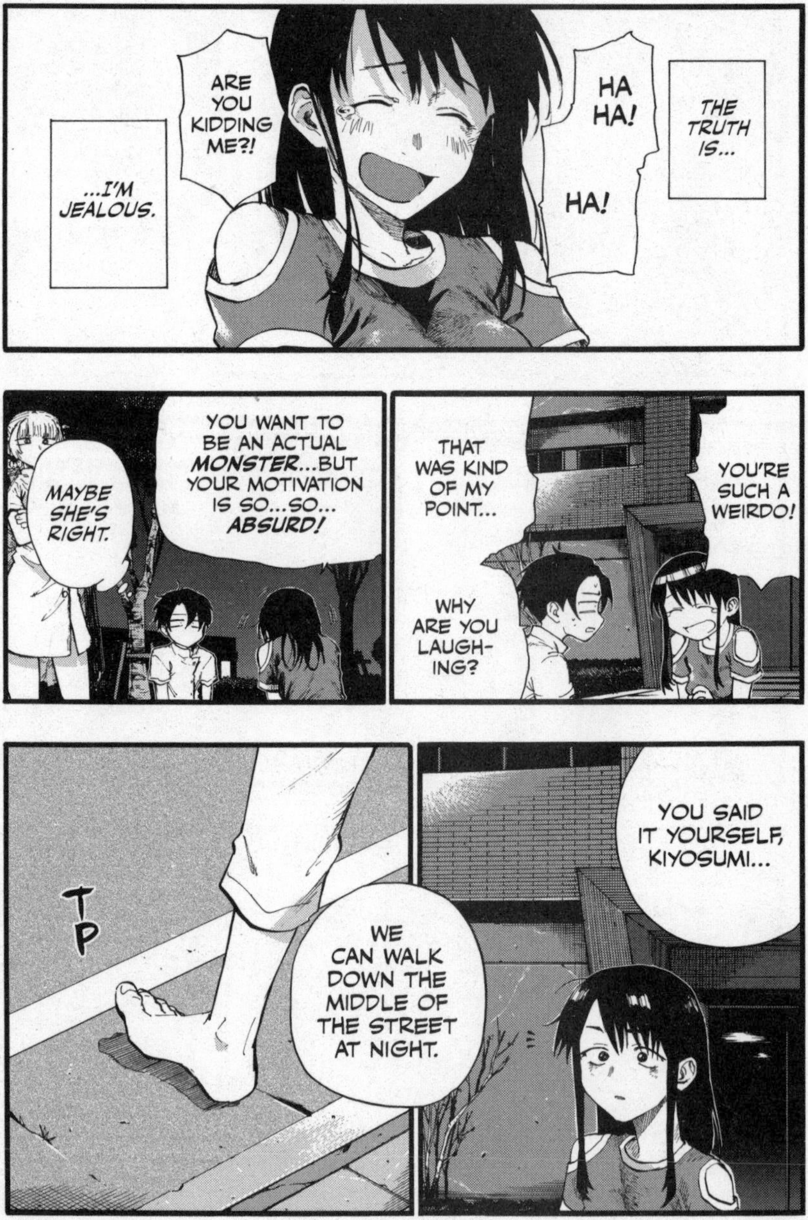
THE TRUTH IS...
HA HA!
HA!
ARE YOU KIDDING ME?!
...I'M JEALOUS.
YOU'RE SUCH A WEIRDO!
THAT WAS KIND OF MY POINT...
WHY ARE YOU LAUGHING?
YOU WANT TO BE AN ACTUAL MONSTER...BUT YOUR MOTIVATION IS SO...SO... ABSURD!
MAYBE SHE'S RIGHT.
YOU SAID IT YOURSELF, KIYOSUMI...
WE CAN WALK DOWN THE MIDDLE OF THE STREET AT NIGHT.
TP

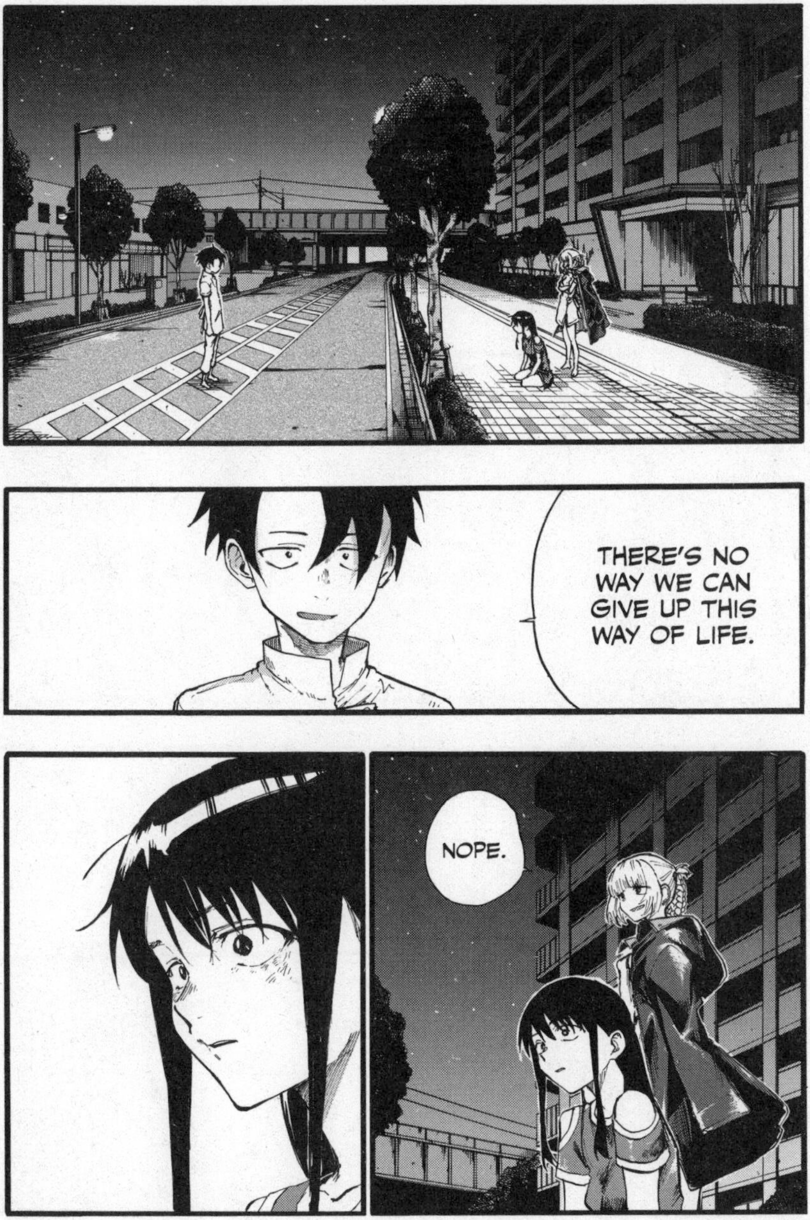
THERE'S NO WAY WE CAN GIVE UP THIS WAY OF LIFE.
NOPE.

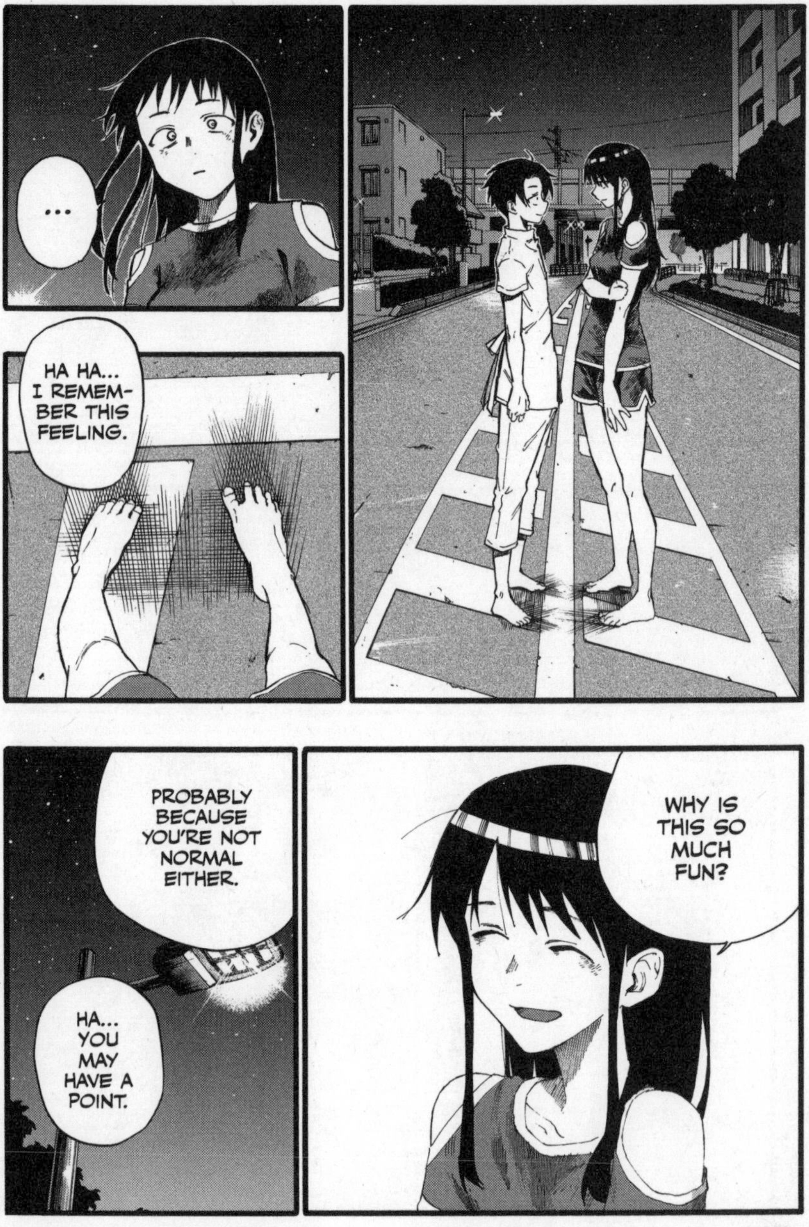
...
HA HA... I REMEMBER THIS FEELING.
WHY IS THIS SO MUCH FUN?
PROBABLY BECAUSE YOU'RE NOT NORMAL EITHER.
HA... YOU MAY HAVE A POINT.

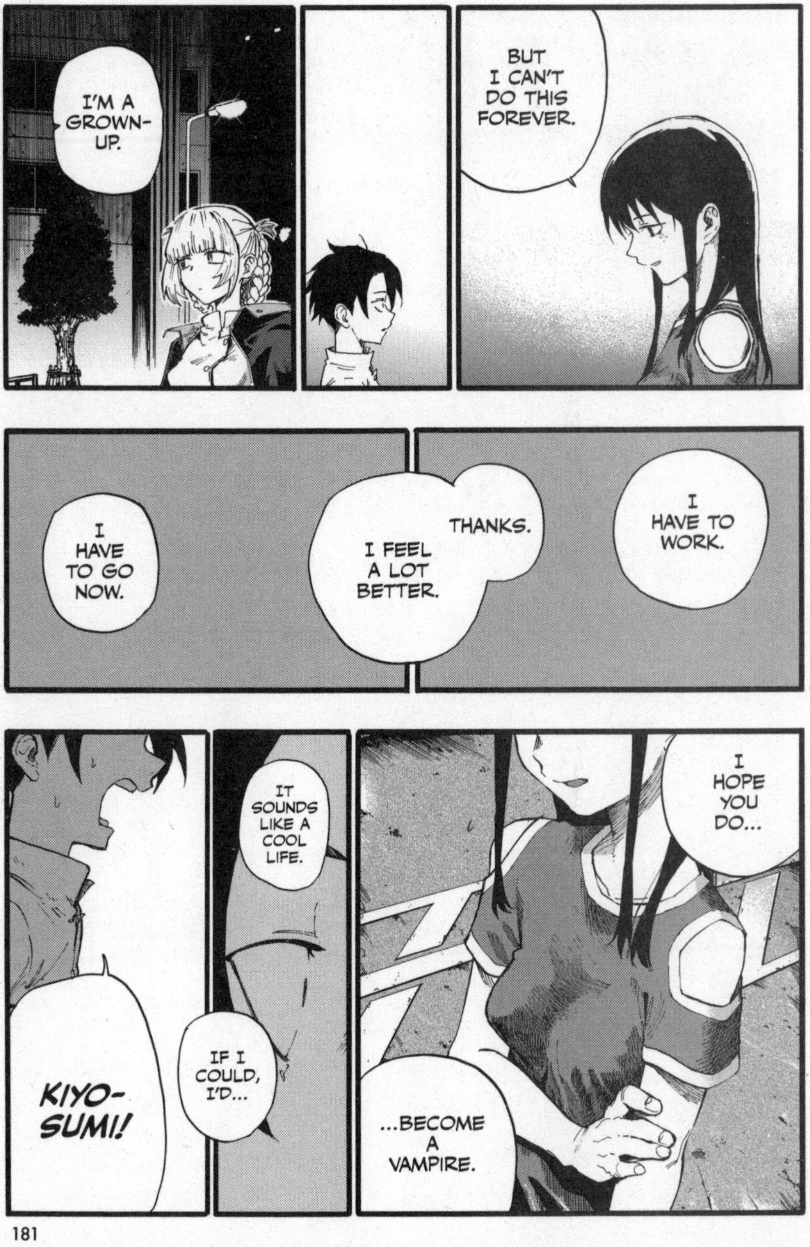
BUT I CAN'T DO THIS FOREVER.
I'M A GROWN-UP.
I HAVE TO WORK.
THANKS.
I FEEL A LOT BETTER.
I HAVE TO GO NOW.
I HOPE YOU DO...
...BECOME A VAMPIRE.
IT SOUNDS LIKE A COOL LIFE.
IF I COULD, I'D...
KIYO-SUMI!

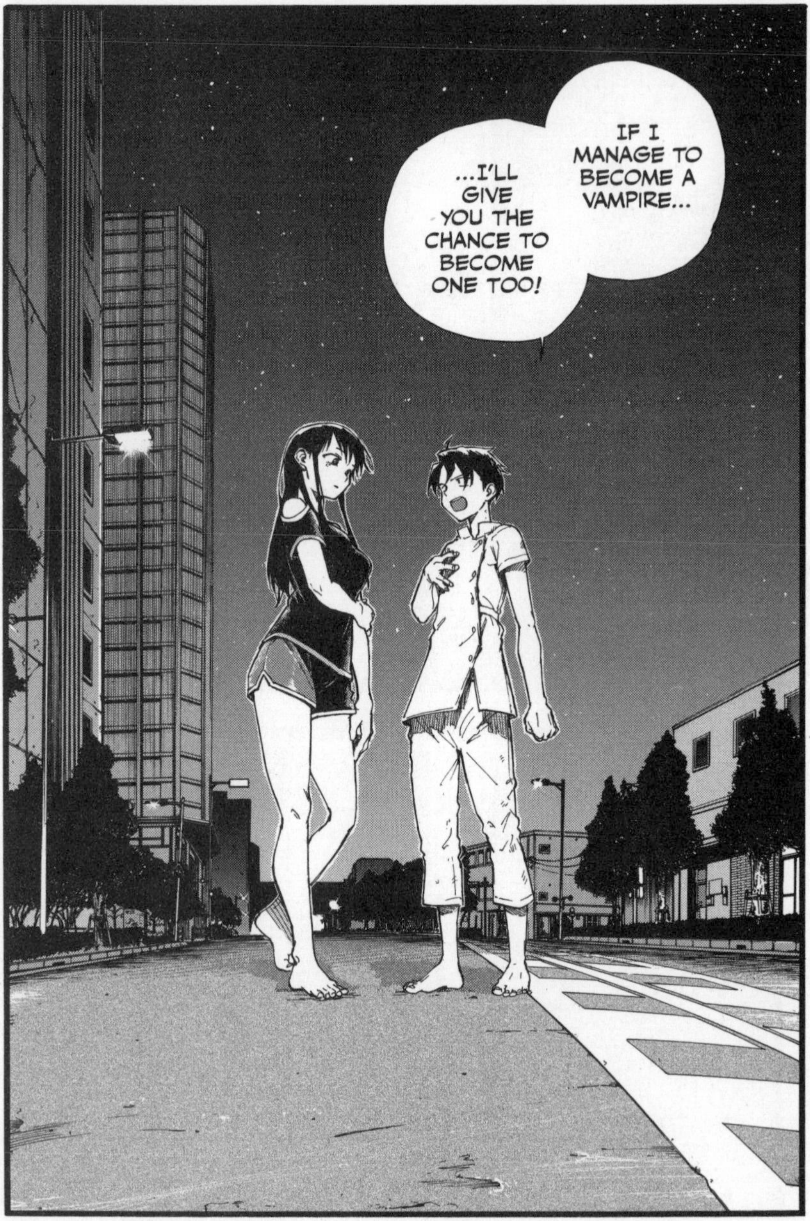
IF I MANAGE TO BECOME A VAMPIRE...
...I'LL GIVE YOU THE CHANCE TO BECOME ONE TOO!

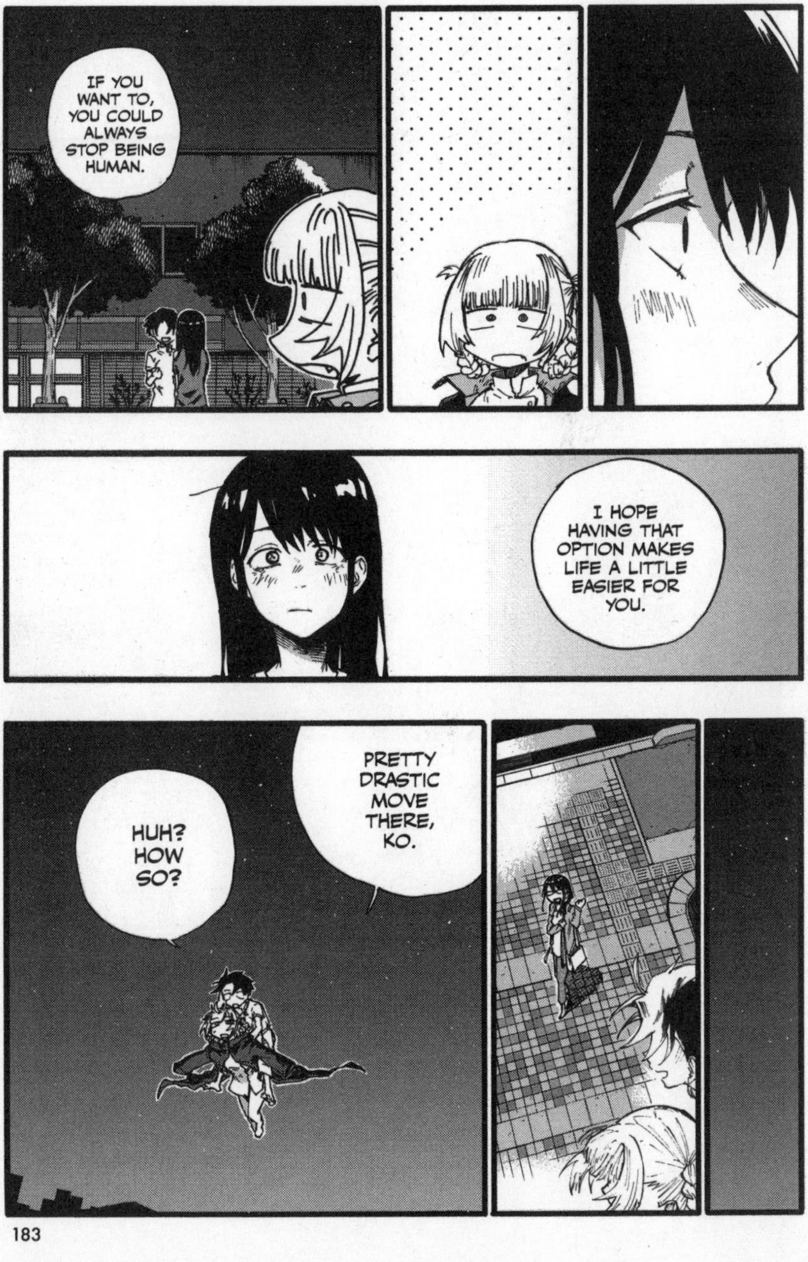
IF YOU WANT TO, YOU COULD ALWAYS STOP BEING HUMAN.
I HOPE HAVING THAT OPTION MAKES LIFE A LITTLE EASIER FOR YOU.
PRETTY DRASTIC MOVE THERE, KO.
HUH? HOW SO?

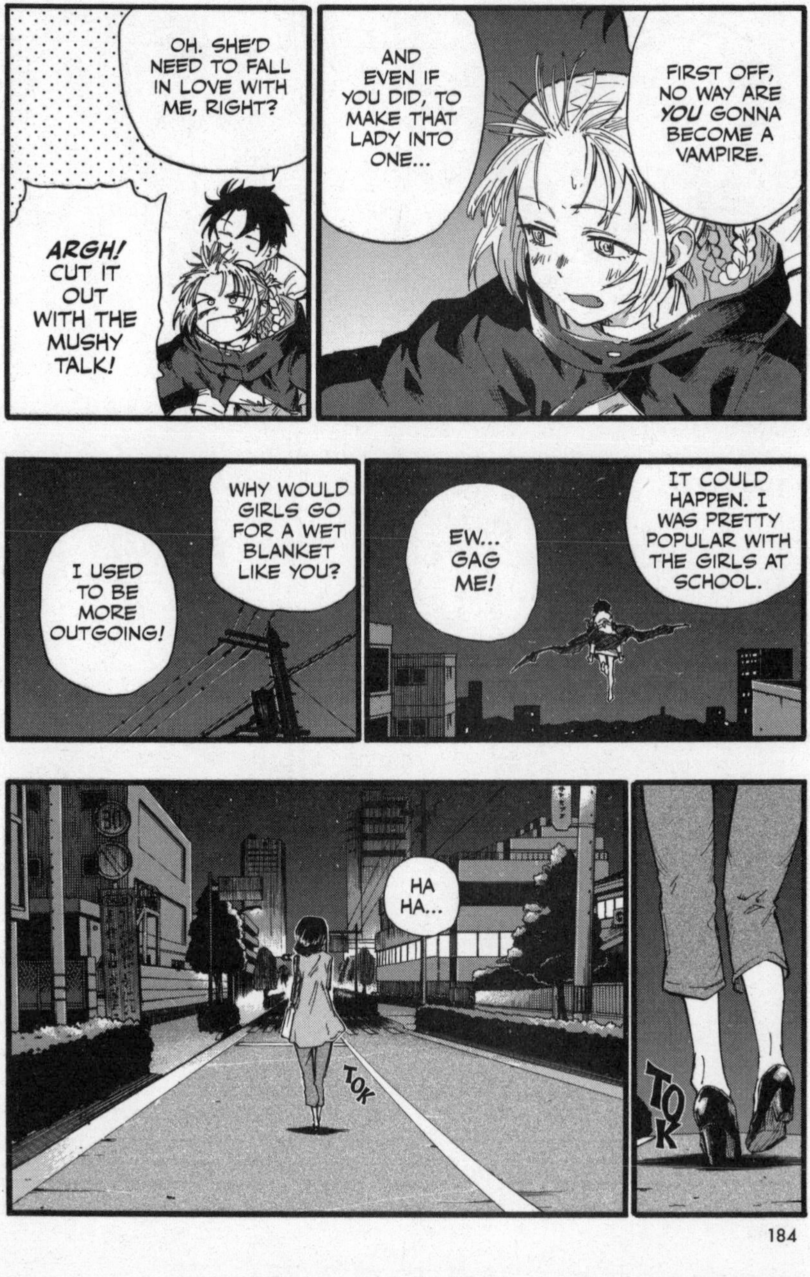
FIRST OFF, NO WAY ARE *YOU* GONNA BECOME A VAMPIRE.
AND EVEN IF YOU DID, TO MAKE THAT LADY INTO ONE...
OH. SHE'D NEED TO FALL IN LOVE WITH ME, RIGHT?
ARGH! CUT IT OUT WITH THE MUSHY TALK!
IT COULD HAPPEN. I WAS PRETTY POPULAR WITH THE GIRLS AT SCHOOL.
EW... GAG ME!
WHY WOULD GIRLS GO FOR A WET BLANKET LIKE YOU?
I USED TO BE MORE OUTGOING!
TOK
HA HA...
TOK

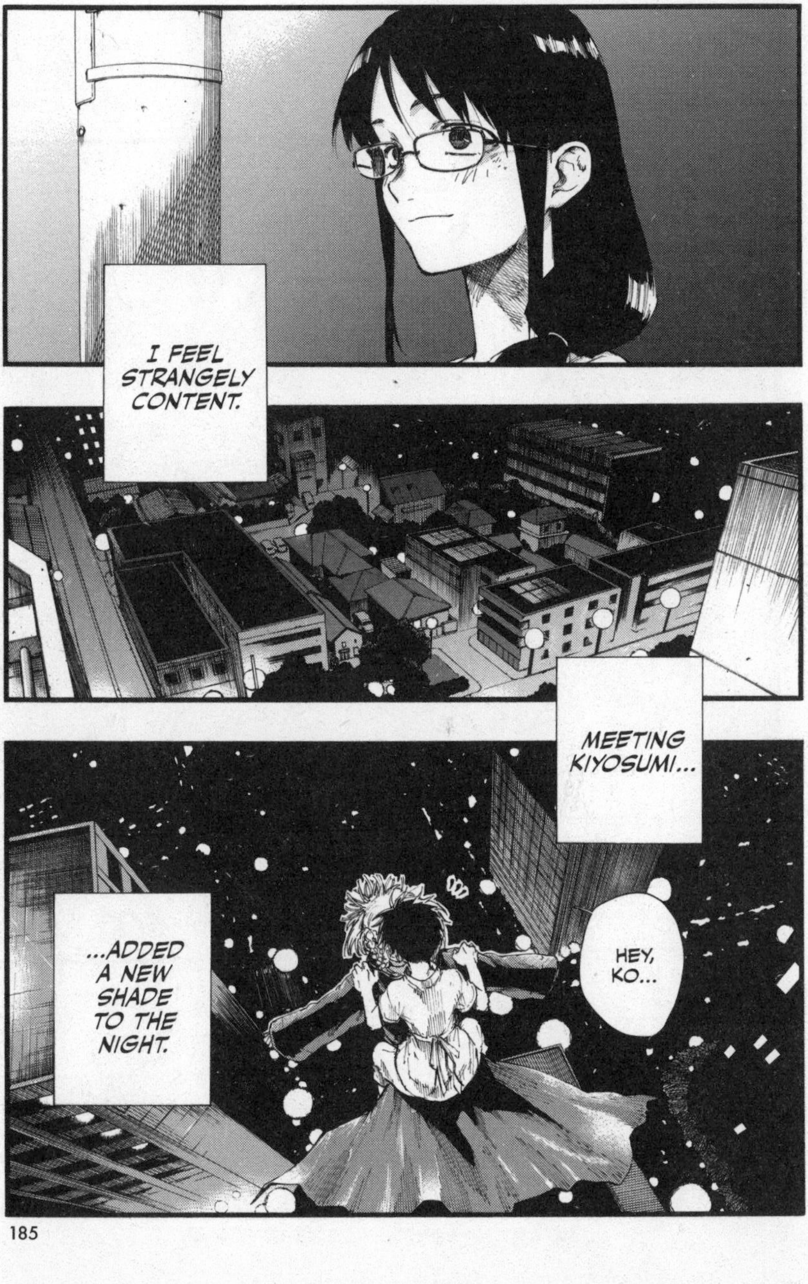
I FEEL STRANGELY CONTENT.
MEETING KIYOSUMI...
HEY, KO...
...ADDED A NEW SHADE TO THE NIGHT.

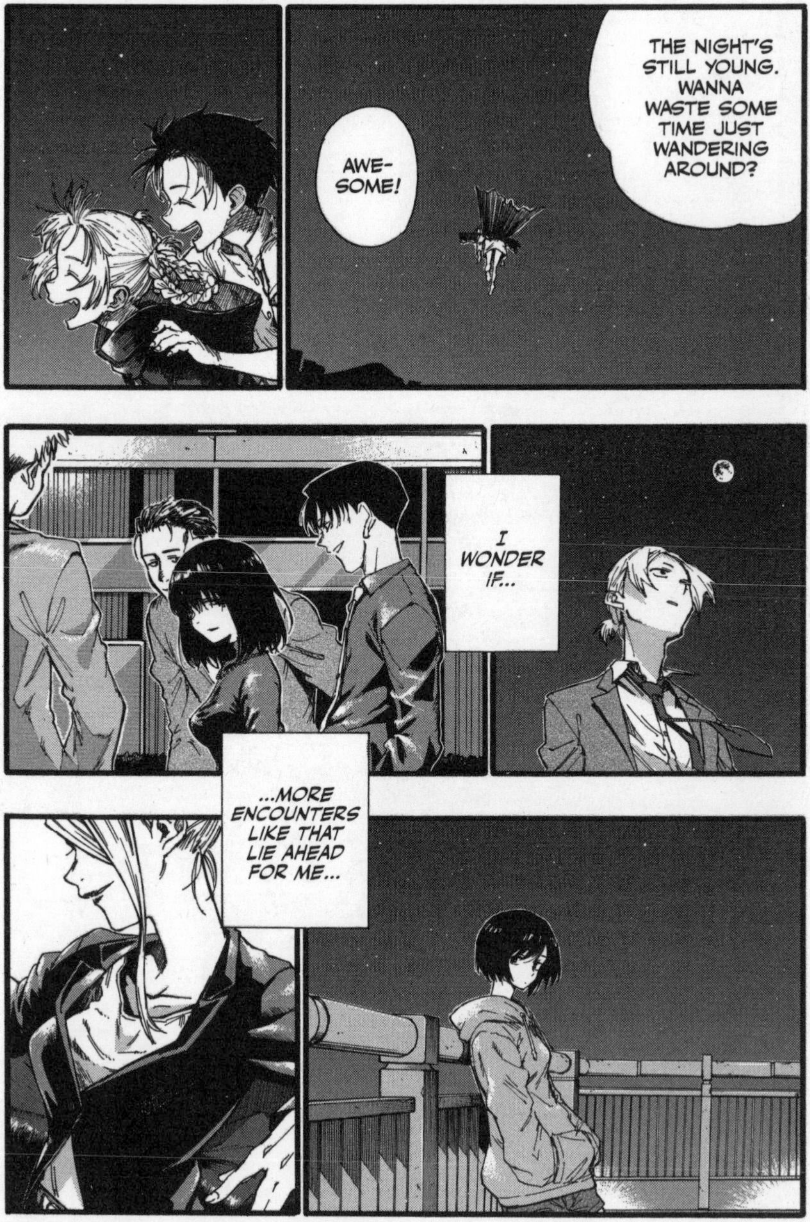
THE NIGHT'S STILL YOUNG. WANNA WASTE SOME TIME JUST WANDERING AROUND?
AWE-SOME!
I WONDER IF...
...MORE ENCOUNTERS LIKE THAT LIE AHEAD FOR ME...

CALL OF THE NIGHT 2 · TO BE CONTINUED...

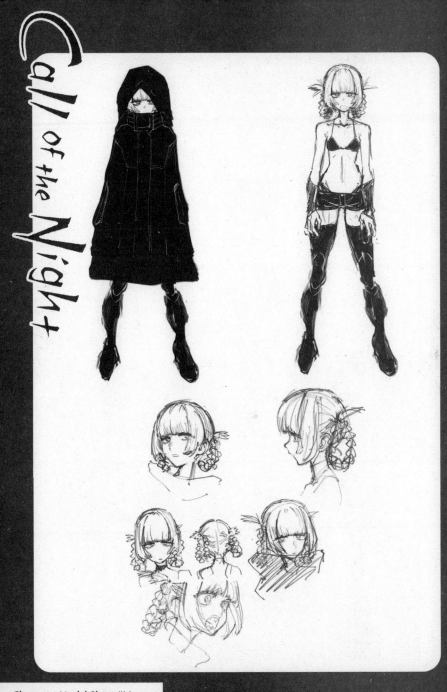

Call of the Night

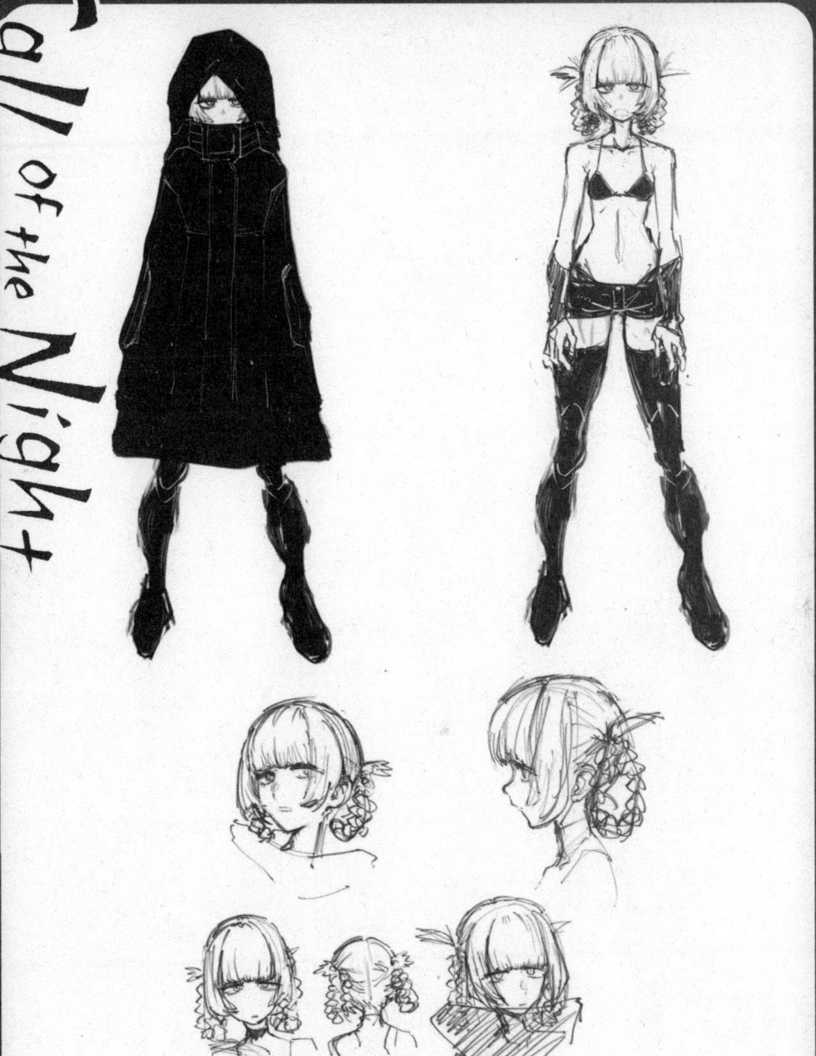

Character Model Sheet #Nazuna

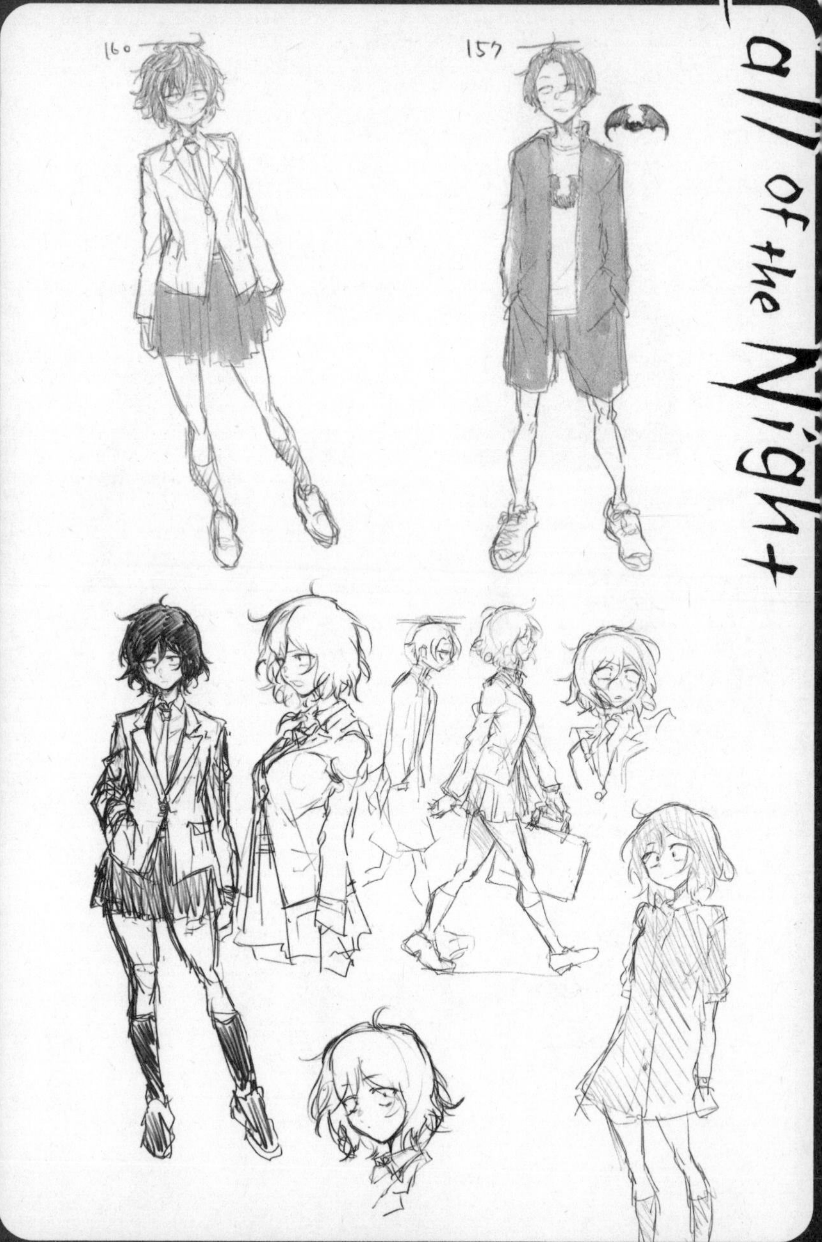
160
157

Character Model Sheet #Ko and Akir

Afterword

It's volume 2.
I can hardly believe it.
Didn't volume 1 just come out the other day?

It's hard to draw people lying down.

When I send a draft to my editor, I think, "This is so funny!"
But when it gets published and I read it, I start to wonder,
"Is this really all that funny?" I guess that's a common problem
for cartoonists. I laugh a lot while drawing, but maybe that's
because it's usually the middle of the night.

Let's look to the night for insight.
See you in volume 3.
KOTOYAMA

These are the tools that I use to work.
Over the last few years, I've settled on these...for now.
This is volume 2!
Thanks for reading.

—KOTOYAMA

KOTOYAMA

In 2013, Kotoyama won the Shonen Sunday Manga
College Award for *Azuma*. From 2014 to 2018,
Kotoyama's title *Dagashi Kashi* ran in *Shonen Sunday*
magazine. *Call of the Night* has been published
in *Shonen Sunday* since 2019.

Call of the Night

⟨ 2 ⟩

SHONEN SUNDAY EDITION

Story and Art by
KOTOYAMA

Translation – **JUNKO GODA**
English Adaptation – **SHAENON K. GARRITY**
Touch-Up Art & Lettering – **ANNALIESE "ACE" CHRISTMAN**
Cover & Interior Design – **ALICE LEWIS**
Editor – **ANNETTE ROMAN**

YOFUKASHI NO UTA Vol. 2
by KOTOYAMA
© 2019 KOTOYAMA
All rights reserved.
Original Japanese edition published by SHOGAKUKAN.
English translation rights in the United States of America, Canada, the United Kingdom,
Ireland, Australia and New Zealand arranged with SHOGAKUKAN.

Original Cover Design – Yasuhisa KAWATANI

Printed in the U.S.A.

Published by VIZ Media, LLC
P.O. Box 77010
San Francisco, CA 94107

10 9 8 7 6 5 4 3 2 1
First printing, June 2021

viz.com   shonensunday.com

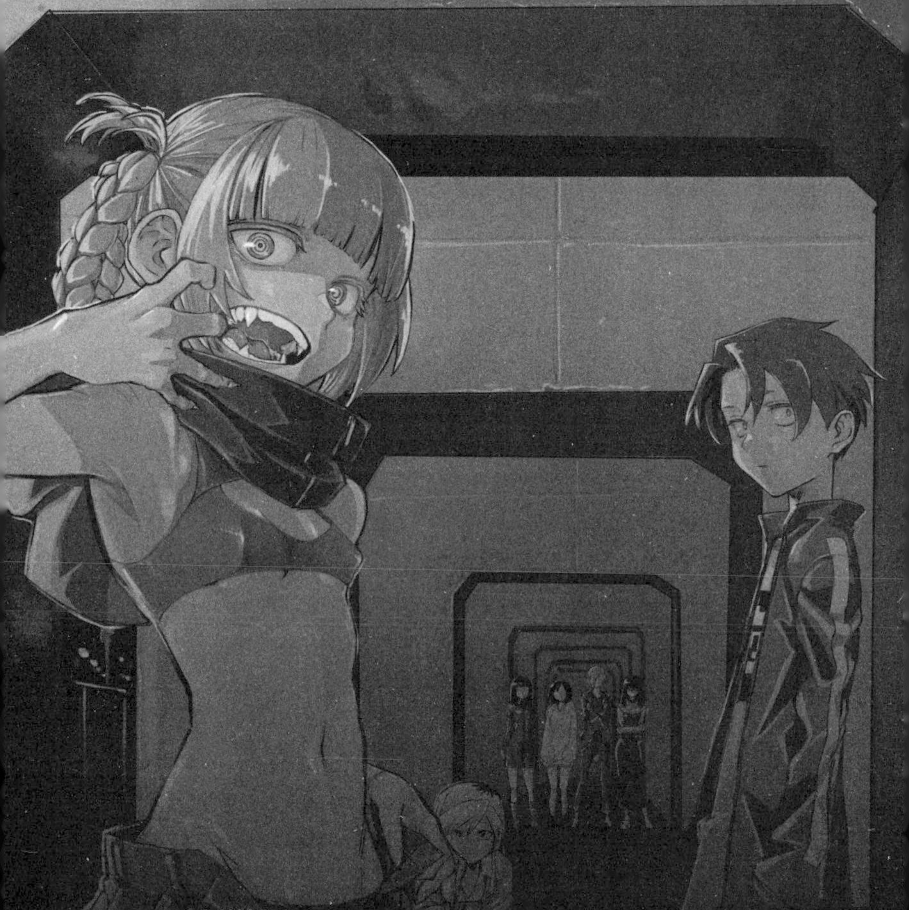

VOLUME 3

Nazuna isn't the only one who thinks Ko is a delicious snack. And he isn't the only one who gets jealous. When Ko draws the attention of four other vampire girls with nefarious intentions, he must fight for his life even though he wants to give it up to become a vampire—but only to a certain special someone. Unfortunately, there's a time limit on being "turned," which raises the...*uh*...stakes. Then, Ko follows some dating advice that backfires. Undeterred, he tries to help another vampire and mortal mend their love/hate relationship.